COLLINS GEM

STAMPS

James Mackay

Consultant: Hugh Jefferies

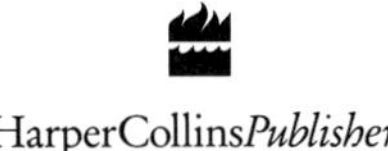

HarperCollins*Publishers*

HarperCollins Publishers
PO Box, Glasgow G4 0NB

First published 1999

Reprint 10 9 8 7 6 5 4 3 2 1 0

© The Foundry Creative Media Co. Ltd 1999

All pictures supplied courtesy of James Mackay,
except pp 36, 38, 44, 45, 48, 50, 53, 107 courtesy
of Stanley Gibbons Ltd.

ISBN 0 00 472345-7

Created and produced by Flame Tree Publishing, part of
The Foundry Creative Media Co. Ltd
Crabtree Hall, Crabtree Lane, London SW6 6TY

Printed in Italy by Amadeus S.p.A.

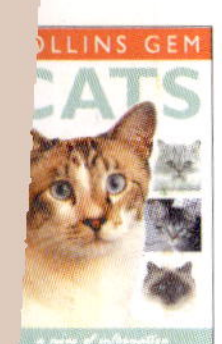

COLLINS GEM
CATS
a mine of information

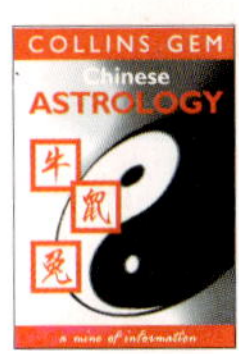

COLLINS GEM
Chinese
ASTROLOGY
a mine of information

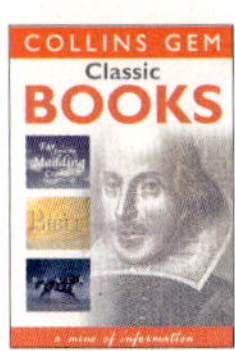

COLLINS GEM
Classic
BOOKS
a mine of information

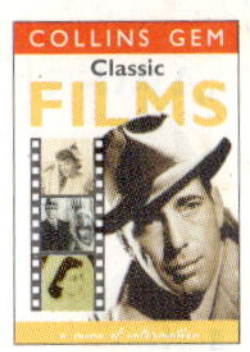

COLLINS GEM
Classic
FILMS
a mine of information

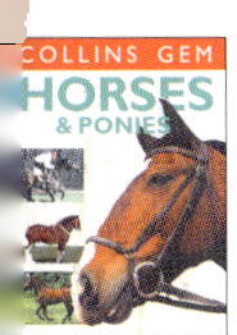

COLLINS GEM
HORSES
& PONIES
a mine of information

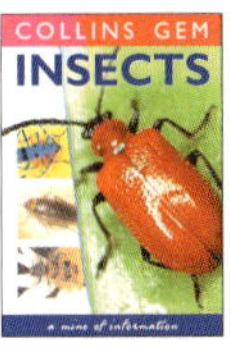

COLLINS GEM
INSECTS
a mine of information

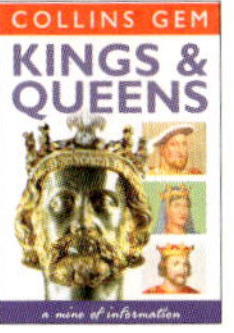

COLLINS GEM
KINGS &
QUEENS
a mine of information

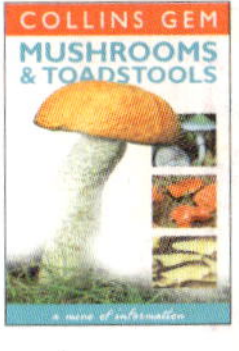

COLLINS GEM
MUSHROOMS
& TOADSTOOLS
a mine of information

COLLINS GEM
SNAKES
a mine of information

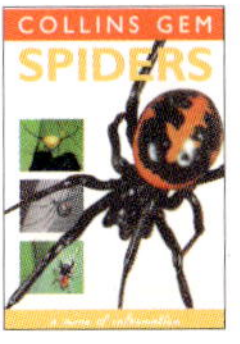

COLLINS GEM
SPIDERS
a mine of information

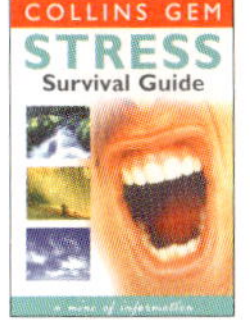

COLLINS GEM
STRESS
Survival Guide
a mine of information

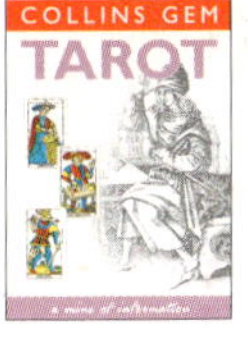

COLLINS GEM
TAROT
a mine of information

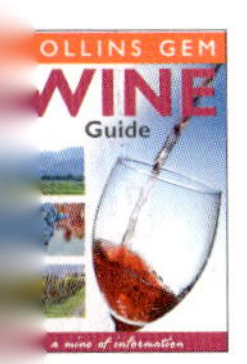

COLLINS GEM
WINE
Guide
a mine of information

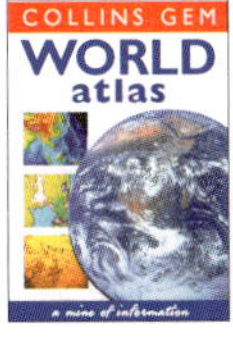

COLLINS GEM
WORLD
atlas
a mine of information

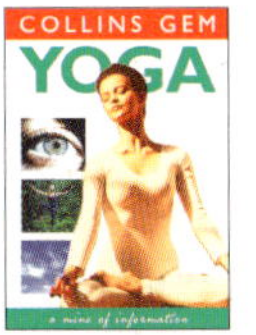

COLLINS GEM
YOGA
a mine of information

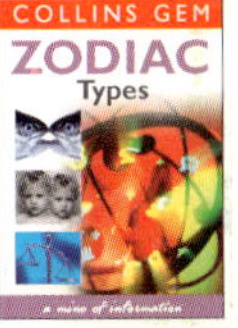

COLLINS GEM
ZODIAC
Types
a mine of information

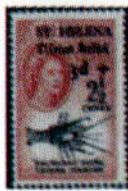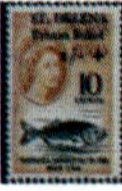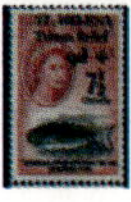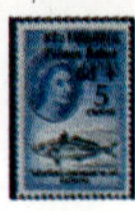

Contents

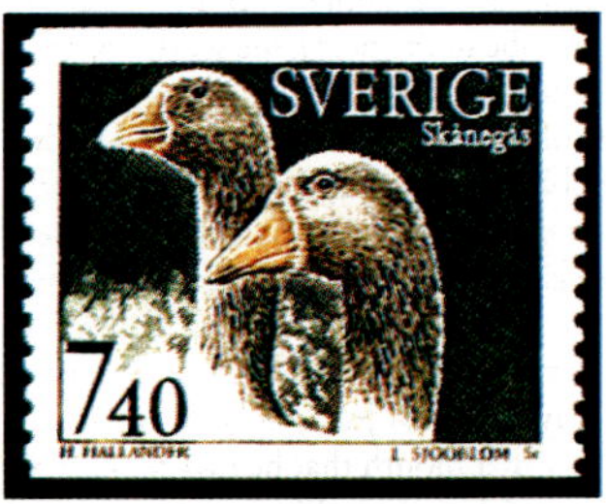

Swedish coil stamp, designed by H. Hallander and engraved by Lars Sjooblom.

Introduction

STAMP-COLLECTING has been called 'the king of hobbies and the hobby of kings' – a reference to the fact that George V of Great Britain, Carol of Romania and Farouk of Egypt were keen collectors. Other famous philatelists were President Franklin D. Roosevelt and the actors Peter Cushing and Yul Brynner. It was – and still is – the king of hobbies, with over three million collectors in the United Kingdom, five million in Germany, 12 million in the USA, and probably up to 100 million worldwide.

Of course there is a wide difference between the millionaires who compete for the great rarities in the saleroom and the schoolchildren who save the stamps off their mail and put them in a drawer, hoping that some day they will find the time to sort them and put them into a proper album. In between there are the people who buy new issues across the counter of their friendly neighbourhood post office, perhaps buy a stamp magazine occasionally, send first-day covers to themselves, subscribe to the new issue service of a philatelic bureau or join a local stamp club.

The beauty of stamp-collecting is that it is so flexible. It is an absorbing hobby for young and old alike. You could spend millions of pounds chasing the great rarities, but you would probably have just as much fun tracking down nicely used examples of the latest commemoratives from your office mail.

Stamp-collecting began almost as soon as stamps appeared in Britain, in May 1840. Dr John Gray of the British Museum noted in his diary that month that he had purchased examples of Penny Blacks and Twopenny Blues, not to put on his mail but to keep for their historic interest, so he can fairly be regarded as the first stamp collector. As early as 1842 *Punch* was noting that young ladies were saving used stamps to decorate plates, screens and even entire walls.

By 1852 a Belgian schoolmaster was advising his pupils to collect stamps as a means of learning geography. Within a decade the first magazines, catalogues and dealers were established. The Philatelic Society of London (now the Royal)

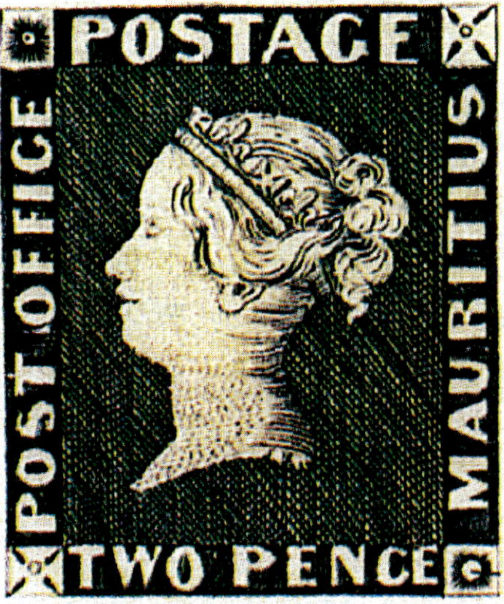

The Mauritius 'Post Office' 2d, 1847.

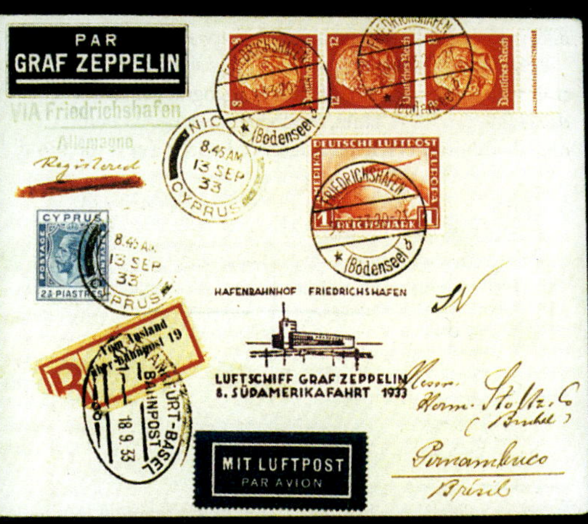

A souvenir cover from one of the Graf Zeppelin *flights.*

was founded in 1869 and has flourished ever since.

Stamp-collecting even acquired a pseudo-scientific name –
philately, coined by the Frenchman Georges Herpin from two
Greek words and literally meaning 'a love of no tax'. The
Greeks themselves have dropped the negative *a* and prefer the
word *philotelia*, a love of taxes!

How To Use This Book

THIS BOOK contains a wide variety of information about stamps of all kinds, from 1840 to the present day, arranged in a dozen sections; together with a final reference section providing a guide to identification of inscriptions, foreign alphabets, useful addresses and a glossary of terms.

Each section is colour-coded for easy reference and takes the reader through the basics of the hobby, step by step, from starting a rudimentary collection to aspects of specialised philately. Along the way, helpful advice is given on joining a club, choosing the right album and equipment, as well as the techniques of preparing stamps for mounting and writing up in the album.

Because differences in the technical aspects of stamps can have a dramatic effect on their value, it is important to master the basics of the various printing processes, watermarks, perforation and the other minutiae which distinguish rare or elusive stamps from their common and therefore less valuable counterparts.

There are tips on buying and selling stamps, and on how to use a stamp catalogue. The various approaches to stamp-collecting are explored and the pros and cons of general and specialised collecting, thematics and postal history are outlined. The book goes far beyond government-issued adhesive postage stamps, taking a look at local stamps,

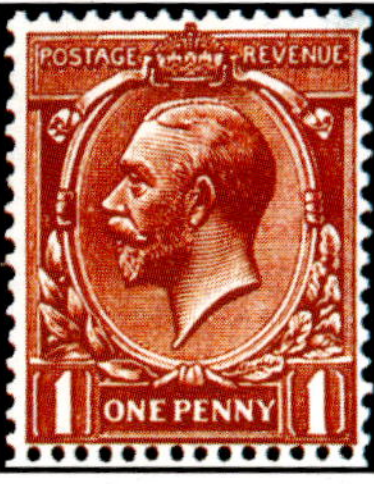

British stamp printed by the letterpress method.

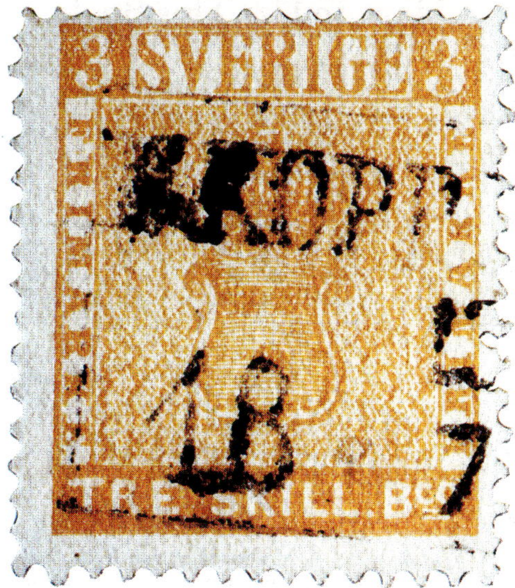

The Three Skilling Yellow of Sweden, the world's most valuable stamp.

revenues and other Cinderellas of philately, postal stationery and postmarks.

The factors which make a stamp valuable are considered, and there is a section dealing with the pitfalls of fakes and forgeries. Finally there is an index which lists every subject covered in this book.

INTRODUCTION TO STAMPS

History of Postage

Adhesive postage stamps and postal stationery with impressed or embossed stamps have been around only since 1840, although the postal services, of which they are an outward symbol, go back much farther.

BEFORE 1840, WHEN adhesive stamps were adopted in the United Kingdom, there were marks struck by hand on letters to indicate that the postage had been prepaid, although it was more common for the postmaster to endorse the letter in manuscript, usually in red ink. As a general rule, however, letters were transmitted unpaid, and it was left to the recipient to pay the postage. The amount of postage depended

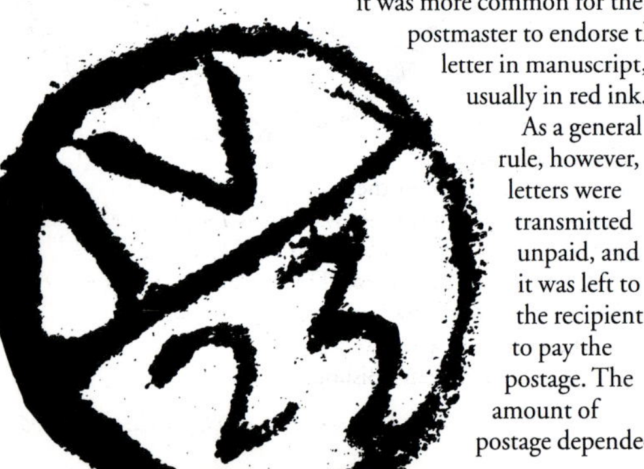

largely on how far the letter had travelled. Weight was not as important as the number of sheets comprising the letter, two sheets meaning double postage, three sheets treble postage and so on. Envelopes counted as an extra sheet, and for that reason very little use was made of them before 1840.

Postal services developed gradually all over western Europe in the fifteenth and sixteenth centuries. In England the Royal Mail was just that, a service used exclusively by the king and his court. The service was thrown open to the general public by King Charles I in 1635, in a bid to raise revenue without recourse to Parliament. This service was disrupted during the Civil War (1642–49), but resumed at the Restoration in 1660. The datestamp (see p.148) was invented in 1661 by Colonel Henry Bishop.

The Bishop mark, the world's first datestamp, 1661.

CHEAP POSTAGE AND THE UPU

By 1800 many countries had a local postal service. There was even an international service, operated by the Counts of Thurn and Taxis in the Holy Roman Empire and even as far afield as Poland and Spain; but international mail was slow, cumbersome and expensive.

IN THE EARLY nineteenth century, after the Napoleonic Wars, Europe entered an era of relative peace in which trade developed rapidly. Rising standards of literacy and greater mobility of population encouraged letter writing, but charges were excessive. Britain led the way in reforming the posts: Rowland Hill (1795–1879) instigated Uniform Penny Postage

German stamp portraying Heinrich von Stephan.

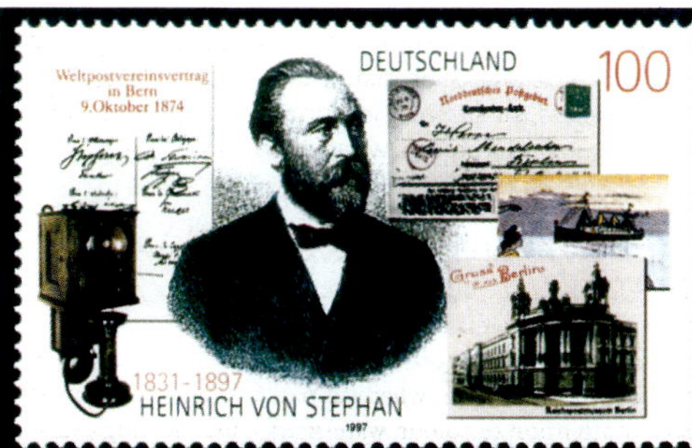

in 1840, together with adhesive postage stamps which made the system much more convenient. Other countries soon followed suit. By 1860 the system of cheap postage, calculated by the weight of the letter, was well established.

The Postmaster General of Prussia, Heinrich von Stephan, organised the Universal Postal Union in 1874. The UPU, with its headquarters in Berne, Switzerland, coordinates international postal services to this day. It introduced a system of international accounting (1875), with uniform colours for stamps according to their purpose (1891), registration (1880), parcel post (1881), international reply coupons (1907) and labels for airmail and customs declaration (1920). It also sanctioned the use of bulk posting prepaid in cash as well as meter marks (1922) and adopted aerogrammes (1947).

The Anatomy of a Stamp

Stamps, which often look alike, may be quite different in minor details. Such distinctions may greatly affect their value, so it is very important to understand the anatomy of a stamp, what it consists of and how it was printed.

MAIN FEATURES OF A STAMP

THE FIRST thing you will notice about any stamp you acquire is whether it is mint (unused) or used. Every stamp incorporates certain information in its design: its country of origin and its face value (what was paid for it). Collectors will also pay attention to colour, watermarks, the printing process used and the type of paper the stamp is printed on.

In Britain, the Royal Mail tends to issue stamps in sets of four or five different denominations covering the main postal rates. The higher values therefore occur mostly on bulky or registered packets or on airmail, so are seen less often. Other countries, notably the USA, prefer to issue stamps at the basic domestic rate, either one at a time or, increasingly, in booklets or even whole sheets containing a variety of different designs.

Nowadays there are so many other ways of prepaying postage that adhesive stamps are not as common as they once were. On the other hand, most countries now issue new stamps virtually every month, so that the variety on ordinary mail is infinitely greater.

COLOUR

THE MOST readily detected difference between two similar stamps is the colour, as stamps produced over many years may run to numerous printings and the printer might not be concerned about using ink of exactly the same shade and composition. Different shades and tints enable collectors to place stamps in chronological order. Accurate identification of colour can be very important. For example, the George V halfpenny stamp in green (1912) is worth 50p mint; in the distinctive yellowish shade known as Cyprus green (1914) it would be worth £1,500.

PAPER

LESS APPARENT are the different types of paper that may have been used, and quite an interesting collection could be formed to illustrate the range of papers on which stamps have been printed. You would find blue sugar-bag paper (British Guiana, 1852), rice paper (Japan, 1872), newspaper (Jersey,

1943), goldbeaters' skin (Germany, 1872) and transparent paper (Saxony, 1946). Paper can vary in type and quality from expensive handmade rag paper to modern machine-woven paper produced from vegetable fibres; this has a high kaolin content which gives it the bright, white glossy surface necessary for multicolour printing. Paper may be tinted right through or may be white on the front and coloured on the back, and range in thickness from pelure (very hard and thin) to cartridge (soft and thick).

WATERMARKS

A WATERMARK is the most common type of security device used on stamps. Watermarks are impregnated into the paper when the pulp is rolled out. The sheets are squeezed out under a roller made of wire gauze to which are attached the water-mark bits – usually made of brass in various shapes and sizes.

These bits make the paper slightly thinner at that point, hence their watermarks can be seen when held to the light. At one time fear of forgery induced most countries to use watermarks, but nowadays they are largely confined to Malta

Examples of British watermarks.

(Maltese Crosses) and the countries handled by the Crown Agents (a crown over the letters CA). Nowadays fluorescent patterns have largely taken their place.

Britain's Victorian stamps have various types of watermark: a crown, a cross, an anchor or even heraldic flowers. In 1912 a watermark showing a crown over the royal cypher was adopted. The stamps of George V may look the same, but the watermarks tell a different story: Simple Cypher (August 1912), Multiple Cypher (September 1912) or Block Cypher (1924). The watermark changed for each succeeding monarch until the present reign, when there were the Tudor crown and E2R (1952), St Edward's crown and E2R (1955) and Multiple Crowns (1958–65). Finally the watermark was abandoned in 1967–68, thus producing four different versions of the Elizabethan definitives (ordinary stamps in permanent use).

Other security devices include embedded silk threads (Switzerland), embossed grilles (USA), imitation watermarks printed on the back (Greece, New Zealand, Sweden) or serial numbers (Spain and colonies).

PERFORATION

The earliest stamps were issued imperforate and had to be cut apart with scissors. Various methods of piercing paper were attempted before true perforation, in which small holes are punched out, was developed from 1854 onwards.

IT WAS AN Irishman, Henry Archer, who pioneered effective methods of separating stamps. In 1848 he began experimenting with a rouletting machine, which used tiny knife-blades to produce a pattern of cuts. Rouletting usually consists of short dashes in a straight line, but there have been many fancy patterns, such as serpentine, arc or saw-tooth. Rouletting was extensively used in many countries and, indeed, has survived fitfully to the present day, although it is now mainly used for postal labels for airmail, registration or special delivery.

True perforation, in which tiny discs of paper are actually cut out, was perfected by Archer in 1850 and was finally adopted by the British Post Office, after extensive trials, in 1854. Thereafter it spread rapidly to all parts of the world.

Early perforations were made by a blade mounted with pins, the stamps being perforated a line at a time. Nowadays sheets are perforated by a comb which cuts out holes along the line and down the sides as well. Sometimes similar stamps may be line- or comb-perforated at different times. Line-perforated stamps have irregular 'teeth' in the corners, whereas comb-perforated stamps always have regular teeth.

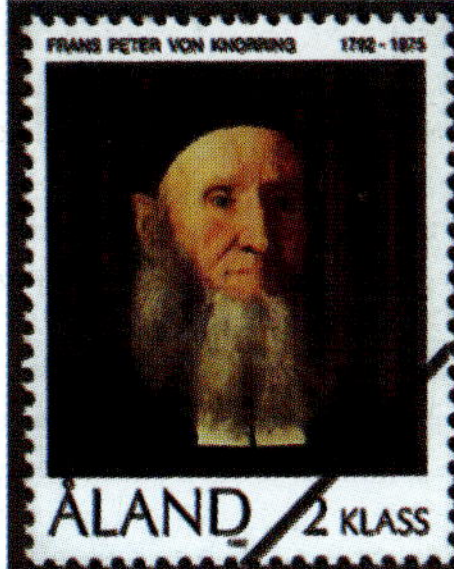

Example of line perforation with irregular corners.

Example of comb perforation with regular corners.

PHOSPHOR BARS

IN 1959 British stamps began to appear with vertical phosphor bands on their face to facilitate electronic sorting and facing of mail (ensuring that letters and cards were the right side up for cancellation by machine). While these phosphor bands can usually be seen with the naked eye – if the stamp is tilted slightly off the horizontal – collectors soon discovered that there were different kinds of phosphor, distinguishable by the colour emitted under ultraviolet light – first green, then blue and later violet.

Since the 1970s, however, things have become very complicated. The penny stamp, for example, was printed on original coated paper (OCP), then fluorescent coated paper (FCP), advanced coated paper (ACP) and latterly non-fluorescent coated paper (NFCP). It may also be found with phosphor bands, all-over phosphor, phosphorised paper and latterly bands with yellow or blue fluor, so an ultraviolet lamp (see p. 48) is indispensable in identifying them.

PRINTING PROCESSES

Since 1840 five major printing processes have been used. As there are many instances of two or more different processes being used at various times during the currency of a series it is important to be able to distinguish them.

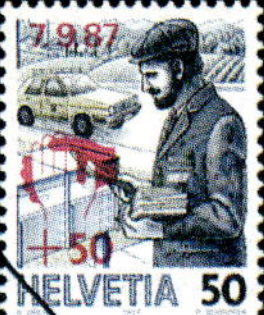

Intaglio

The earliest process was called intaglio, copperplate or recess-printing. The term 'line-engraving' is sometimes loosely used, but should strictly apply only to the die or plate from which the stamps are printed.

In the intaglio process, lines, grooves and recesses bite into the surface of the plate. Ink is then forced into these recesses and the surface of the plate wiped clean. The paper is then forced, under great pressure, into the recesses where it absorbs the ink lying there. This gives the paper of such stamps its characteristic ridged surface. Most banknotes are produced by this method, hence their crisp surfaces on which the tiny ridges can be felt with the fingertips.

In Britain this process was used for low-value stamps until 1880 and for the high values of 1913–77 and 1988 onwards. Until recently all US stamps were recess-printed and it is still used for most definitives. Canada, Austria, the Czech Republic, Slovakia, France, Denmark and Sweden continue to use this process extensively.

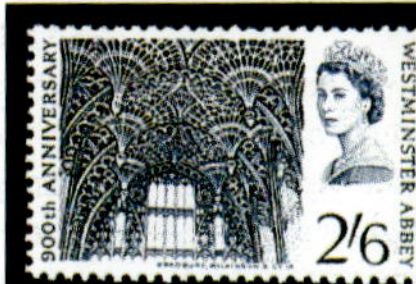

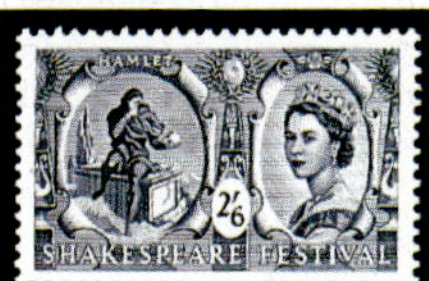

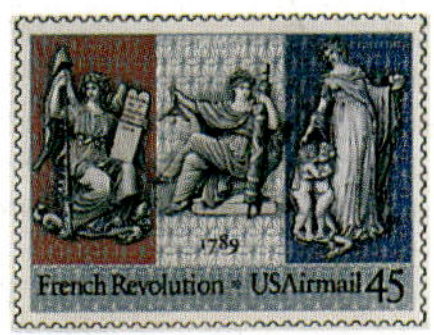

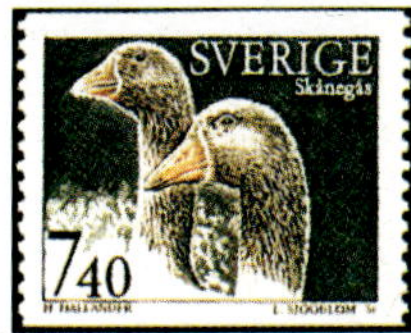

Examples of intaglio stamps from Switzerland (left), Great Britain, the United States of America and Sweden (above).

Letterpress

Letterpress, relief or surface printing is sometimes known to collectors as typography, and stamps made by this method are said to be 'typographed'. It is the opposite to intaglio, since the surface of the plate is cut away, leaving ridges on which the ink is spread. The paper is pressed against the raised lines of the plate and picks up the image from them. The chief merit of this process was the cheapness with which printing blocks and stereos – printing blocks used in letterpress – could be cast, but it could not

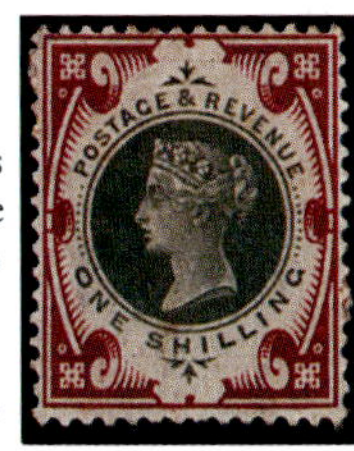

produce such fine and sensitive results as intaglio, and careless over-inking tended to produce a blurred effect.

It was widely used in early European stamps and in Britain was employed by the De La Rue printing firm for stamps above 2d in denomination from 1854, for all stamps from 1880 to 1913 and for the low values until 1934. It survived longest in the postage due labels (1914–70).

A variant of this was typesetting, using loose type, ornament and printer's rule to create a design (used in early British Guiana, Fiji, Lithuania and Uganda).

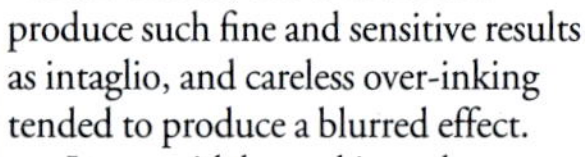

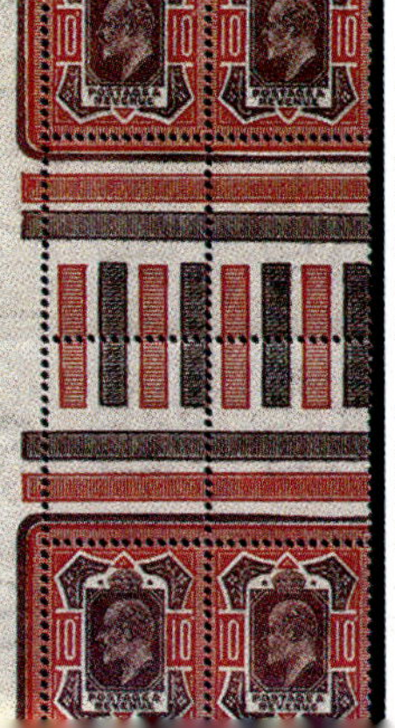

Letterpress stamps of Great Britain.

Embossing

This technique was introduced by Britain in 1841 for postal stationery (see p.90) and was used on stamped envelopes until the 1970s. Paper is struck between two dies to produce a raised design, usually in colourless relief. Adhesive 6d, 10d and 1s stamps (1847–54) were embossed, as were many early stamps of Austrian Italy, Portugal, the German states, the German Empire (1872–75) and Bavaria (1867–1911). Embossing returned in the 1960s, the Queen's head being embossed in gold foil on many British stamps. Very recently thermography, which looks like embossing, has been widely used to give a three-dimensional effect to multicoloured stamps.

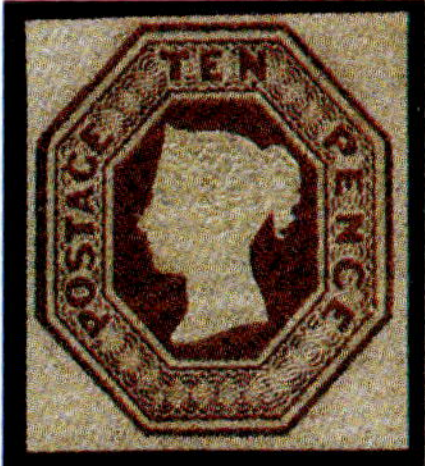

Embossed 10d stamp of Great Britain.

Lithography

Lithography (from Greek *lithos*, stone, and *graphein*, to write) derives its name from the fact that slabs of finely polished limestone were used in the process.

In 1798, an Austrian-born actor and music publisher, Alois Senefelder, discovered that the limestone from the Solenhofen quarries near Munich could be polished to a very smooth surface and that a drawing made on it with a substance known as 'fat ink' could be used to print impressions on paper. The image is laid down on the stone in greasy ink, or by means of transfers, in reverse. After fixing by acid, the stone is continually dampened in the course of printing, but the

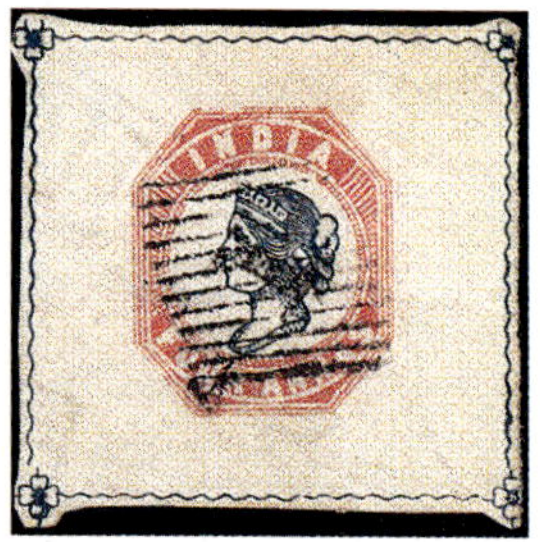

India 1854, 4 annas red and blue (left); Austrian stamp of 1998 marking the bicentenary, and showing an actual lithographic stone (below).

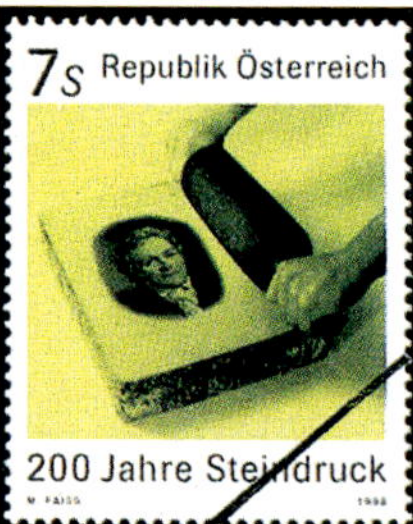

printing ink only sticks to the greased image which repels the water. A printed impression is made when paper is brought into contact with the inked stone. The paper placed over the stone would then take up an impression from the inked area.

The process has since been refined and mechanised, thin zinc plates replacing the cumbersome stones, but the basic principle remains the same. A modern variant is offset lithography, in which the design is not printed directly from the plate but is transferred to a rubber roller which then comes into contact with the printing surface. Lithography is now often combined with intaglio to create startling multicolour effects, retaining the incisive quality associated with recess printing.

Photogravure

Known also as rotogravure or heliogravure, this photographic process is cheap, efficient and technically versatile, capable of the most subtle and complex multicolour reproduction.

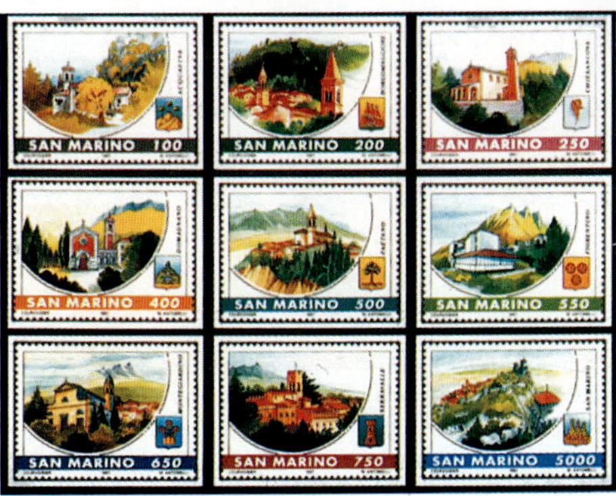

Photogravure stamps of San Marino by Courvoisier.

As the name suggests, photogravure relies heavily on photography. A photogravure plate or cylinder bears a photographic image etched into its surface. The ink goes into the recesses which, in this case, are composed of fine dots of varying density, and the paper picks up the impression in much the same manner as in intaglio. Under a magnifier one can see the fine pattern of dots which are always present in photogravure.

A screening process is also used in modern offset lithography and it is not always possible to tell them apart, though photogravure generally has greater depth and tonal qualities than the other methods and is capable of much finer results.

Photogravure was widely used in magazine illustration from the 1890s to the 1930s, but was first applied to stamps in 1914 in Bavaria. Harrison and Sons were the first British firm to recognise the potential of photogravure, and printed stamps for Egypt (1923) and the Gold Coast (1928) by this method, before changing the British low-value definitives to photogravure in 1934. Courvoisier of Switzerland and Enschedé of Holland are also leading exponents of this process, though it has, to some extent, given way in more recent years to multicolour offset lithography.

ERRORS

Stamp-collecting is virtually unique in that something which is less than perfect is often worth a great deal more than a perfect specimen. A stamp showing an error is usually much scarcer than the correct version, and the law of supply and demand ensures that the error commands a high premium.

PROBABLY THE most common type of error is the error in design, but this only becomes valuable if it is speedily rectified. There are many examples of design errors which are more widespread than the

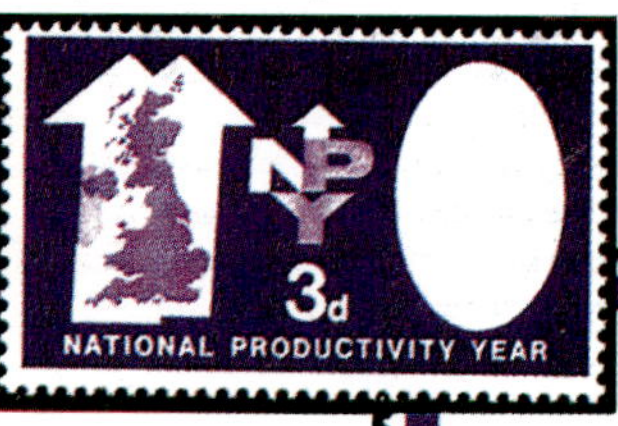

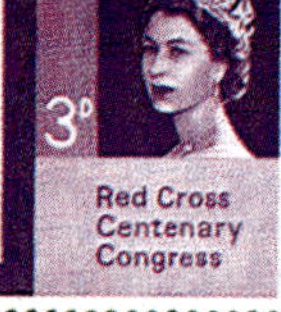

British stamps with missing colours.

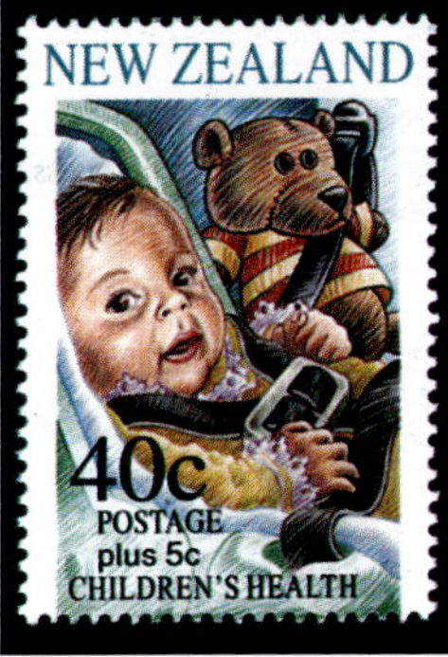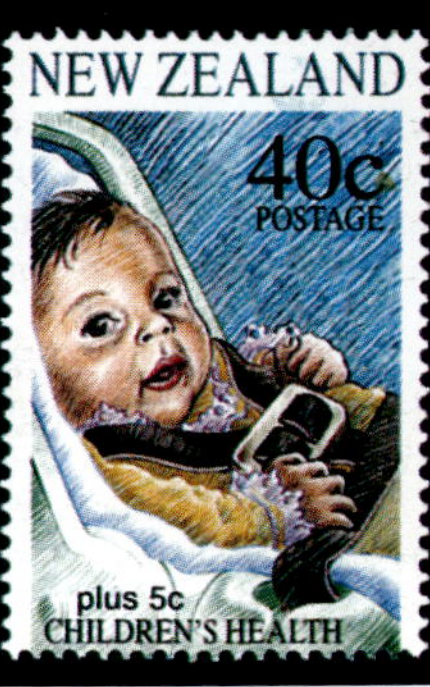

Design error: New Zealand 40c Health stamp. The Teddy Bear design was scrapped after printing, but a few got into circulation by mistake.

amended version. As a rule, these errors consist of spelling mistakes, and it is possible to collect matched pairs, showing the mistake and the correction side by side.

Errors in production, being accidental, are invariably much rarer. The most common is the partial or total omission of perforations. Stamps may turn up without any perforations at all, but more frequently they are found imperforate horizontally or vertically and are best collected in pairs, or singles with adjoining marginal paper to show the lack of perforations in between – otherwise it would be a simple matter to trim off the perforations with scissors.

Errors in printing usually arise where two or more colours are involved, requiring two or more passes through a press. This can result in stamps with the centre inverted in relation to

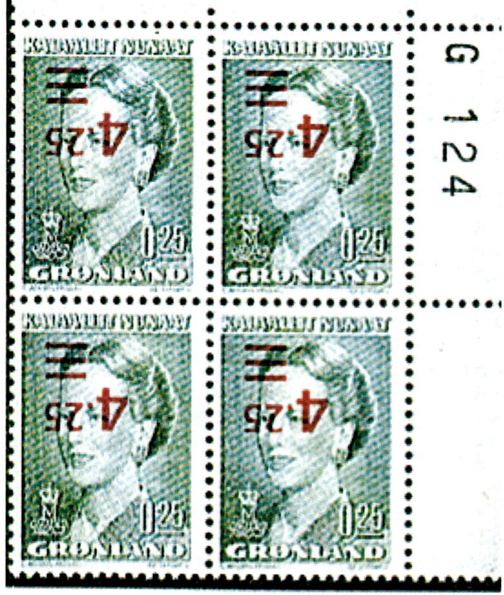

Greenland: Queen Margrethe stamps with inverted surcharge.

the frame, or the colours badly out of register, or even one or more colours missing, often with spectacular results.

Overprints and surcharges, applied to stamps to alter their face value or purpose, may be found inverted, sideways or double.

Starting a Collection

Stamp-collecting is one of the few hobbies that need not cost anything once you have the basic equipment. The stamps from your mail and the letters and postcards of family and friends would make a start.

STARTER KITS

YOU COULD start with a ready-made beginner's outfit containing an album, hinges, tweezers, magnifying glass and perhaps a booklet with basic hints and a glossary of inscriptions to aid identification. Some philatelic bureaux now produce starter kits to encourage people to take up the hobby and these follow a similar pattern.

Before you start, be warned that there are right and wrong ways of handling stamps, from the raw material clipped off mail to the album page neatly mounted and written up. Stamps should always be handled with tweezers, except when they are wet, in which case plastic tongs are safer. Whichever method you choose, ensure it is employed with extreme care!

ACQUIRING STAMPS

TELL YOUR friends that you are collecting stamps and you will soon be surprised at the range and diversity of material that comes your way. This method can be augmented by purchasing stamps in packets. Most dealers sell packets containing 100, 500, 1,000 or more stamps, either one-country or a whole-world mixture, or even by subject such as animals, birds, trains and ships. Many dealers also sell kiloware – stamps on pieces of envelopes as collected by charities and sold by the kilo, hence the name. The drawback about kiloware is that you invariably end up with a lot of duplicates, though it is a good source for postmarks.

When begging for stamps from friends and relatives it is best to acquire them intact on the envelope or card if possible. This is because there might well be an interesting slogan, postmark or some other marking or label alongside the stamp. Try to educate your sources of supply: persuade them not to remove stamps from envelopes, as doing so may tear or thin the stamp.

REMOVING STAMPS FROM PAPER

WHEN YOU have decided to remove stamps from their covers, cut the backing paper carefully, at least a centimetre clear all round. The pieces can then be floated (never soaked) in a basin of lukewarm water, face upwards, until they part easily from the paper adhering to them. Many stamps nowadays are printed on glossy paper with fugitive inks (inks that run) and phosphor bands, so that their appearance may be spoiled by total immersion, especially in hot water.

The stamps should be lifted from the water and laid face down on sheets of clean white blotting paper to dry. Once dry they can be pressed flat between two or three books. Leave for at least 24 hours before removing them. There are now patent drying-books and even electric stamp-driers for the serious enthusiast.

Avoid steaming a stamp off an envelope – you run the risk of the gum filtering through the paper, to give it a translucent 'oiled-paper' appearance. Non-collectors also have a distressing tendency to clip stamps off mail too closely for comfort, resulting in stamps with their perforations trimmed or cut into.

MOUNTING USING STAMP HINGES

Next to the stamp album, the stamp hinge or mount is the most important accessory. Do *not* use adhesive tape to fix stamps to the page, even on the marginal paper around a stamp. It has a rubber fixative which stains and ruins both stamps and album pages and is very difficult to remove.

THE TRADITIONAL stamp hinge is made of very thin, strong transparent paper, double-gummed for easy peeling so that it can be removed, if required, without damaging either the stamp or the page. Hinges may seem fiddly to use, but once you have mastered the art it is a very simple operation.

Place the stamp face downwards, take the hinge and, if not already folded, fold it into a third and two-thirds with the gummed side outwards. Moisten the lesser portion and attach it lightly to the upper part of the back of the stamp, close to, but not protruding beyond, the perforations. Moisten the other part of the hinge near the bottom end and attach the stamp and hinge to the appropriate place on the page. Hinged stamps should lie perfectly flat, but they can be gently raised without difficulty to examine the backs if necessary.

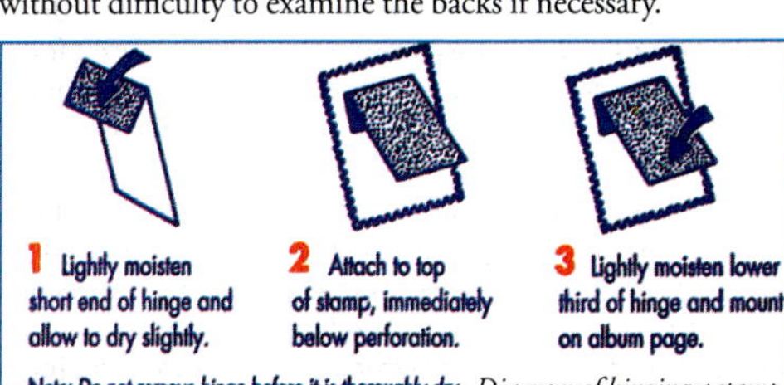

1 Lightly moisten short end of hinge and allow to dry slightly.

2 Attach to top of stamp, immediately below perforation.

3 Lightly moisten lower third of hinge and mount on album page.

Note: Do not remove hinge before it is thoroughly dry. *Diagram of hinging a stamp.*

Developing a Collection

JOINING A CLUB

There are more than 350 stamp clubs in the UK and most towns have one. They offer the best way of getting on in the hobby. In addition, there are nationwide or international clubs devoted to a particular country or aspect of stamps, such as airmails (see p.70) and Cinderellas (see p.156).

YOUR PUBLIC LIBRARY or local museum should have details of the nearest stamp club: the name, address and telephone number of the club secretary, how often the club meets and where. Stamp-collectors are only too ready to help beginners and you will be assured of a warm welcome.

Most clubs meet once a month, but many meet fortnightly and some meet every week, mainly during the season from September to the end of May. Club subscriptions are usually very modest and cover the hire of a meeting-room and perhaps the expenses of occasional visiting speakers.

Meetings take the form of talks and displays of stamps. Members' nights, where everyone is expected to show a few pages of stamps, are a good way of breaking the ice and encouraging newcomers.

Above all, clubs are the ideal way to get to know other collectors and swap your unwanted duplicates. Some clubs hold regular auctions, but the chief methods of exchanging stamps are either informally before or after the main meeting, or through the club packet.

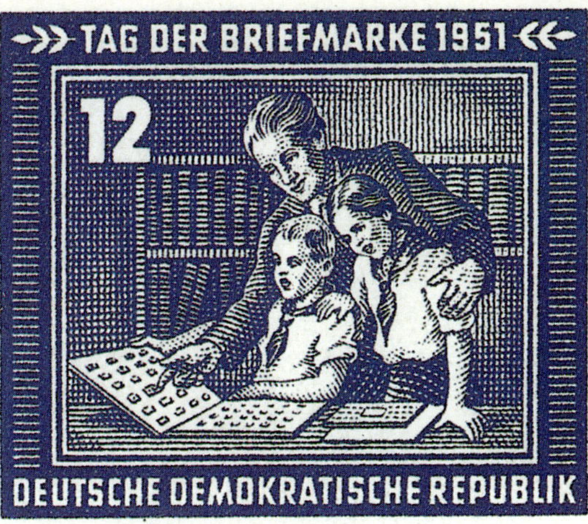

East German stamp depicting stamp collectors, 1951.

The packet is a box containing a number of booklets in which members arrange their duplicates and put a price on them, usually at a good discount from the catalogue prices. These boxes circulate among the members and offer an inexpensive way of adding to your collection.

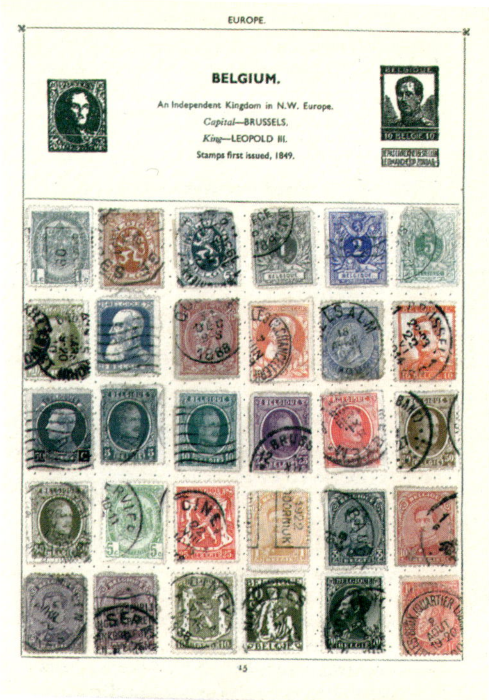

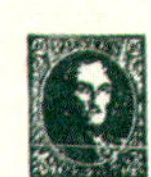

Typical page of a printed fixed-leaf album.

STAMP ALBUMS

You will soon progress beyond the elementary level, and the first thing you will need next is a good album. Eventually you will need to consider loose-leaf albums that give you the space to display and annotate your growing collection.

Fixed-leaf Albums

These have fixed pages and printed headings, often including illustrations of representative stamps, partly for decoration and partly to aid identification. The main drawback of fixed-leaf albums is that both sides of the page are meant to be used and this can cause stamps to rip each others' perforations as the pages are turned. Also, you will soon find that your stamps (particularly from the more important countries) outgrow the space available.

Loose-leaf Albums

Sooner or later you will have to graduate to a loose-leaf album. At one end of the scale there are albums with plain leaves, where it is entirely up to you what headings and other inscriptions you wish to write on them. Many of the plain albums are spring-backs, which means that additional pages can be inserted easily without having to dismantle the binder. The snag about this system is that the album does not lie flat when open, and if too many pages are inserted the springs are weakened and then the leaves may fall out.

Peg-fitting albums have the advantage that they lie flat when opened and there is no fear of pages being dislodged. The main disadvantage is that if you wish to insert a new page you have to unpeg the binder and remove all the leaves up to the required place. The task of replacing the pages correctly can be tedious. The solution is to use a multi-ring binder which enables the album to lie flat but facilitates the replacement or addition of pages by means of the patent catches at the top and bottom of the spine.

Printed loose-leaf albums for British stamps.

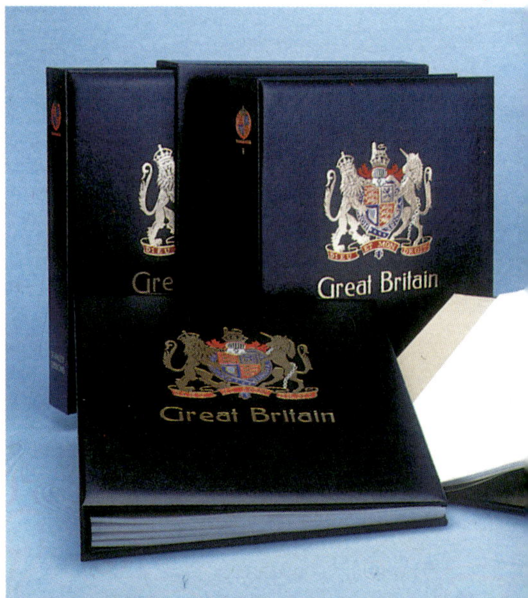

One-country Albums

Many nineteenth-century albums had a printed space for
every stamp. This idea still survives in the form of one-country
albums, for which annual supplements are published. They
are ideal for the collector content with single stamps, although
there are matching blank leaves to cope with pairs, strips,

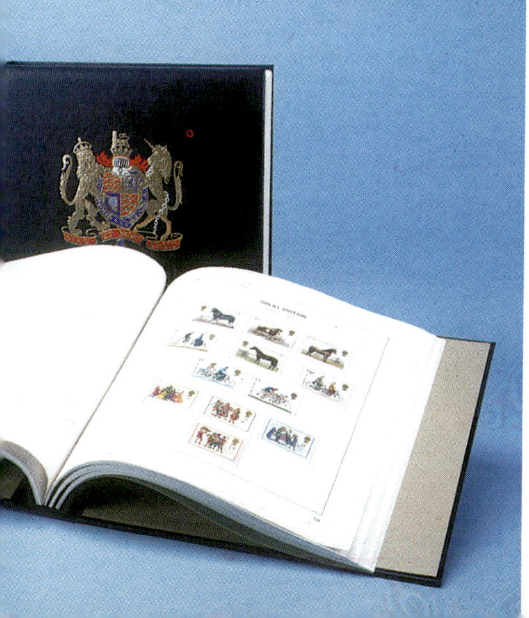

blocks and covers. The main publishers are Schaubek, Ka-Be, Lindner and Michel (Germany), Minkus and Scott (USA), Stanley Gibbons (UK) and Yvert (France). Between them they cover every country in the world.

DISPLAYING STAMPS

If you are using a loose-leaf album with blank pages, rather than a printed album, you will want to lay out the page of stamps in an attractive manner. Do not overcrowd the page but aim for a balanced effect.

FIRST OF ALL, it is a good idea to lay your stamps on the blank page to try to make a layout with maximum eye appeal. It is better to have too few than too many stamps on each page. An ideal number for the average page would be about 20 small-format definitives or 12 to 15 large stamps, or even fewer if they are really big, as many modern stamps are.

If you have 16 stamps, all of the same size and format, it is tempting to take the easy road and lay them out in four rows of four. This may be

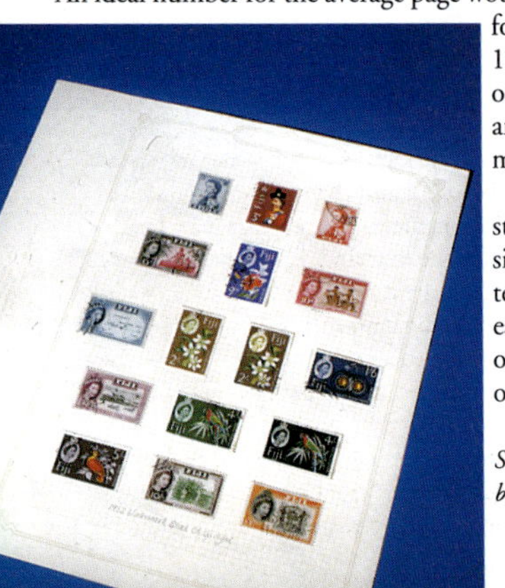

Sample page to show a balanced layout.

symmetrical but it is monotonous. A pyramid layout is more interesting, and permits the easy rearrangement of a row, should additional stamps be issued later on.

A page devoted to several commemorative issues may pose other problems, but it is advisable to group single stamps in the same row, either horizontally or vertically, and allow one or two rows for a set of four or five stamps. You should aim for symmetry as far as possible. Allow a generous space between rows and between each stamp in the same row.

Modern sheets of 10, 12, 16, 20 or even more stamps of different designs side by side can be affixed to the page with transparent photographic mounting corners.

WRITING UP

Opinions vary as to how much annotation is ideal, and it is usually a matter of personal preference. The main thing is not to clutter the page with so much writing that the stamps are swamped.

THE ACTUAL method of annotation varies from person to person, depending on their skill and the neatness of their handwriting. Some collectors prefer copperplate handwriting, while others prefer to print the lettering. A draughtsman's pen or mapping pen and black india ink are the best materials for calligraphy, but an ordinary fountain pen is infinitely better than ballpoint, which is liable to smudge and may affect the stamps. Pencil should be avoided unless the layout is at a transitional stage.

There are various forms of stencil, such as Letraset, which result in a highly professional job though they are relatively expensive to buy and very time-consuming to use.

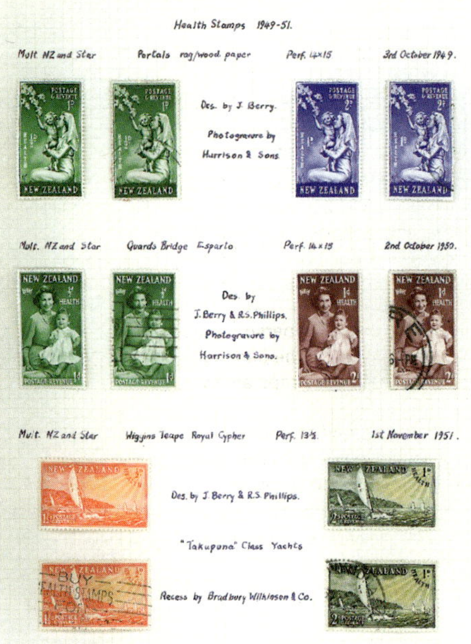

Page from a collection showing the arrangement and annotation of stamps.

Nowadays, however, many collectors use the page-making facilities available in PC software packages and this, combined with laser printing, results in an effect every bit as good as the best printed album pages, yet tailored to individual requirements.

HINGELESS MOUNTING SYSTEMS

THE HAWID STRIP, deriving its name from its inventor, Hans Widemeyer, is a thin plastic strip with an adhesive backing and a transparent 'window'. The stamp is placed inside the strip which can be trimmed to size and affixed to the page. Strips come in many sizes, from 21 mm to 50 mm high and even larger, to accommodate all sizes and shapes of stamps. This system is particularly useful for mint stamps, preserving them in an unmounted mint state.

BUYING AND SELLING STAMPS

While it is possible to collect stamps for little or no outlay, a meaningful collection, likely to appreciate in value, is only possible if some costs are involved. You can purchase stamps from a dealer, bid at auction or buy direct from the philatelic bureau of the issuing country. Most collectors probably use all three methods in varying degrees according to the level of their interest and what they can afford to spend.

Dealers

The number of stamp shops in the high streets of Britain has dwindled sharply in recent years owing to increased overheads. Many dealers now prefer to operate by mail order, or attend the fair circuits which are now immensely popular.

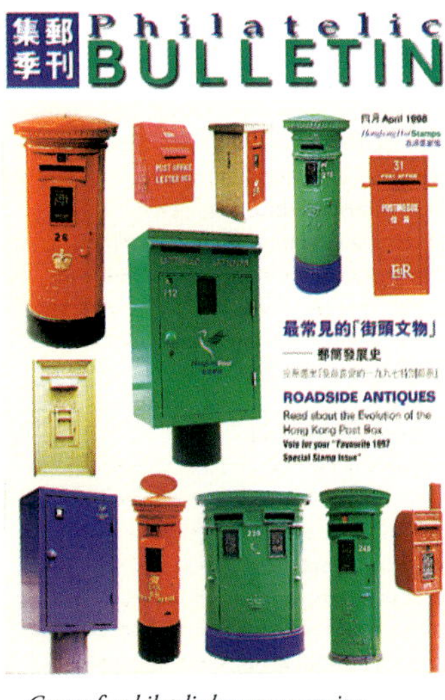

Cover of a philatelic bureau magazine.

In pricing their stock, dealers are influenced to a large extent by the catalogues, such as Gibbons in Britain, Scott in the USA or Michel in Germany. Many British dealers in European stamps, in fact, prefer to use Michel as their guide, with the result that some material may appear more expensive than by Gibbons' standards; but here again the law of supply and demand operates. More details on the use of catalogues is given on p.52.

Remember that a dealer's selling price is also governed by many other factors. This is often overlooked by collectors when they come to sell their stamps and are offered less than they paid for them. A dealer, however, has to discount the majority of the cheaper stamps and bases his offer on the few better items.

Auctions

These offer the best method of purchasing a collection intact as the basis for further expansion. If you attend a stamp auction, go with a firm idea in mind of how far you are prepared to go and do not get carried away. Remember also that most auctioneers now add a buyer's premium of 10–15 per cent, and this can greatly increase the cost. Selling at auction is often preferable to selling direct to a dealer, as dealers are competing with private collectors, and a fairer price should result. Against that, you have to offset the auctioneer's commission and a delay of weeks or months between consigning for sale and the receipt of the cheque in payment.

Direct Purchase

If you are concentrating on the stamps of a few countries, or even a single country, you may prefer to purchase direct from the appropriate philatelic bureau. An enquiry to the General Post Office in the capital city generally elicits a response, outlining the methods of payment and terms of despatch.

Most bureaux these days will accept the major credit cards, which makes purchasing very simple. They also operate a standing order system for subscribers, who automatically receive all new issues in a manner specified by them: whether a set of singles and/or first day covers, maximum cards (picture postcards whose design incorporates that of the stamp and/or postmark, to be fixed on the decorated side), postal stationery, mint or used, or blocks of four and even complete sheets. Bureaux also publish regular newsletters and brochures which often contain background information unavailable in the general stamp magazines. Some even give regular customers free gifts of choice items not available to the general public.

Equipment

As well as a supply of storage and display materials such as mounts and albums, tweezers and some form of magnifier are essential equipment for any collector. In addition, other items have been specifically designed for the enthusiast.

TWEEZERS

STAMPS SHOULD never be handled with the fingers as even the cleanest hands have a tiny film of grease or perspiration which can result in fingerprints adhering to the surface. For this purpose tweezers have been developed and can be purchased from stamp dealers. Do not use the type of tweezers used to pluck eyebrows: many of these have pointed ends which could damage a stamp. Stamp tongs have flattened 'spade' ends which make the safe handling of stamps easy.

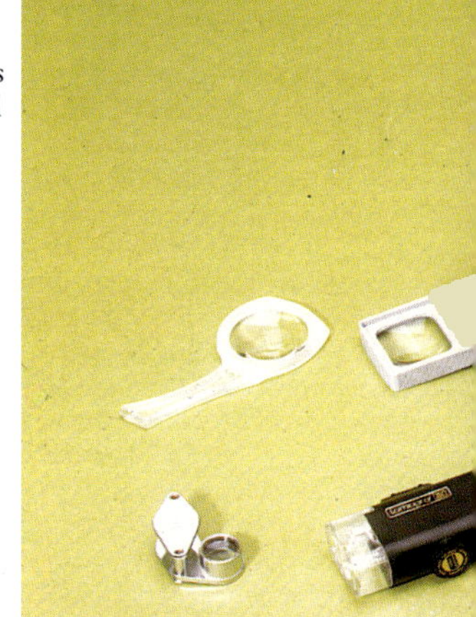

A range of magnifiers.

MAGNIFIERS

FOR THE examination of stamps in great detail some form of magnifier is necessary. These come in all shapes and sizes, from an inexpensive plastic magnifier costing a pound or two to battery-operated illuminated glasses and the highly professional Eschenbach magnifiers with adjustable focus and an accurate measuring scale calibrated in tenths of a millimetre. There are folding magnifiers that can be carried in the purse or pocket and there are magnifiers for highly detailed study which will show up the very fibres of the paper. The better magnifiers, giving up to x 10 magnification, cost in the region of £20–£30.

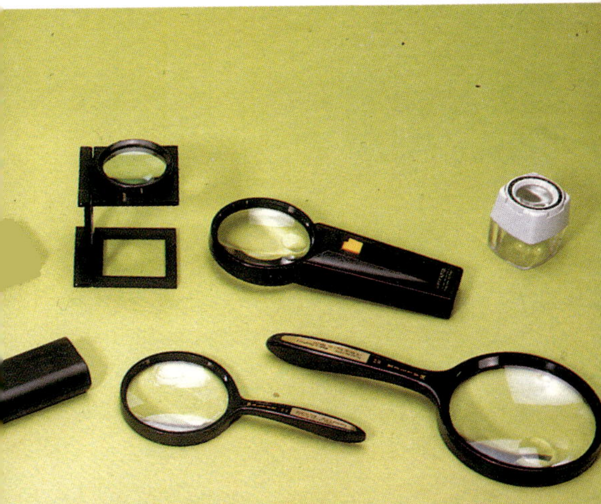

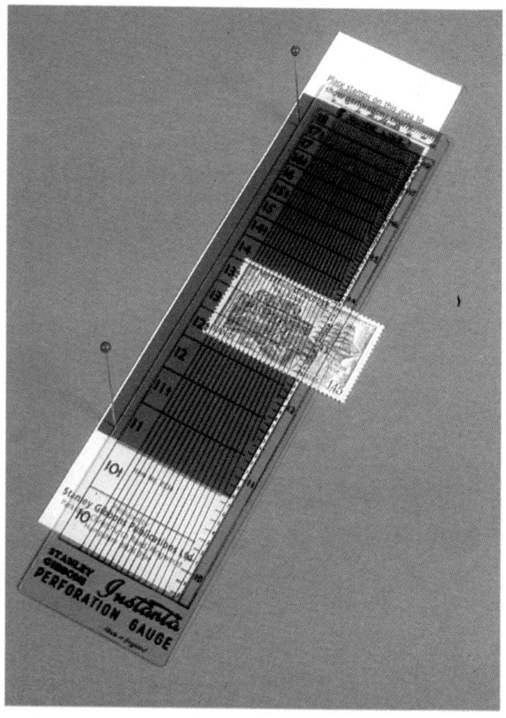

The 'Instanta' perforation gauge.

PERFORATION GAUGES

DR JACQUES-AMABLE Legrand invented the Odontometre, or perforation gauge, in 1862. Suddenly, stamp-collecting became much more scientific as collectors learned to distinguish between apparently similar stamps by their perforations.

Legrand counted the number of holes in a length of 2 cm. Thus a stamp gauging 14 all round would have 14 holes in a length of 2 cm on each side. A stamp gauging 15 x 14 would have 15 holes along the top and bottom and 14 at the sides. Oddly enough, for a scale based on the metric system, Legrand adopted vulgar fractions to denote intermediate gauges, e.g. 13¾ x 12½, and this has survived to the present day, although many collectors now use the decimal system. Modern Australian stamps, for example, usually gauge 13.86 x 14.6.

Similarly, while many perforation gauges continue to have black dots of varying sizes printed on card or white plastic, just as Legrand devised them, more precise gauges in transparent plastic now rely on intersecting lines, permitting measurement to two decimal points.

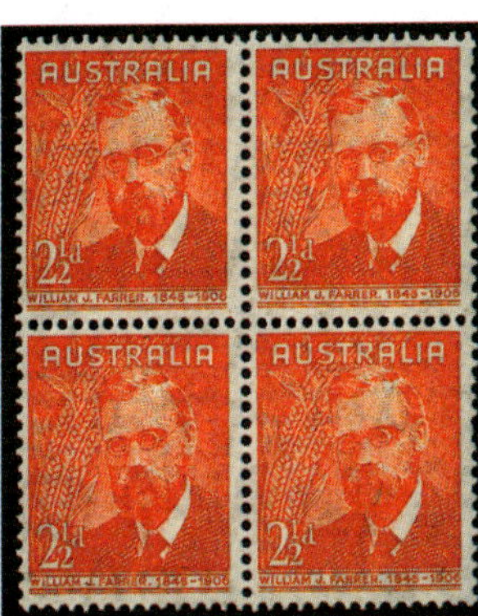

Block of comb-perforated stamps.

WATERMARK DETECTORS

AT THEIR simplest, these are small black metal or plastic trays on which the stamp is laid face down. A drop or two of benzene momentarily renders the stamp transparent, and then the watermark can be seen clearly. Note that children should not handle benzene. More advanced versions are battery-operated with lights and filters and are particularly effective in showing up the watermarks on chalk-surfaced or thick-paper stamps.

COLOUR CHARTS

MOST CATALOGUE publishers produce charts with up to 200 colours and shades, identifying the colours of the stamps in their catalogues. They are useful at an advanced level in distinguishing between subtle shades which indicate different printings of a stamp over a period of months or years.

ULTRAVIOLET LAMPS

ULTRAVIOLET lamps may be battery- or mains-operated, and the best have interchangeable short- and long-wave bulbs. There are hand-held models as well as the larger desk-top versions.

Until the 1950s the UV lamp was used by collectors to detect tampering and faking. For example, a stamp

Ultraviolet lamp.

exposed to ultraviolet light would reveal evidence of cancellation by pen and ink, rubber stamp or postmark, which had been washed off or chemically removed in order to pass the stamp off as an unused specimen. The lamp would also reveal repairs to thins or tears, since the original state of the stamp showed up clearly under the ultraviolet rays.

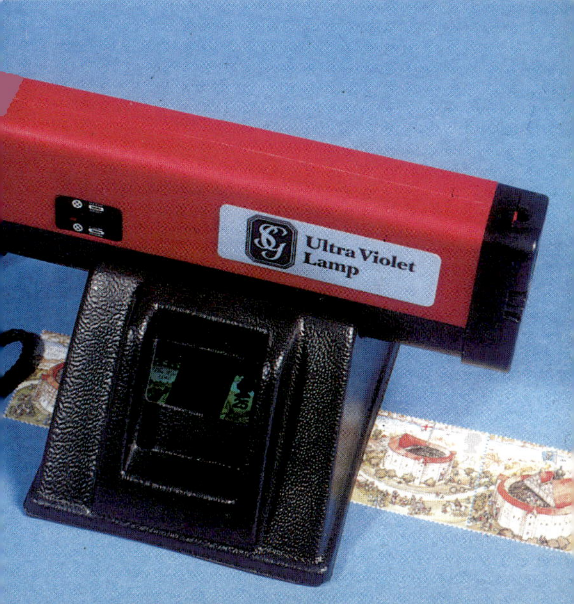

IDENTIFYING STAMPS
Introduction

IT HAS BEEN estimated that, even on a simplified basis (ignoring differences in perforation, watermark, shade and printing process) about 350,000 different stamps have been issued by postal administrations throughout the world since 1840. The annual output is now about 12,000 and is steadily rising from year to year.

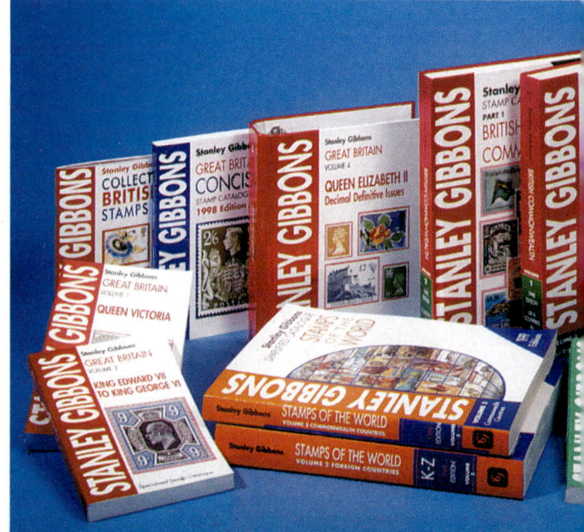

This section deals with the different types of stamp and describes the various ways in which they can be collected. The identification of stamps, whether by the country of issue, the date or even the reason for the issue, relies on the stamp catalogue.

The earliest catalogues, appearing in the 1850s, were merely dealers' price lists, but pioneer collectors, such as Alfred Potiquet and Oscar Berger-Levreult in France and Dr John Gray in Britain, were already at work compiling their own handbooks, from which the highly detailed, well-illustrated catalogues of the present day gradually evolved.

For the general collector Stanley Gibbons' *Stamps of the World* (three volumes) is ideal. Gibbons also publish two paperbacks, *Collect British Stamps* and *The Great Britain Concise Catalogue*, as well as a massive five-volume specialised catalogue devoted to British stamps in the greatest detail. In between come the famous 'red' Gibbons, two large volumes covering the Commonwealth, as well as the 10 'green' volumes (European countries) and 11 'blue' books (rest of the world).

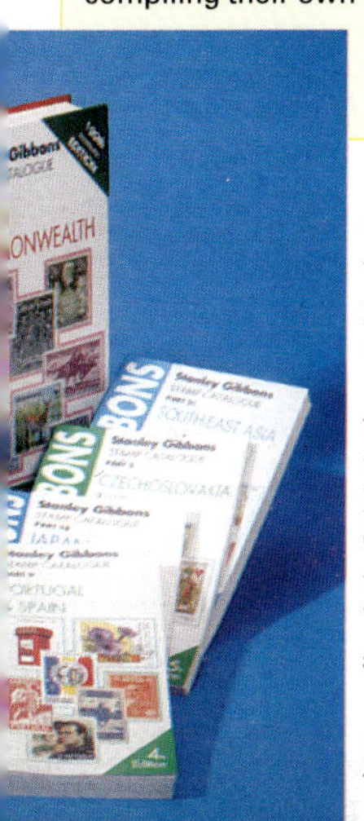

A selection of catalogues ranging from simplified to advanced titles.

Catalogue Prices

CATALOGUES LIST stamps in chronological order, with brief descriptions. Opposite each entry are at least two columns giving prices in mint and used condition. Many catalogues now also include a column for stamps in unmounted mint (never hinged) condition and some even quote prices for stamps on cover. The prices quoted are based on current market values, and represent the price you would expect to pay if you bought from a dealer. Quite often, however, dealers sell the commoner stamps at a discount from the catalogue price. Conversely, the more elusive material may cost well above the catalogue price, if the dealer considers the catalogue to be out of step with the market. These prices are therefore merely a rough guide for dealer and collector alike.

USING THE CATALOGUE

THE MAIN purpose of the catalogue is to identify your stamps so that you can arrange them in your album in the correct order and annotate them properly.

The first step is to identify the country of issue. British stamps do not bear a country name, in deference to Britain having invented stamps, but the UPU requires all other member countries to include an inscription, in the Roman alphabet, denoting the country name. Prior to the 1970s, this was optional, but a key to identification will be found in the Reference Section.

Having found the country, it is then a matter of scanning the pages until you find an appropriate illustration or description of it. The datestamp on a used stamp helps, while the face value of mint stamps may be a clue and you will usually be able to locate the period when that value was the basic letter rate, and thus narrow down the search.

Pages from the Australian section of the Commonwealth 'red' Gibbons catalogue, showing the layout of text and illustrations in three columns. Note the enlargement of details from the ½d kangaroo stamps to show flaws and retouches. Prices are given for stamps in mint and used condition.

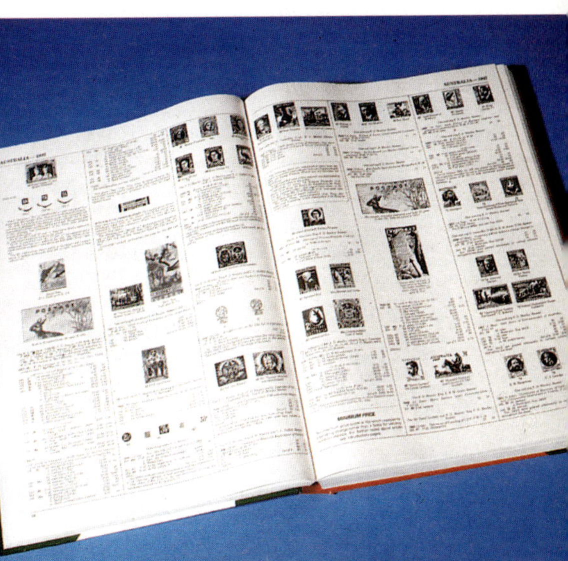

Types of Stamp

In the beginning, there was only one kind of stamp, prepaying the postage on letters. Such stamps, known as permanent or definitive stamps, still form the basis of the current series, but over the years many other kinds of stamp have evolved.

THE IDEA of using adhesive stamps to denote the prepayment of postage spread slowly at first, but by the 1860s these small pieces of paper were in universal use. The size and format of the Penny Black were based on the

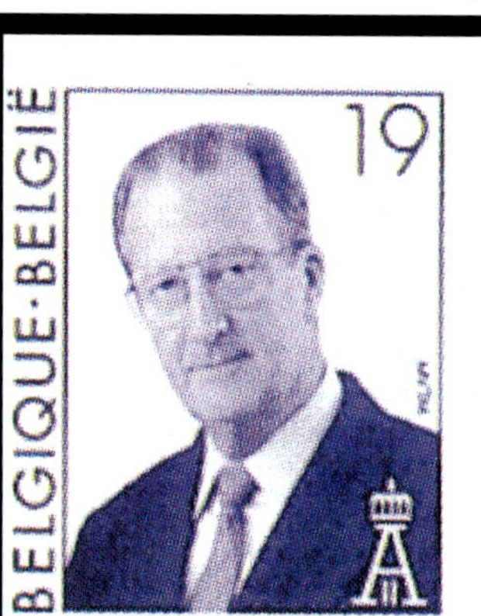

small pieces of paper used to secure the lead staples by which embossed stamps were affixed to parchment legal documents from 1694 onwards, and this has been retained not only by Britain but many other countries right down to the present day.

The first British stamps bore the profile of Queen Victoria, and this convention was adopted by many other monarchies. Britain has adhered to this convention since 1840; the Machin series (see p.122) since 1967 has consciously gone back to the simplicity of the Penny Black. Royal portraiture is also favoured by Spain and the Scandinavian countries, though often combined with numeral or armorial designs.

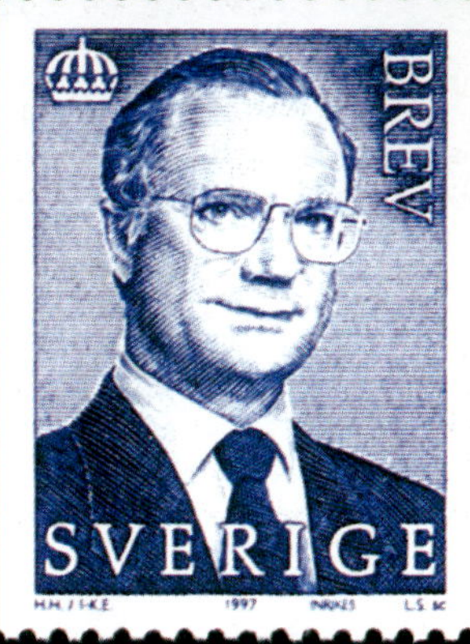

France and Switzerland chose heraldry or allegory, and this set the pattern for other republics. National emblems and heraldic shields are other alternatives which have been widely used. This genre has also been used effectively by Jersey in recent years, depicting the arms of the 12 parishes in full colour.

The USA opted for portraits of Benjamin Franklin (first Postmaster General) and George Washington and to this day famous Americans provide abundant subject matter. In the late 1930s there was even the Presidential Series in which every denomination, in 1-cent stages from 1c to 25c, portrayed the first 25 presidents.

Portrait definitive stamps of Belgium and Sweden.

Definitive Designs

PICTORIALISM crept in around the turn of the century, with New Zealand, Tasmania and the Latin American republics setting the trend. At the same time many of these stamps became larger; hitherto a larger format was mainly reserved for the higher values. Britain's sole concession to pictorial definitives has consisted of the 2s 6d and 5s stamps of 1951 and the Castle high values since 1955.

At the turn of the century the majority of colonies and protectorates made use of standard keyplate designs, only the country name and denomination being distinctive. This system was used not only in the British Empire but also in the French, German, Portuguese and Spanish empires. A reaction to the monotony of these stamps was the growth of pictorialism

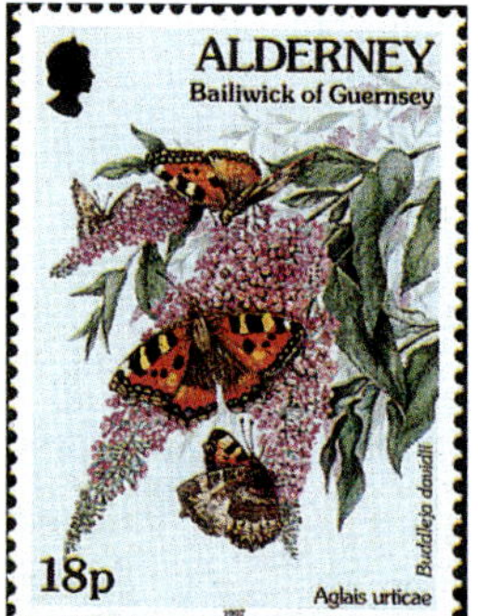

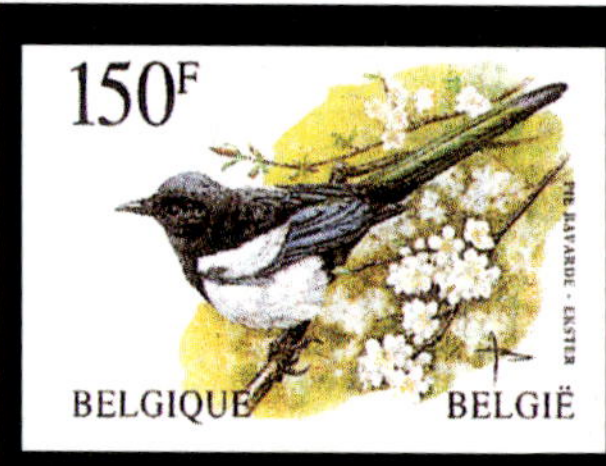

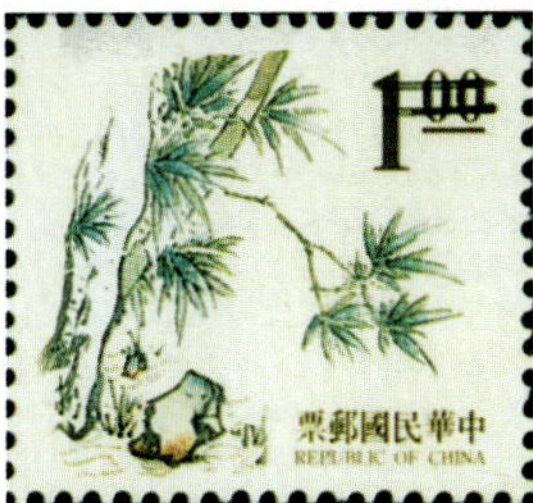

in the late 1920s and 1930s, often tastefully engraved with frames and vignettes in contrasting colours.

The smaller countries of Europe also appreciated the advantage of pictorial designs, and it is significant that the most attractive definitives in the prewar period came from Andorra, Liechtenstein, Monaco and San Marino. Today, both Germany and Russia prove that pictorial designs are possible in a small format.

Nowadays the most conservative countries are the Scandinavian group whose definitives include a high proportion of royal portraits and allegorical or numeral motifs. Denmark currently uses a numeral design introduced in 1933 and an armorial type dating from 1946, but Norway's Posthorn design has been in continuous use since 1871. Sudan (1898–1951), Ireland (1922–68) and Tonga (1897–1953) also had long-running definitive designs.

Pictorial definitive stamps of Alderney, Belgium, Taiwan and Germany.

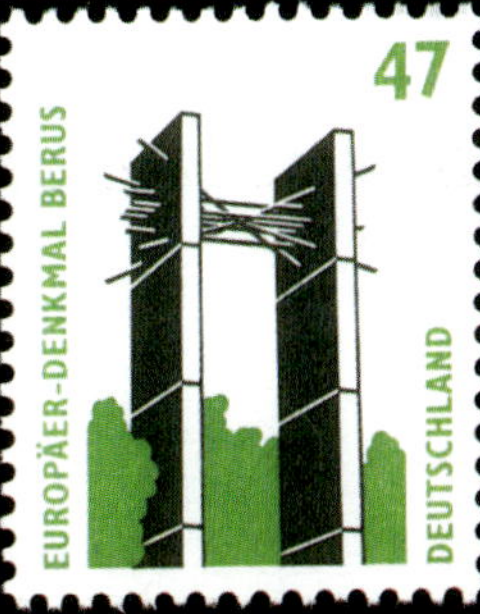

Commemorative Stamps

A commemorative stamp is one that is issued to mark a historic anniversary or personality, or to publicise a current event. Such stamps are generally on sale only for a brief period.

THE IDEA of using stamps to celebrate an anniversary arose in 1876 when the USA issued stamped envelopes to mark the centenary of the Declaration of Independence. In 1887 a local post in Germany issued a stamp to celebrate a shooting contest and the following year New South Wales released a long series inscribed 100 YEARS to mark the centenary of the colony. Hong Kong overprinted 2c stamps (1891) to celebrate the Golden Jubilee of the British colony, and Montenegro overprinted its definitives (1893) to mark the quatercentenary of printing in that country. The first commemoratives in America were issued in 1892–93 to celebrate the 400th anniversary of the first voyage of discovery by Columbus. Africa's first commemorative appeared in 1895, when the Transvaal marked the

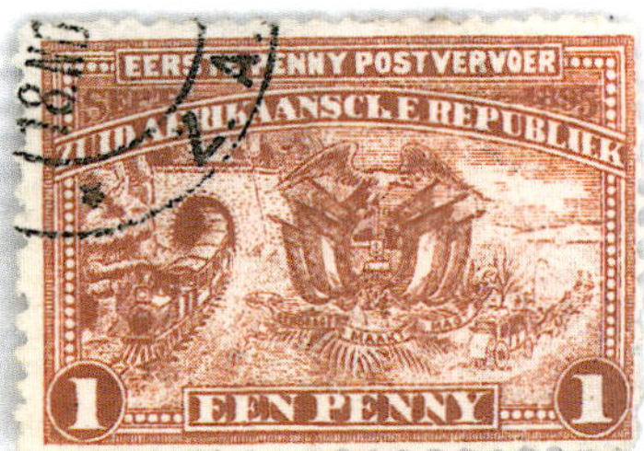

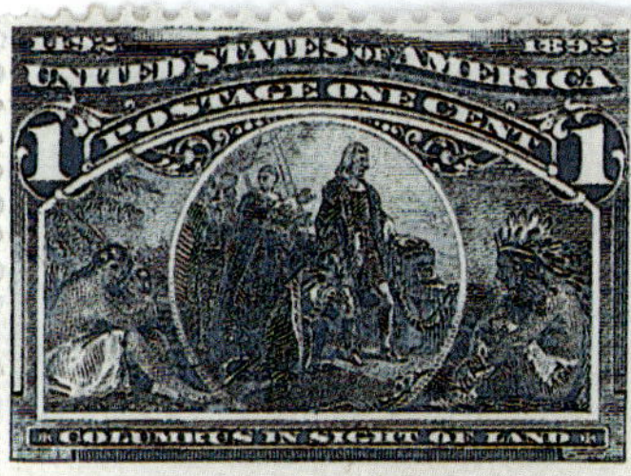

introduction of penny postage.

By the beginning of the twentieth century the concept of commemorative stamps was quite well established. Although Britain issued commemorative stationery in 1890 for the Jubilee of Penny Postage, it was not till 1924 that the first adhesive stamps appeared. Although German private posts (1887–1900) issued many commemoratives, Germany itself did not do so until 1919. France's first appeared in 1923.

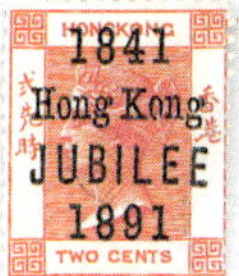

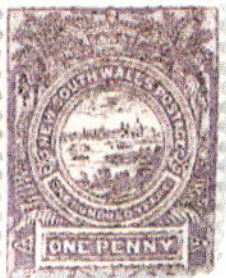

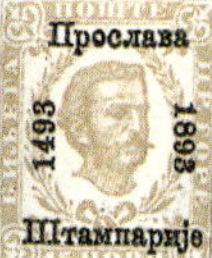

The world's first commemoratives: Transvaal, Africa (1895); USA Columbus (1893); Hong Kong Jubilee (1891); New South Wales, Australia (1888) and Montenegro (1893).

Omnibus Issues

IN 1898, Portugal and her colonies issued stamps in uniform designs to mark the 400th anniversary of Vasco da Gama's discovery of the sea route to India. Known to collectors as an omnibus issue, this practice did not spread to other areas until 1931 when France publicised the Paris Colonial Exhibition in this way. France repeated the exercise with colonial issues marking the International Exposition in Paris (1937) and the New York World's Fair (1939).

The British colonies, whose stamps were produced under the aegis of the Crown Agents, released an omnibus issue in 1935 for the Silver Jubilee of King George V and followed this with the Coronation issue in 1937. From then until 1965 colonial omnibus issues in identical designs became increasingly frequent, but declining sales forced the Crown Agents to rethink their policy. As a result, the pattern since then has been to use distinctive designs for each set, even if released for a common purpose with an underlying theme. Thus recent issues marking the

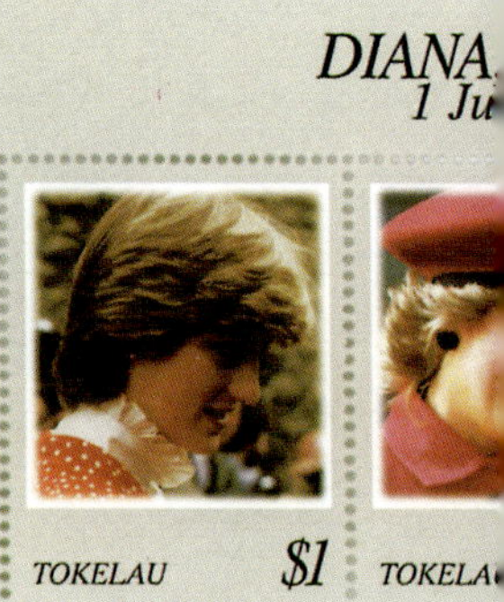

80th anniversary of the RAF have consisted of four stamps and a miniature sheet of four, showing different aircraft, the whole building into a veritable gallery of aviation. The memorial omnibus issues for Diana, Princess of Wales, have likewise opted for a wide range of different photographs.

Omnibus issues now loosely encompass stamps by many countries for the same anniversary, such as the centenary of the Universal Postal Union (1974), or a UN-sponsored event such as the International Year of the Ocean (1998).

Diana miniature sheet, Tokelau Islands, 1998.

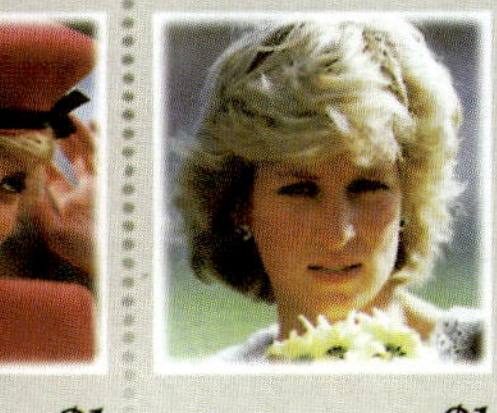
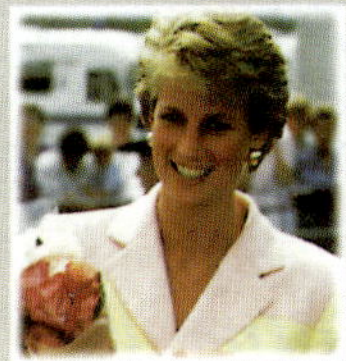

Special Issues

A MODERN tendency is to issue short pictorial sets from time to time without the pretext of an anniversary or current event. This policy was adopted by Britain in the 1960s as a means of catching up with the rest of the world which had used the medium of commemoratives to promote a national image or to educate people about a country's achievements.

As a rule, there is some commemorative element, however tenuous, but the main intention is to provide a range of material for the thematic collector. Thus the tercentenary of Winstanley's Tower was the excuse for a set of five stamps depicting British lighthouses and the centenary of the death of Lewis Carroll the occasion for five stamps devoted to scenes and characters from children's literature.

Special issues are also produced for seasonal occasions, such as Christmas and Easter, to which, in recent years, have been added stamps for St Valentine's Day and even the Chinese New Year (including issues as far afield as New Zealand, Jersey and the Isle of Man).

Christmas and St Valentine's Day have also inspired the release of stamps for general use on greetings cards. Stamps of this kind, specifically inscribed 'Happy Birthday',

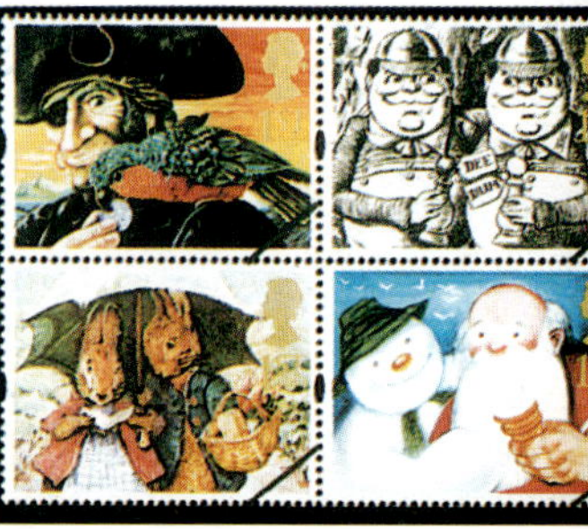

'Write Soon', or 'Congratulations' have been issued by the USA, Ireland, Israel and New Zealand, whereas Britain's stamps, issued in booklets of 10, tend towards a theme such as smiles, lovers, nostalgia and good luck symbols.

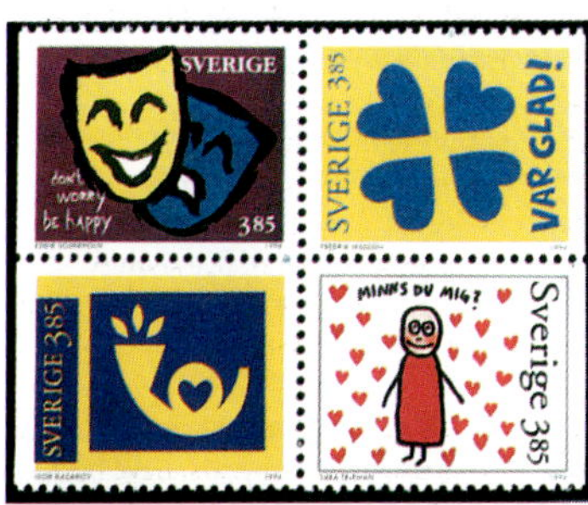

Greetings stamps of Sweden and Great Britain.

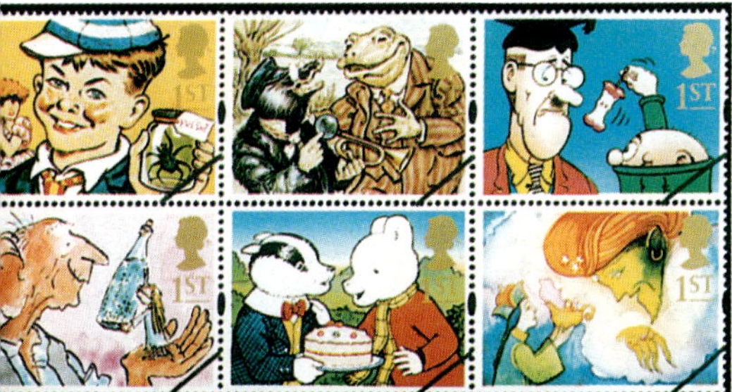

Joint Issues

Stamps issued by two or more countries acting jointly, and often using similar designs, differ from omnibus issues in being produced by independent states not tied by colonial affiliations.

JOINT ISSUES originated in the late 1930s when the countries of the Little Entente and the Balkan Entente issued stamps simultaneously, although the designs tended to have little in common. In the postwar period political alignments inspired an extension of this concept under the generic name of Europa issues.

Since 1956 stamps inscribed EUROPA have been issued each year. At first they were confined to the countries of the European Coal and Steel Community, but in 1960 the concept was taken over by the

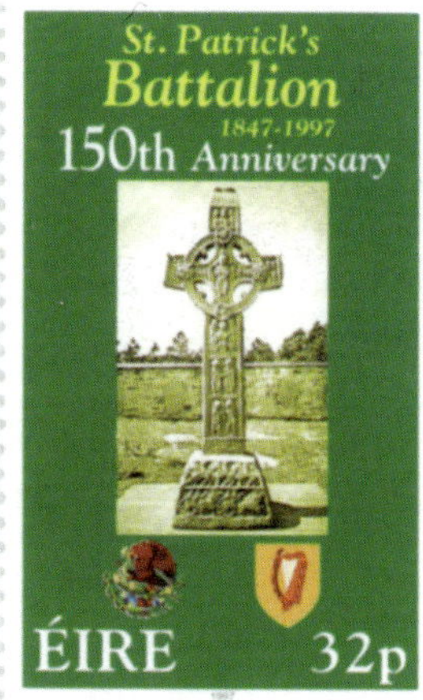

European Conference of Posts and Telecommunications (CEPT). More or less uniform designs were used until 1974 but since then a common theme, interpreted widely, has been adopted. The organisation, renamed PostEurop, now embraces *all* European postal administrations.

Similar issues are made by the Scandinavian countries (Norden) and by Spain and the American countries (UPAEP or Espamer). There have also been numerous joint issues since 1959, involving two or more countries celebrating a common event or personality. The first was an issue by Canada and the USA marking the opening of the St Lawrence Seaway. In 1965, Romania and Yugoslavia issued identical stamps with both country names and denominations, and this has since been followed by Italy and San Marino (1996) and Switzerland and Liechtenstein (1997).

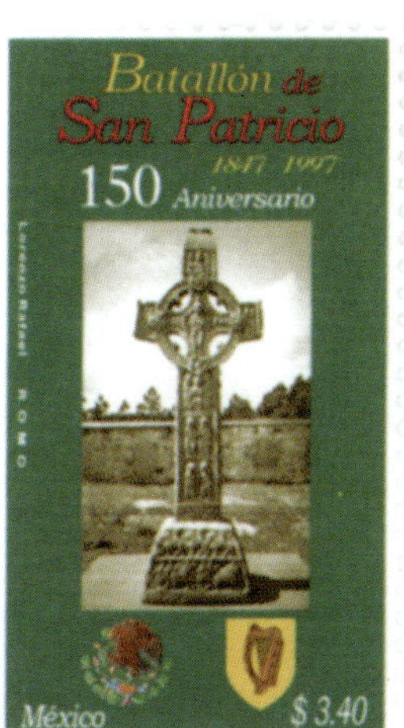

Joint issues from Mexico and Ireland for the St Patrick's Battalion, 1997.

Charity Stamps

Known in the USA as semi-postals, charity stamps are stamps bearing a premium over postal value, the additional sum going to charity, sometimes in general though more usually for a specific good cause.

THE CONCEPT of charity stamps originated in Britain in 1890 when a pictorial envelope celebrating the Jubilee of Penny Postage was sold for 1s but only represented postal duty of 1d, the remaining 11d being given to the Rowland Hill Benevolent Fund for Post Office Widows and Orphans. At the time of Queen Victoria's Diamond Jubilee (1897) labels were produced for the Prince of Wales' hospital charity. These had no postal validity, but the idea was taken up by New South Wales and Victoria, each of which issued 1d and 2 ½d stamps sold at 12 times face value (i.e. 1s and 2s 6d), the massive premium going to charity.

The idea spread to Europe in the 1900s, with both Romania and Russia issuing stamps with a modest charity surcharge. Austria, Belgium, France and Switzerland were prolific issuers of such stamps, while virtually every stamp from Nazi Germany in 1938–40 bore an enormous premium in aid of Hitler's Culture Fund. The practice has moderated in more recent years and the UPU has tried to curb excessive premiums. Britain has only issued such stamps twice (1975 and 1989) and Canada three times (1974–76), while the USA's first semi-postal was issued on 13 August 1998 to raise funds for breast cancer research.

Swiss Pro Juventute *and* Pro Patria *stamps.*

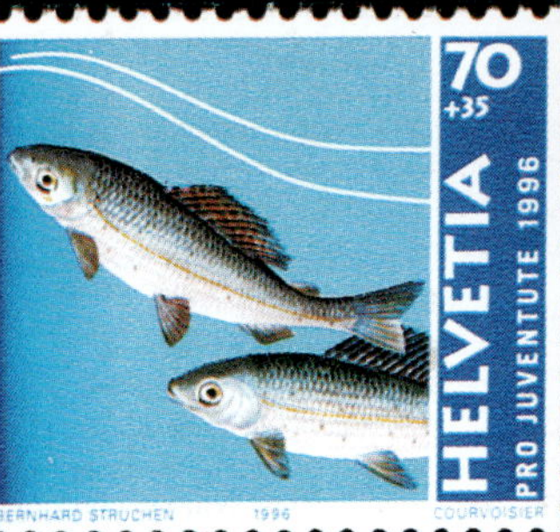
70
+35
HELVETIA
PRO JUVENTUTE 1996
BERNHARD STRUCHEN
1996
COURVOISIER

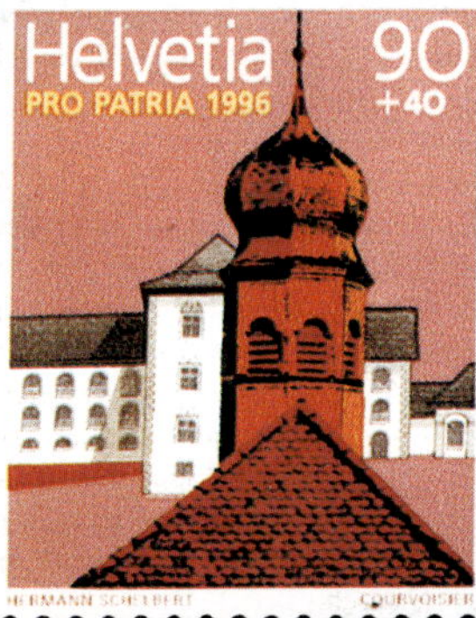
Helvetia
90
PRO PATRIA 1996
+40
HERMANN SCHELBERT
COURVOISIER

ANNUAL CHARITY ISSUES

Charity stamps can be divided into groups and some of these have a large following, despite the fact that their postal value is only part of the price which has been paid to acquire them. These are annual issues of long standing and it is even possible to form specialised collections devoted entirely to them.

FIRST IN this field are the children's charity stamps issued by Switzerland since 1913. Known to collectors as *Pro Juventute* (from their Latin inscription meaning 'on behalf of youth') they began modestly with a single stamp but over the years have expanded to sets of four or five, generally with an overall theme. Inspired by the success of the youth stamps, Switzerland later began issuing annual stamps for national charities, under the banner of *Pro Patria* (meaning 'for the fatherland').

The Swiss set the pattern for other countries. The Benelux countries issue children's stamps around Christmastime and a more general charity issue at midsummer. Germany issues stamps inscribed *Wohlfahrstmarke* (welfare stamp), *Weihnachtsmarke* (Christmas stamp) or *Jugendmarke* (youth stamp) with charity premiums and a wide range of themes.

France and Finland have issued Red Cross stamps since 1914 and 1930 respectively. One of the most popular series comprises the Children's Health stamps issued by New Zealand since 1929, showing all aspects of children's activities and numerous portraits of young Royals.

Portugal and Yugoslavia have had charity stamps whose use was compulsory on all mail on certain days. They even issued special postage-due labels to surcharge uncharitable mail which did not observe this rule!

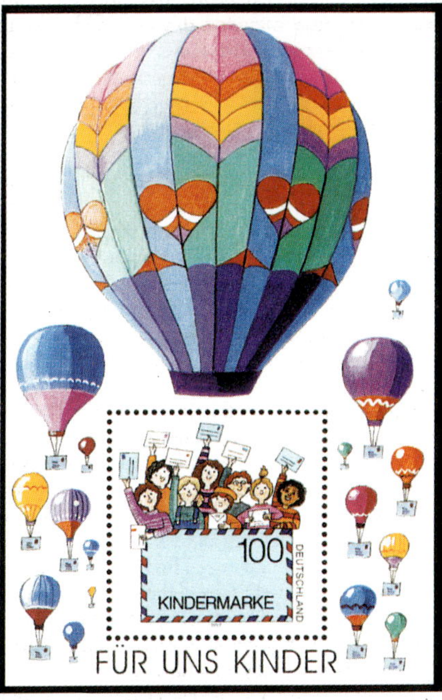

Germany: Kindermarke *miniature sheet.*

Airmail Stamps

Sending mail by air dates back to the balloon flights from Paris when it was under siege in 1870. Mail flights by heavier-than-air machines began in the early 1900s but were in the nature of stunts. Various labels and semi-official stamps, postmarks and souvenir postcards were produced and are now highly prized as airmail forerunners.

EXPERIMENTAL mail flights took place in Italy (1910), India, Britain and the USA (1911), and during the siege of Przemysl in Poland (1915) letters and cards were flown out by

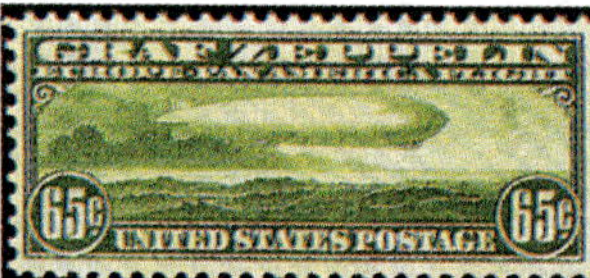

military aircraft. Italy established the world's first regular airmail service between Rome and Turin in 1917 and stamps overprinted for this purpose are regarded as the world's first official airmail issue.

Many of the air stamps up to the late 1920s were semi-official and of limited validity, or were entirely unofficial, being

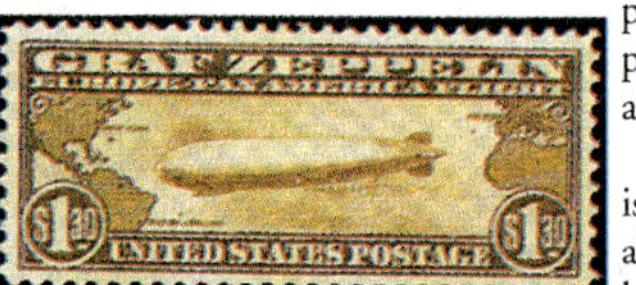

produced by the promoters of private air services.

In 1918 the USA issued a set of three airmail stamps. Austria had an overprinted series the same year and Germany released a distinctive pair in 1919. In many countries specific stamps were confined to airmail. In Britain

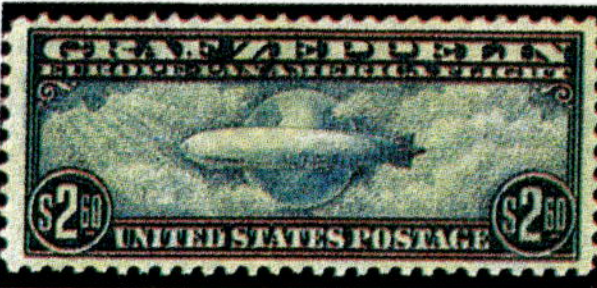

certain denominations were intended for airmail rates, but were never specifically inscribed for that purpose.

With the advent of 'all-up' airmail services distinctive airmail stamps tended to die out, although their place has been taken since the 1940s by aerogrammes.

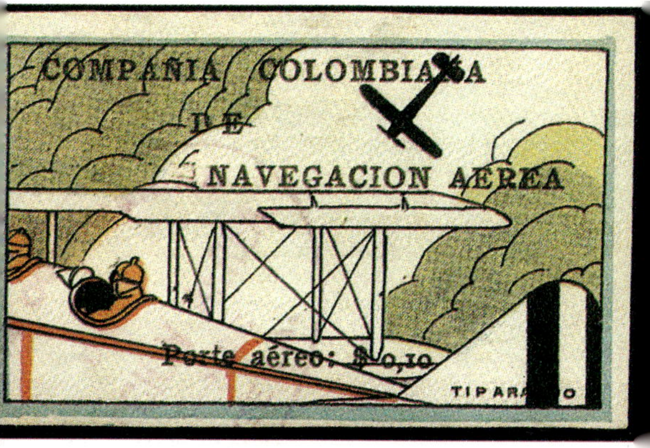

Air stamps: US Graf Zeppelin *set, 1930 (left and top) and Colombia, 1920 (above).*

INTERNAL AIRMAILS

THE GREATEST use of airmail stamps today is in those countries which, because of their size, rely on airmail as a quicker but more expensive way of conveying mail from one

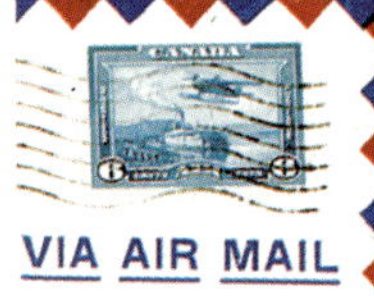

part to another. Canada, the USA, Mexico, Chile and Colombia all have a long history of special stamps for internal airmails, though Canada has dropped this practice in recent years.

Chile issued stamps inscribed CORREO AEREO CHILE for use on external airmails, and similar designs inscribed CORREOS DE CHILE LINEA AEREA NACIONAL (Posts of Chile, National Air Line) for internal airmails. Best-known of the internal air stamps were those issued by a company with the lengthy title of *Sociedad Colombo-Alemana de Transportes Aereos* (Colombian-German Society for Air Transport), usually known from its initials as SCADTA. The company eventually operated external services as well, and issued stamps overprinted with the initials of the destinations, e.g. EU (*Estados Unidos*, USA), A (*Alemana*, Germany) or E (*España*, Spain).

SPECIAL FLIGHTS

STAMPS, postmarks, covers and postcards have been produced for the inauguration of air routes, as well as some of the great pioneering flights across the Atlantic, Pacific and around the world.

There have also been distinctive stamps and covers for mail carried by helicopters, rockets and even by carrier pigeon. Gliders, balloons, parachutes and man-powered flight have had their quota of airmail mementoes.

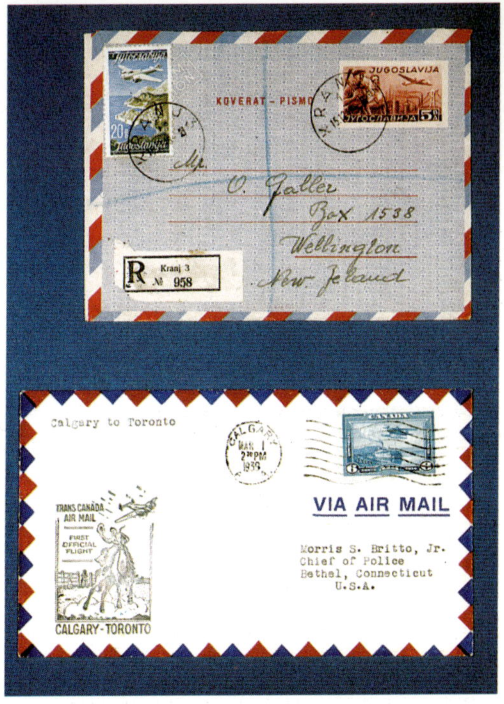

Top: airmail cover from Yugoslavia to New Zealand; bottom: first flight cover from Canada showing an internal 6c airmail stamp and souvenir cachet.

Stamps for Special Purposes

Collectors term them 'end of book' stamps because many catalogues group them at the end of the main country listing. They are stamps whose use is restricted in some way.

POSTAGE DUE AND TO PAY LABELS

STRICTLY SPEAKING these are not stamps at all, but accountancy labels, denoting a charge for underpaid postage or customs duty to be recovered from the addressee. They were introduced by France in 1859. Britain did not adopt them until 1914. Changes in surcharging mail has caused the use of such labels largely to die out.

Because they were purely internal there was no need to express the country name and they can often be identified only by their inscriptions:

A Payer or *A Percevoir* France or French colonies

Bajar Porto Indonesia

Chiffre Taxe France

Deficit Spain or Spanish colonies

Doplata Poland

Doplatit or *Doplatne* Czechoslovakia

Franqueo Deficiente Latin America

Losen Sweden

Multa Portugal

Multada Spanish-speaking countries

Porteado Portugal and colonies

Porto Denmark, Hungary, Yugoslavia and German-speaking countries

Portzegel Netherlands

Postas le n'ioc Ireland

Recouvrement France or Monaco

Segnatasse Italy

Sobreporte or *Sobretasse* Spanish-
   speaking countries
Taxe France
Takca Bulgaria
Takse Albania

Taxa da Plata Romania
Te Betaal South Africa
Te Betalen Belgium or Holland
Vom Empfanger Einzuziehen
   Danzig

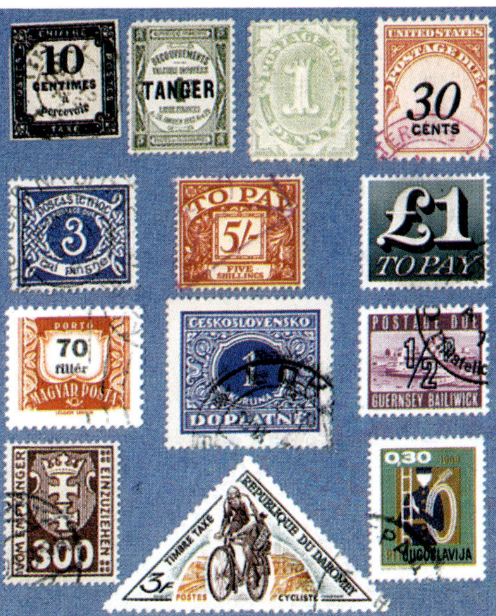

Spread of postage-due stamps.

Stamps have also been issued at one time or another for a number of different purposes, in cases where it was desirable to separate the different services for accountancy reasons. Below are summarised the principal categories, together with inscriptions which help to identify their country of origin.

Newspapers and journals USA, Austria (*Zeitungsmarke*), France (*Journaux*), Italy (*Giornali*), New Zealand and Portugal (*Jornaes*). Czechoslovakia had some stamps inscribed *Noviny*, but others were distinguished only by their designs. The same country also overprinted stamps O.T. (*Obchodni Tiskovina*) for use on commercial printed matter.

Parcels Belgium (*Postcollo* or *Colis Postal*), Bulgaria (*Koletni Pratki*), Mexico (*Buitos*), Italy and San Marino (*Pacchi Postali*) and the USA. Uruguay had an extensive series, including some inscribed *Encomiendas de Granja* (agricultural produce).

Special or Express Delivery Canada, Italy (*Espresso*), Latin American countries (*Entrega inmediata*), Spain (*Urgente*), Colombia (*Extra Rapido*) and the USA (Special Handling).

Registered Mail Canada, Liberia and Colombia. Montenegro and some Latin American countries had stamps inscribed AR (advice of delivery), while Colombia had stamps inscribed A (*Anotado*) and R (*Registro*) respectively, covering the registration fee and notification of delivery.

Official Mail Britain, Argentina, Australia, Canada, Norway (*Offentlig Sak*) and USA. New Zealand's Government Life Insurance Department had its own stamps (1891–1989).

Miscellaneous The Netherlands had marine insurance stamps, letters thus franked being carried in unsinkable safes aboard ship. Stamps for pneumatic post, late fee and personal delivery were issued by Italy, Colombia and Czechoslovakia respectively.

Examples of special-purpose stamps.

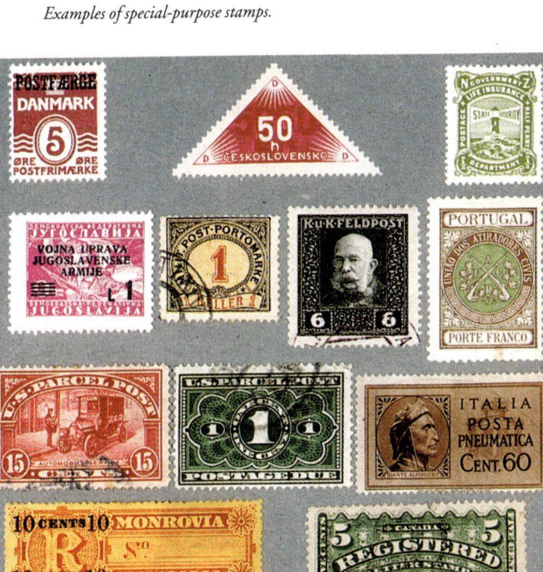

Booklets

The idea of issuing stamps in booklets that would fit
into the wallet or purse was considered by Britain in
1878, but not adopted until 1904. The first booklets
were issued by Luxembourg in 1894 and the practice
is now in universal use.

GERMANY, Belgium, France, the USA and Canada were
among the early users of booklets. Britain delayed their
introduction on grounds of cost and when they were eventually
adopted each booklet contained 2s-worth of stamps but was
sold for an extra ½d. As this proved unpopular the price was
reduced to 2s and the cost of the booklet itself was covered by
replacing one of the ½d stamps with a label bearing a St
Andrew's cross.

Soon, however, postal administrations realised that they
could sell the space on the covers and the pages of interleaving
to commercial advertisers. This proved a lucrative business that
more than covered the cost of producing the booklets.

This advertising matter extends to the panes of stamps
themselves, when non-postal labels are included to make up
the pane without creating an awkward value. In some countries
the outer margins of the panes carry tiny advertisements.

Booklets are produced from special printings of stamps, the
panes of four or six often arranged upside down in relation to
each other. Miscut panes often give rise to *tête-bêche* pairs.
Stamps with inverted watermarks or straight edges often came
from booklets. Stamps of different denominations are often
printed *se-tenant* (side by side) and as an alternative to an

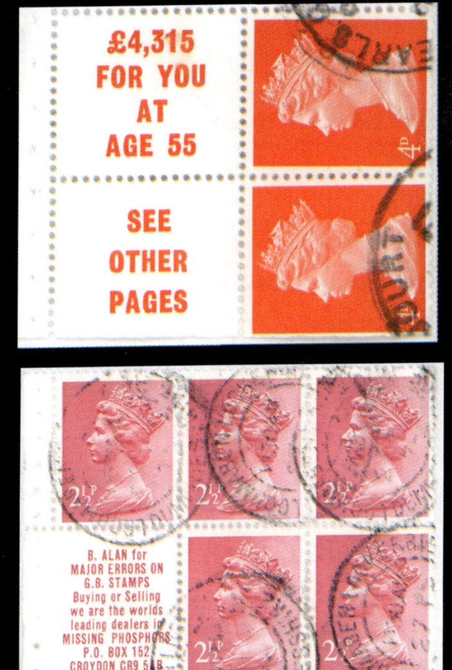

British booklet panes with advertising labels se-tenant.

advertising label some countries favour a label with a diagonal cross or some other ornament, to prevent the perforated paper being used for forging stamps.

FOLDED BOOKLETS

THE EARLIEST booklets had separate back and front covers, stitched together to hold the panes and interleaves. In 1920 Sweden pioneered folded booklets, in which the panes of stamps were simply affixed to the inner side of the cover by the

Pictorial cover of Singapore 'Fragile Forest' stamp booklet.

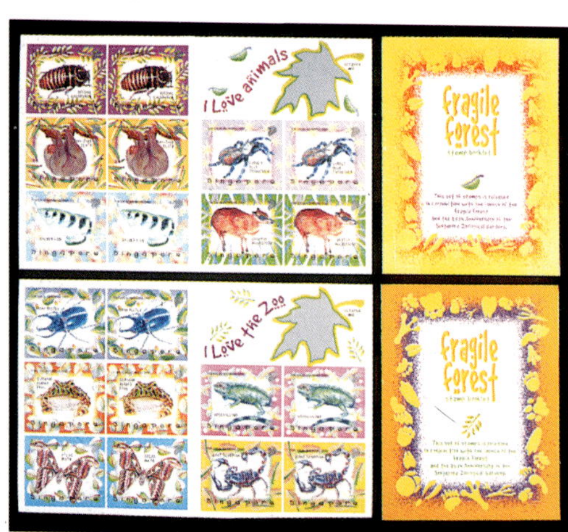

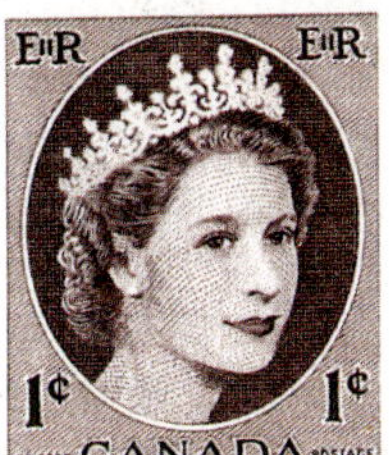
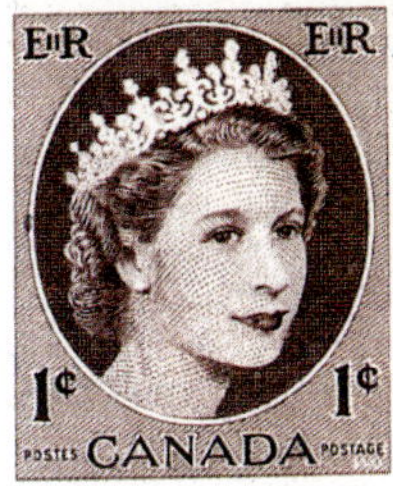
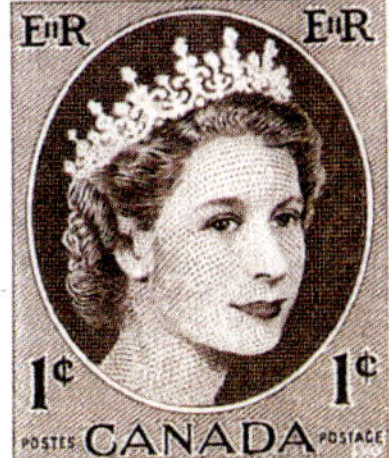

Canadian booklet panes with advertising labels se-tenant.

gummed margin, and then folded over. This concept gradually spread to other countries and is now standard, especially for vending machines and retail outlets. Many special issues of a thematic nature are now released in booklet form, notably in Canada, Finland and the USA.

PRESTIGE BOOKLETS

PRESTIGE booklets, pioneered by Britain in 1969, developed booklets with advertising generated by a single sponsor. They are larger than normal, with panes of up to nine stamps (often in *se-tenant* combinations) attached to descriptive panels and having pages with text and illustrations in between. The concept is now used by many other countries.

Booklet cover: British Greetings stamps (Children's Literature, 1993).

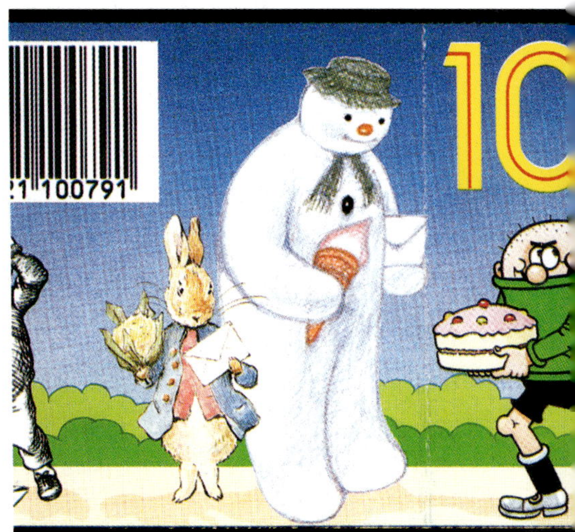

GREETINGS BOOKLETS

BOOKLETS containing a pane of different stamps with various conventional greetings were pioneered by the USA in 1987. They were adopted by Britain in 1990 and have since spread to Ireland, New Zealand and Israel, usually with greetings labels to match. Canada (1994) pioneered greetings booklets in which the stamps could be individually customised with self-adhesive circular labels.

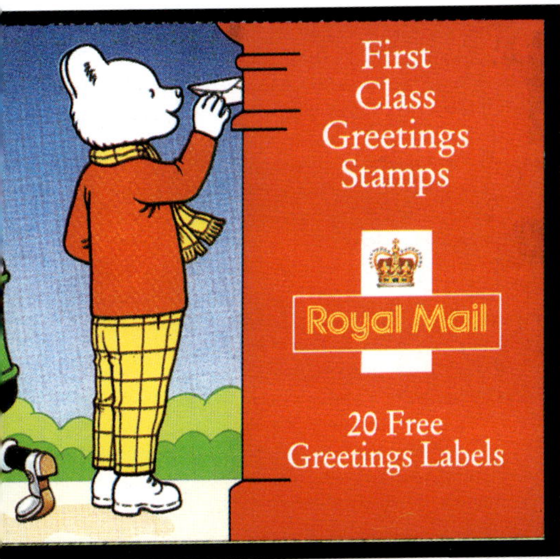

Coils and Automatic Stamps

Stamps in a continuous roll were designed for use in coin-operated slot machines or mailroom dispensers. The earliest coils were produced from strips of stamps taken from sheets, a portion of the sheet margin being used to join one strip to the next. Coil-join pairs are much sought after by philatelists.

A LATER DEVELOPMENT was to print stamps in continuous coils of several hundred stamps. British coil stamps were perforated on all four sides, but individual stamps can be recognised by their sideways watermark. In most countries, however, coils are, or were, imperforate on the outer edges and often serially numbered on the back of every tenth stamp. As coils were best suited to small-format definitives some countries, such as Austria, Gibraltar and New Zealand, which normally have large pictorial definitives, had to introduce small-format stamps specifically for slot machines.

Nowadays many countries issue packs of self-adhesive stamps in rolls of 100 – easier to handle and more hygienic than the traditional 'lick and stick' variety.

Coil stamps in coin-operated machines have largely been replaced by automatic stamps, pioneered by Frama of Switzerland in the 1970s. These dispense a preprinted label with the value added by the customer, using a key-pad. Originally prosaic, they are often quite colourful, especially the stamps manufactured by the Klussendorf company (Germany).

Automatic stamps from Switzerland and Portugal.

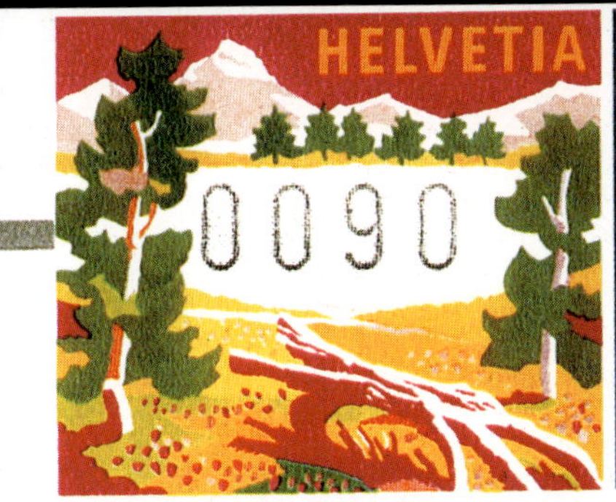
HELVETIA
0090

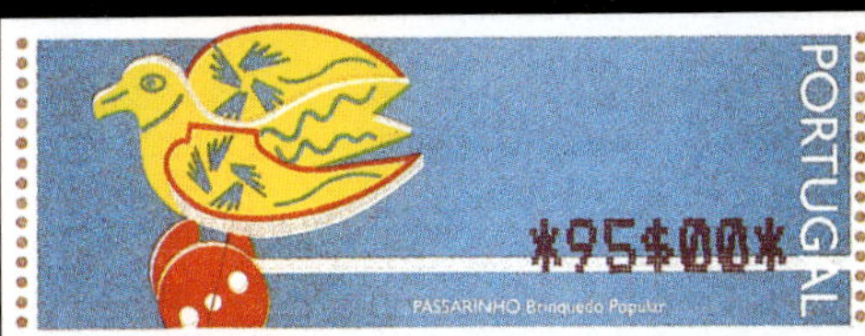
PORTUGAL
95$00
PASSARINHO Brinquedo Popular

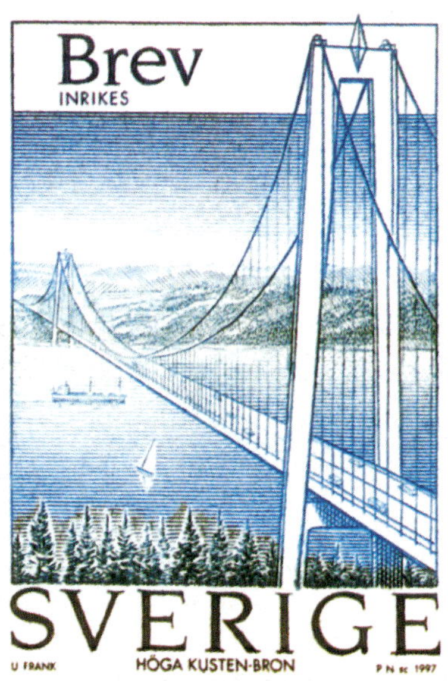

Brev
INRIKES
SVERIGE
U FRANX
HÖGA KUSTEN-BRON
P N sc 1997

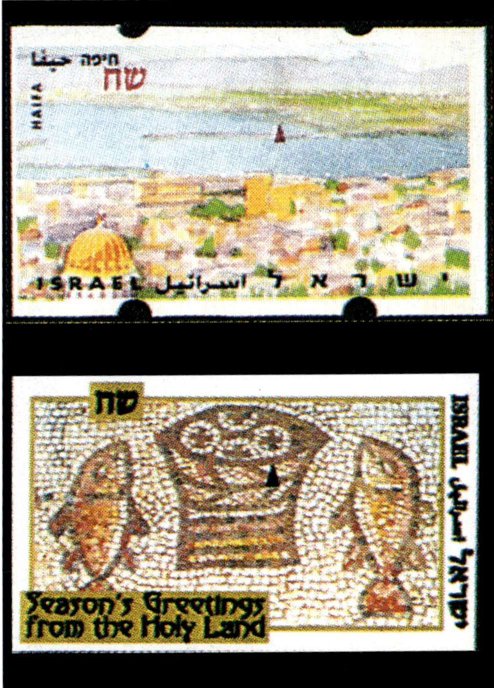

Left: Swedish coil stamp; above: automatic stamps from Israel.

Miniature Sheets
and Composite Stamps

Conventional sheets of stamps may contain 50, 100, 240 or some other large multiple. A miniature sheet, on the other hand, may contain a single stamp, a pair, strip or block of four.

A S MINIATURE sheets increase in size, and conventional sheets decrease (as few as 10 stamps is now the norm in Germany and Holland), the distinction tends to become blurred, especially as the small sheets from these countries often have decorative margins, with a view to encouraging philatelists to collect entire sheets rather than single stamps.

Miniature sheets containing a single stamp, with plain sheet margins, originated in Luxembourg in 1923. In the early period definitive stamps, sometimes in pairs or blocks of four, were issued in this form as souvenirs of philatelic exhibitions. In the postwar period these sheets became increasingly decorative, the motif of the stamp often being projected into the sheet margins.

Composite strips of definitive stamps were produced as coils for slot machines, but in more recent years this concept has spread to sheets in which each stamp either has a distinct, self-contained design, or forms part of a larger picture. At one extreme are the sheets of 50 from the USA showing flags, flowers or wildlife of the 50 states; at the other extreme are the 'sheetlets' of many emergent nations with 10 to 20 stamps.

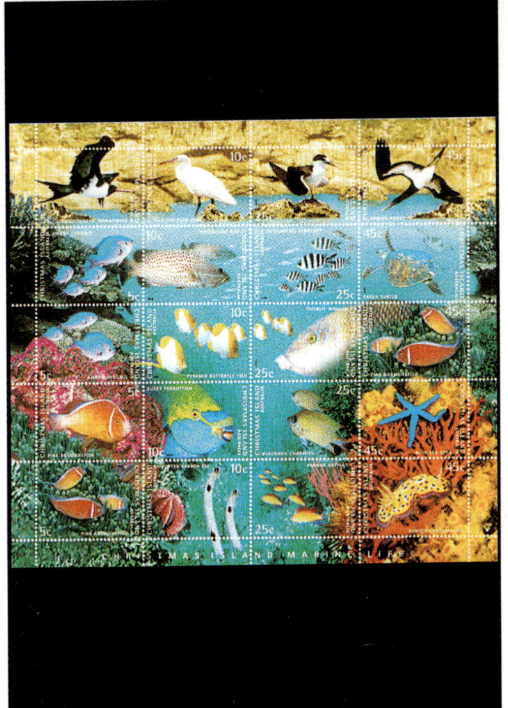

Composite sheetlet from Christmas Island, 1998.

Postal Stationery

Rowland Hill originally envisaged the prepayment of postage by means of pictorial envelopes and wrappers designed by William Mulready. Adhesive stamps were an afterthought.

WILLIAM Mulready's pompous design was derided and soon replaced by plainer envelopes and wrappers with an embossed stamp, a concept that survived in Britain till the 1970s. This pattern was also widely used elsewhere, though gradually the tendency has been to use stamps printed by letterpress or lithography. Special envelopes for registered mail, produced from linen-backed paper with

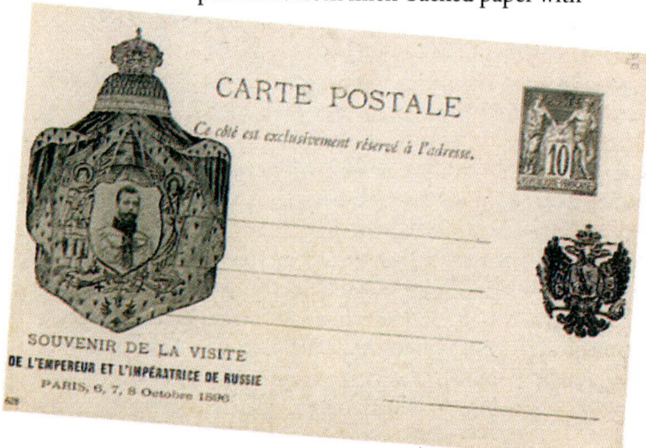

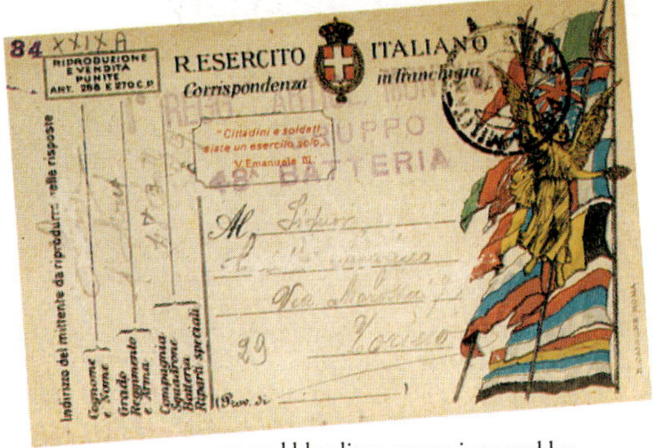

crossed blue lines, were pioneered by
Britain in 1878, but few countries now use them.

Newspaper wrappers, sometimes known as 'bandalettes',
date from the 1850s, although they were not adopted by
Britain until 1870. In that year Britain also adopted the
stamped postcard, which had been pioneered by Austria a year
earlier. Reply-paid postcards were widely used in the 1880s and
1890s and, in fact, survived till the 1960s. Letter-cards
developed at the turn of the century and in the 1980s Britain
briefly had stamped letter-sheets known as 'Postnotes'.

France, Germany and Italy had special stamped envelopes
for pneumatic post. Others produced distinctive envelopes for
telegrams, and in Britain today the equivalent is the bright red
and yellow envelope for telemessages.

Examples of early postal stationery, from France (left) and Italy (above).

Below: telegram postcard (France); right: the world's first stamped postcard (Austria).

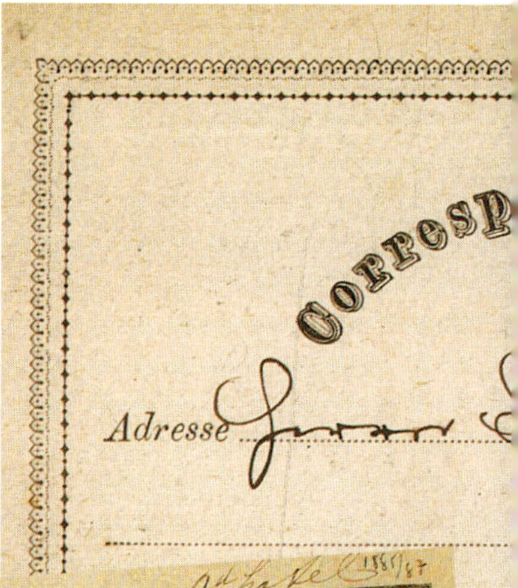

CORResP

Adresse

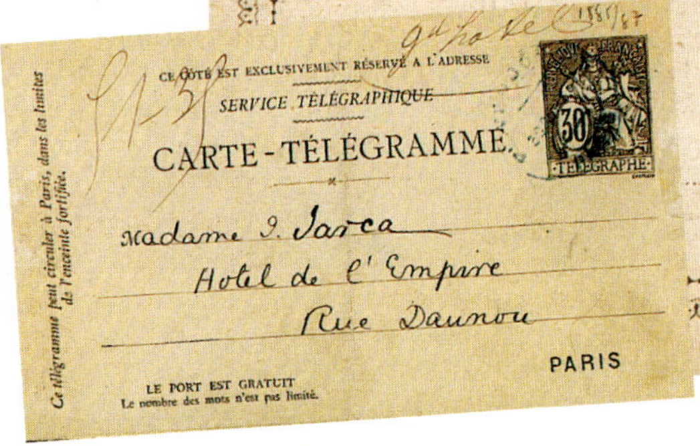

CE CÔTÉ EST EXCLUSIVEMENT RÉSERVÉ A L'ADRESSE

SERVICE TÉLÉGRAPHIQUE

CARTE-TÉLÉGRAMME

30
TÉLÉGRAPHE

Madame J. Jarca

Hôtel de l'Empire

Rue Daunou

PARIS

LE PORT EST GRATUIT
Le nombre des mots n'est pas limité.

Ce télégramme peut circuler à Paris, dans les limites de l'enceinte fortifiée.

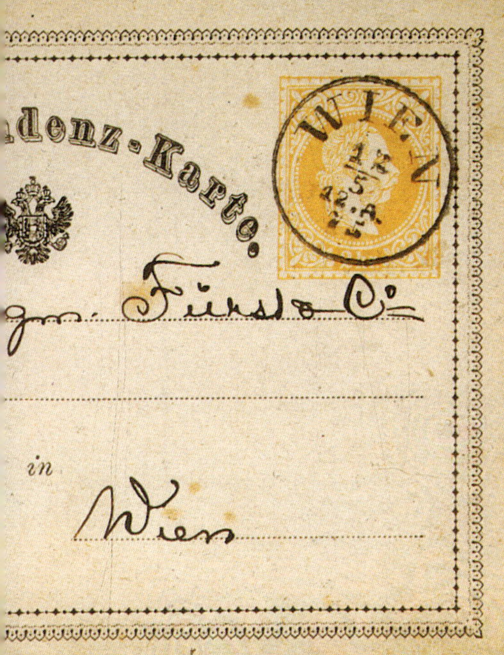

Pictorial and Commemorative Stationery

MANY COUNTRIES issue pictorial stamped envelopes and postcards, either as an adjunct to sets of adhesive commemorative stamps, or as part of an on-going policy of

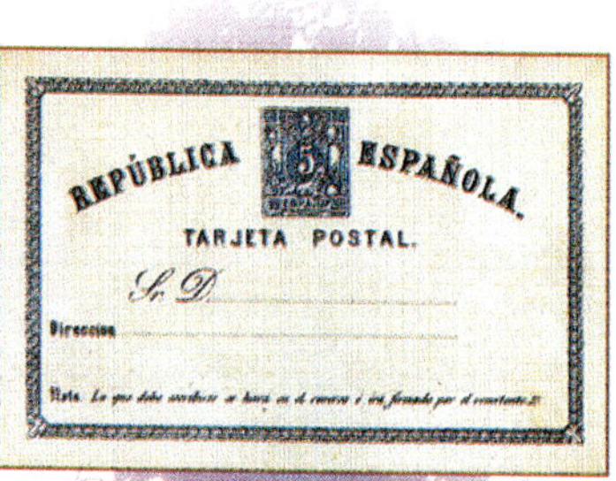

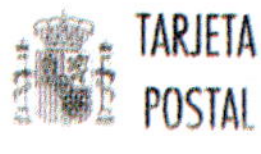

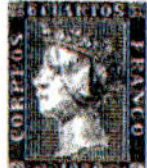

125 ANIVERSARIO
1er ENTEROPOSTAL ESPAÑOL
1873 - 1998

REMITENTE

providing an attractive souvenir for tourists. In many cases the postcards reproduce on the stamp the same motif that occupies the whole of the picture side.

AIR LETTERS AND AEROGRAMMES

AIR LETTERS, invented by Douglas Gumley and first used in Iraq in 1933, were adopted by Britain during the Second World War, initially as a forces air letter and subsequently extended to civilian use. There were even special versions for prisoners'-of-war mail. After the war air letters were adopted by many other countries and are now in universal use. In some countries (such as New Zealand) they were produced by the post office without impressed stamps and therefore required adhesives, but almost everywhere else they are part of the range of official postal stationery.

MODERN DEVELOPMENTS

CONVENTIONAL postal stationery has all but disappeared in Britain, its place taken by the plastic packs designed for special services. Because of their awkward size and material they have been largely ignored by collectors, though they could well prove a good investment for the future.

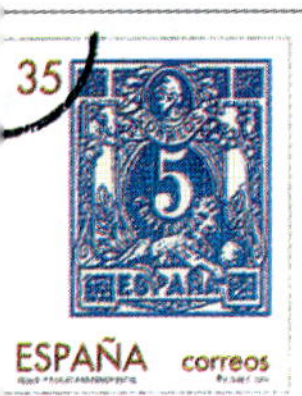

Pictorial stamped postcard of Spain, 1998, celebrating the 125th anniversary of Spanish postcards.

TYPES OF COLLECTION
Introduction

PHILATELY CAN be divided into several broad types of collection: general, thematic or specialised, while postal history is becoming increasingly popular.

Everyone starts off with a general collection, containing everything and anything that remotely resembles a stamp. Gradually, as collectors' knowledge and discernment improve, the non-philatelic items are weeded out.

Not so long ago, collectors would have discarded labels, stationery cut-outs, local stamps, revenue and telegraph stamps, but nowadays these and other 'sidelines' have a steady following and are discussed in the section on Cinderellas.

Even if you are left with just the government-issued adhesive postage stamps, this is such a vast subject that most philatelists try to limit the scope of their collection as they advance in the hobby.

Nevertheless there are still many who cannot resist the appeal and allure of stamps, pure and simple, and who maintain a general, whole-world collection, even if certain parts of it are more specialised than others.

There is no denying the pleasure that can be gained from general collecting. There are many philatelists of long standing, eminent authorities on some specialised aspect or other, who also maintain a general collection which gives them a proper perspective on the hobby and prevents them from becoming too obsessive about one specific area. Everything is grist to your mill; whatever takes your fancy will find a place in your album.

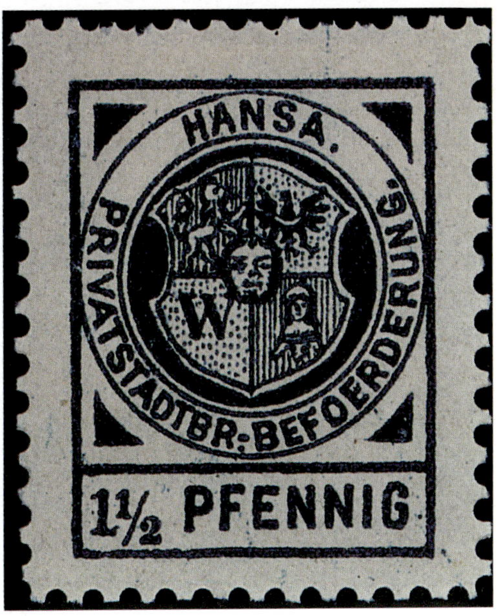

The stamps of the Hansa local post in Germany (1893–1900) featured the arms of the towns in which they were used. This 1½ pf was issued in Breslau (now Wroclaw, Poland).

Narrowing the Field

ONE OF THE bugbears of stamp collecting is the obsession with completeness which often assails the specialist. The general collector, on the other hand, is never troubled by this. Nevertheless, the time often comes when even

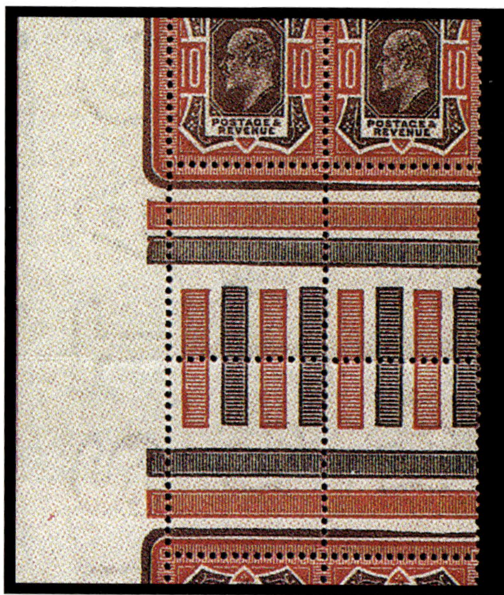

the general collector realises the impossibility of forming a meaningful collection on a general, simplified basis and some limit has to be set.

If the whole world is too much, and a single country too restricting, the answer lies somewhere in between. Thirty years ago most general collectors would have attempted to collect the stamps of the British Commonwealth as a whole. At that time definitives were changed once a decade and commemoratives were produced very sparingly. Today definitives change every three or four years, if not more often, while it seems as if commemoratives are produced every other month at the very least.

Even the smallest territory now issues stamps for all manner of international events, for lack of anniversaries and events of its own to celebrate. Consequently the Commonwealth has become too unwieldy a group for all but the wealthiest, and this area has tended to be divided into more manageable segments.

British collectors, for example, tend to collect the stamps of the United Kingdom, the 'offshore islands' – Guernsey, Jersey and the Isle of Man – and, to a growing extent, the Irish Republic, since these are the five independent postal administrations of the British Isles. Australians collect Australia, Antarctica, Christmas Island, Cocos (Keeling) Islands and Norfolk Island, while New Zealanders concentrate on New Zealand, Ross Dependency, Niue, Samoa and the Tokelau Islands.

Portion of a sheet of British 10d stamps of King Edward VII, showing Jubilee lines, marginal rule and interpane pillars, filling the spaces between the panes.

Other Alternatives

YOU COULD concentrate on all the stamps of a particular reign. Britain and the Commonwealth from the reign of King George VI, for example, is an increasingly popular field because it is both wide-ranging geographically and finite chronologically.

Other collectors turn their attention to the 'dead countries' – those that were absorbed politically and ceased to issue their own stamps. Germans concentrate on the stamps of Bavaria, Baden and the other former kingdoms, principalities and duchies, while Australians have the stamps of New South Wales, Queensland, South Australia, Tasmania, Victoria and Western Australia, and South Africans the former issues of the Cape of Good Hope, Natal, the Orange Free State and the Transvaal.

Sometimes dead countries spring to life again, as, for example, Bosnia, Croatia, Slovenia and Macedonia in the

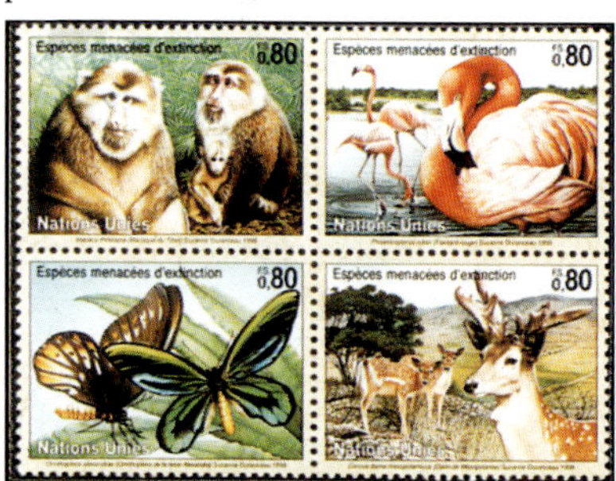

former Yugoslavia, or the republics of the Baltic and Caucasus which were absorbed by the Soviet Union and are now independent again.

Indeed, the new countries of Europe and Central Asia, including Belarus, Moldova, Kazakhstan, Kyrgystan, Tadjikistan, Turkmenistan and Uzbekistan which never had stamps before, have immense appeal for collectors looking for a new area where they do not have a long track-record of elusive older issues to contend with.

Another interesting group consists of the United Nations which has had its own stamps in New York since 1951, in Geneva since 1969 and Vienna since 1979. In addition there are the stamps of the League of Nations (1922–44) and its specialised agencies, as well as the supranational issues for the Council of Europe (Strasbourg), UNESCO (Paris) and the International Court of Justice in The Hague.

Stamps of the United Nations for use in Geneva and New York.

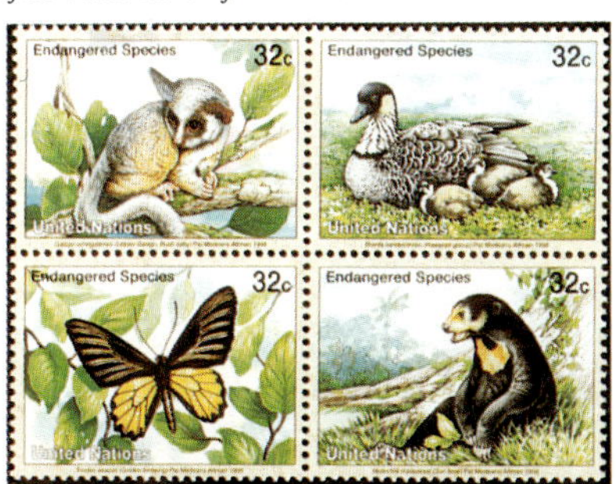

Thematic Collecting

This term embraces all forms of collecting stamps and stationery according to their subject or purpose of issue instead of by the more conventional geographic or political boundaries.

IN THE EARLY years of the hobby there was little scope for forming a collection on thematic lines. Apart from 'crowned heads' and coats of arms, pictorialism was slow to develop. Nevertheless, the first stamp to feature a bird (a dove with a letter in its beak) was issued by Basle in 1845, and by the 1860s there were several stamps showing trains and ships (New Brunswick, USA).

Greater pictorialism developed in the 1890s and within two decades stamps in general were becoming more attractive. Besides, there were, by that time, many more to choose from.

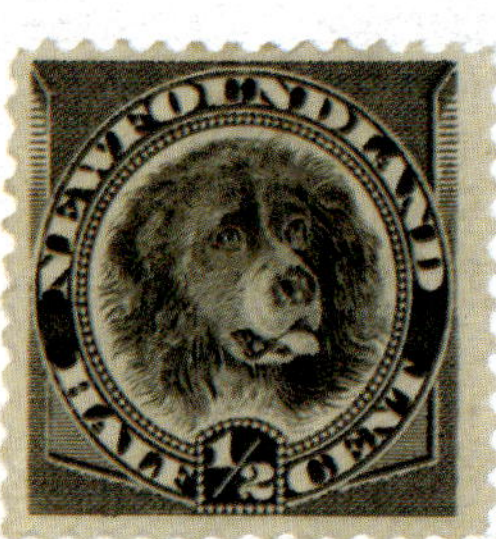

By 1920, therefore, the first collections developed on thematic lines were beginning to emerge.

In addition to the old favourites, such as portraiture and heraldry, ships, trains and maps became popular themes, to which could be added stamps depicting aircraft. It should be noted that many of the stamps of this

period showing an aeroplane were not intended for airmail.
Often enough the issue of a stamp featuring a plane was merely
wishful thinking on the part of a government which had not
yet the means of establishing an air service. Even then, stamps
were beginning to be regarded as a status symbol which could
be used to project an image of a country to the world at large.

Nineteenth-century pictorial stamps (left and below).

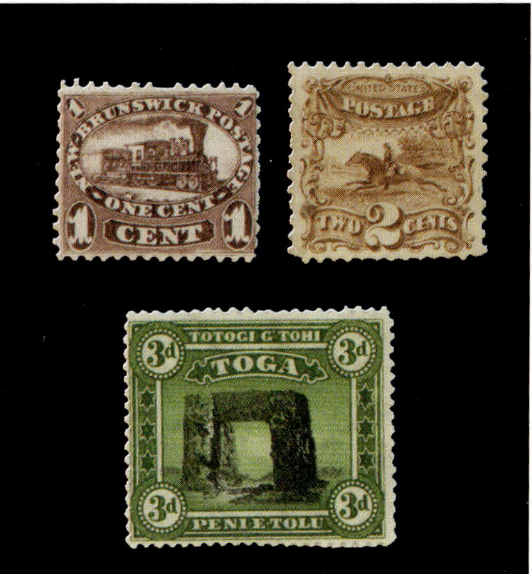

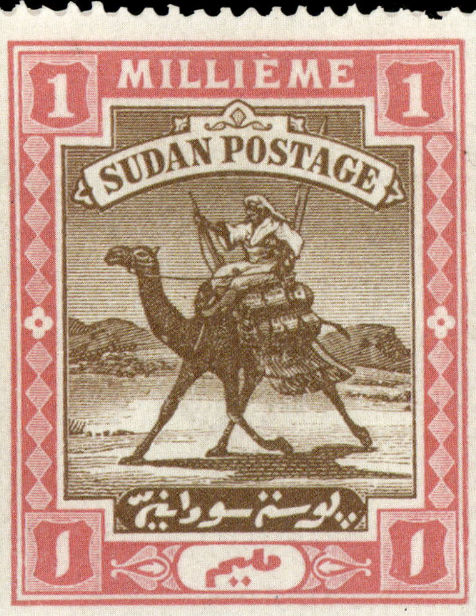

Sudan: the camel postman (1898).

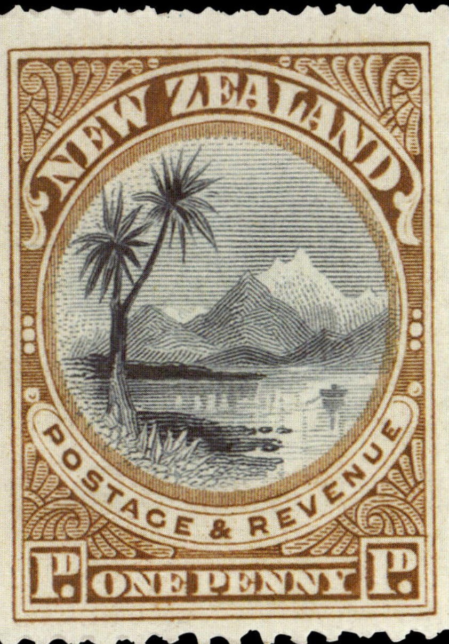

New Zealand: Lake Taupo and Mount Ruapehu (1898).

Arranging stamps according to their subject seems to have developed gradually in the interwar period. Many collectors formed sideline collections of this sort but were regarded as puerile or eccentric by their traditionalist colleagues. After the Second World War, however, this branch of the hobby became more respectable and even acquired distinctive names: *Motiv-Sammlung* in Germany, thematic collecting in Britain and topical collecting in the USA.

In 1949 the American Topical Association was formed; today the ATA has almost 50,000 members in over 100 countries. It has helped to make topical or thematic collecting easier by publishing numerous checklists and handbooks of stamps depicting specific subjects, as well as monthly digests and annual summaries of the stamps of the world classified by their subject.

At the same time detailed and well-illustrated catalogues have been published in the USA and Europe devoted to the more popular subjects such as fauna and flora, religion, fine art, space exploration, the Europa theme, the Red Cross, Boy Scouts and aspects of sport such as the Olympic Games and the World Cup football championship.

In Britain, Stanley Gibbons have produced a separate series of priced catalogues, including volumes devoted to aircraft, birds, butterflies and insects, railways and shells. Among other recent titles are handbooks on bicycles, bees, the World Wide Fund for Nature and Elvis Presley.

Thematic catalogues and handbooks.

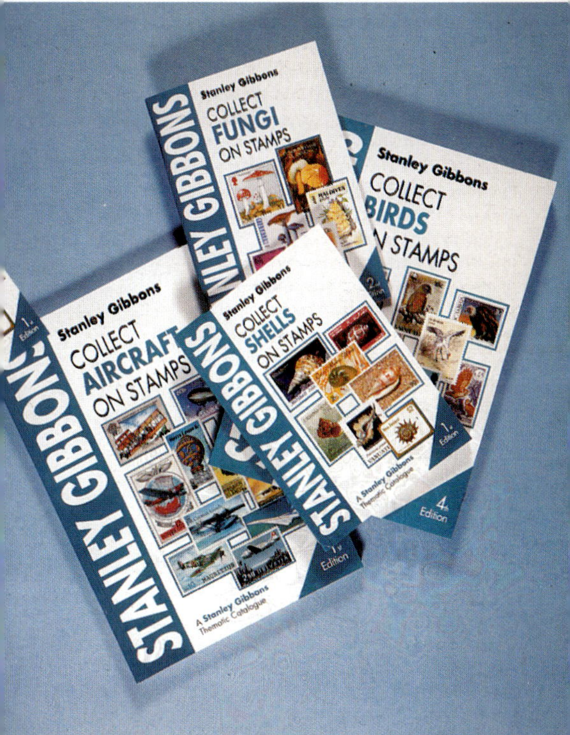
Stanley Gibbons
COLLECT
FUNGI
ON STAMPS
Stanley Gibbons
COLLECT
BIRDS
ON STAMPS
Stanley Gibbons
COLLECT
AIRCRAFT
ON STAMPS
STANLEY GIBBONS
Stanley Gibbons
COLLECT
SHELLS
ON STAMPS
STANLEY GIBBONS
1st
Edition
2nd
Edition
1st
Edition
4th
Edition
1st
Edition
A Stanley Gibbons
Thematic Catalogue
A Stanley Gibbons
Thematic Catalogue

Thematic collecting is now the fastest growing branch of philately. Significantly, many newcomers to the hobby have been drawn to it by forming collections that reflect their professional, sporting or leisure interests.

At one time postal administrations tended to issue sets of stamps with a mixture of themes. Even pictorial definitives would invariably range over a wide field. This made life difficult for the collector who might require only one or two stamps in a set for his theme. Dealers were reluctant to split sets, and stamps surplus to requirement were difficult to dispose of. Nowadays, however, there are even clubs devoted to thematic collecting, and members can swap surplus material easily.

Furthermore, since the 1960s, postal administrations have increasingly tended to oblige the thematic collector by sticking to a single subject. At one time a set of stamps might have depicted pets or animals, for example, but nowadays separate issues showing breeds of dogs, cats or horses are more common.

Similarly, wildlife stamps ranged far and wide, but today we have a situation where the World Wide Fund for Nature stamps concentrate on a single endangered species, depicting every aspect of adults

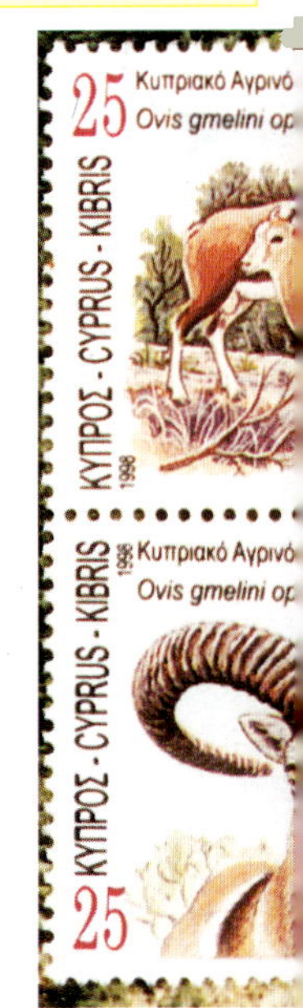

and young, both general views and close-up details. This has helped to create a more mature, more precise treatment of individual themes.

WWF set of four wildlife stamps for the Cyprus Mouflon, 1998.

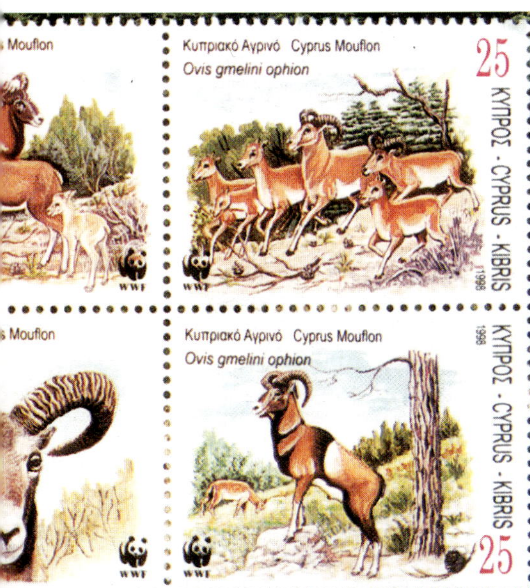

Choice of Theme

The combination of much more frequent issues and the use of modern multicolour printing processes has widened the scope of stamp design enormously and there is now hardly a subject under the sun that has not had stamps devoted to it.

IDEALLY you want to find a subject that has not been overdone, but offers a reasonable amount of variety. Thematic collectors are becoming more and more selective. One collector, for example, has formed a collection of stamps showing bicycles and umbrellas and has even come across stamps that show both: one from Laos featuring a cycle rickshaw and a bystander carrying a parasol, and another from Russia portraying the writer Chekhov carrying an umbrella, with a bicycle just visible in the background.

Having chosen a subject, it is not sufficient to work your way through the stamp catalogues to compile a list of the stamps which feature the subject; that is the easy part. The fun really begins when you start studying stamps in microscopic detail, seeking out that tiny, secondary motif, perhaps tucked away in the frame, which is relevant to your theme.

How many collectors with electricity as their theme are aware of the fact that the US 1c stamp of 1902 portraying Benjamin Franklin has tiny lightbulbs in the upper corner, as a tribute to Thomas Alva Edison, the inventor of electric light?

US 1c stamp, 1902.

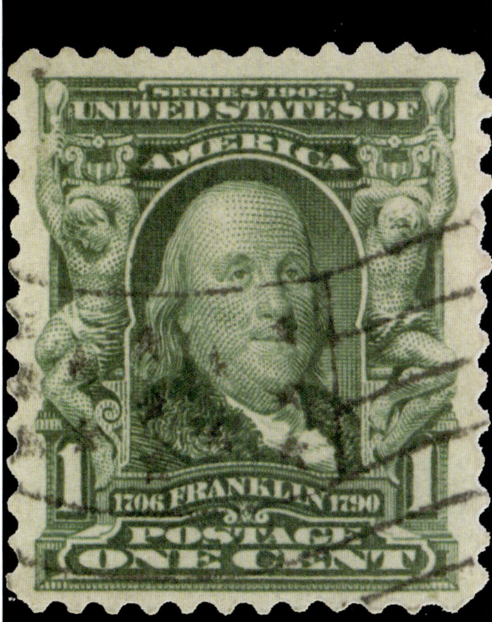

LATERAL THINKING

THEMATIC COLLECTING has now developed to the point at which it is not even necessary for the stamp to show a picture or even a detail which obviously links it to the chosen subject.

Judaica is a popular subject, shared by Jews and Gentiles alike. This topic received a tremendous boost in 1996–97 with stamps from many parts of the world celebrating Jerusalem 3000 – the third millennium of Jerusalem as the capital city of King David. You might not expect to find stamps on this theme from Egypt, but two recent issues would prove you wrong. The first was released in 1993 to mark the 800th anniversary of the death of Saladin, and showed the Saracen leader with the Dome of the Rock, Jerusalem in the background. In 1997 Egypt marked the 50th anniversary of the Arab Land Bank with a stamp showing its emblem, which incorporates the Dome of the Rock.

Eagle-eyed collectors would soon

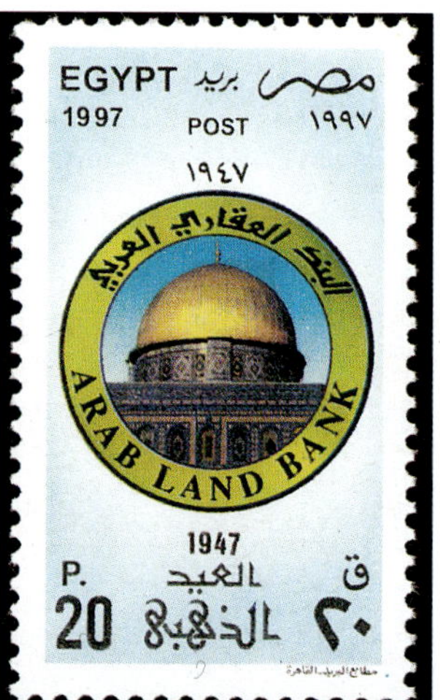

spot these stamps, but how many would include a stamp issued in 1998 by Sweden in the annual series devoted to domestic architecture? This shows the Red Hen Cinema in Halmstad, but the press notice accompanying this issue noted that the first film screened there was *Jerusalem*, based on the novel by Selma Lagerlof. On that score, however tenuous, this stamp would merit inclusion in a collection of Judaica.

Similarly collectors of stamps with a Scottish theme include many flower issues because their scientific names allude to Scottish botanists; not just the obvious ones like forsythia and gardenia but thomandersia (Gabon), baikiaea (Botswana), the ballantinia orchid (Guyana) and many others.

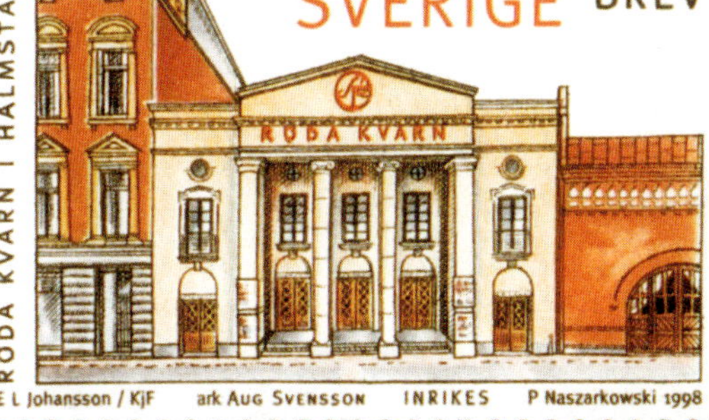

Egypt: Arab Land Bank, 1997; and Sweden: Red Hen Cinema, 1998.

Subject Collecting

Thematic collecting is now divided into three broad
categories, each of which has a large following and
even its own set of rules, at least so far as competitive
exhibitions are concerned.

THE MOST POPULAR category is known as subject
collecting which consists of arranging stamps according to
the subject depicted on them. The ATA checklists or the various
thematic catalogues will give you the basic groundwork for the more
popular subjects, but if you decide on something original there is no
short cut. You will have to work your way through a whole world
stamp catalogue from Abu Dhabi to Zululand, making notes of all
the stamps that seem to come within your scope.

You will end up with extensive lists of stamps, in country
order, and the next stage is to regroup the data so that your
subject is divided into its various aspects. Supposing you have
decided to collect stamps featuring cats. You would find that the
subject can be broken down into the following groups:

Wild Cats
The cat in Pharaonic Egypt
Cats in mythology and
  folklore
The black cat as a good-luck
  symbol or mascot
Caricature or cartoon cats
Cats in literature

Cats in paintings, sculpture
  and other aspects of fine art
Pantomime cats
Cats in general
Kittens
Breeds of cat
Real, identifiable cats such as
  Socks (Bill Clinton's cat)

To this you could add slogan postmarks, pictorial handstamps, metermarks, covers, Louis Wain postcards, labels from the Cats Protection League and other cat charities.

Sheet of cat stamps from Guyana.

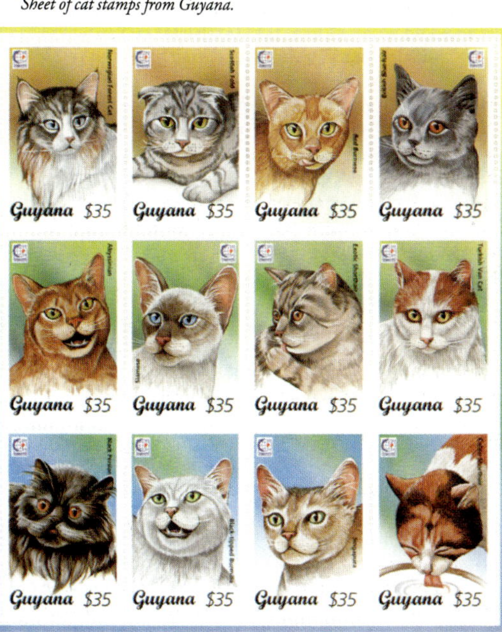

Purpose-of-issue Collecting

Known in America as 'incidental philately', purpose-of-issue collecting denotes stamps marking a particular incident or event. The omnibus issues come into this category, but it has been widened to encompass everything issued in connection with a specific event, whether as part of an omnibus series or not.

IT COULD BE argued that the stamps of 1892–98 honouring the discovery of America or the issues from various colonies to celebrate Queen Victoria's Diamond Jubilee (1897) are the earliest in the purpose-of-issue category.

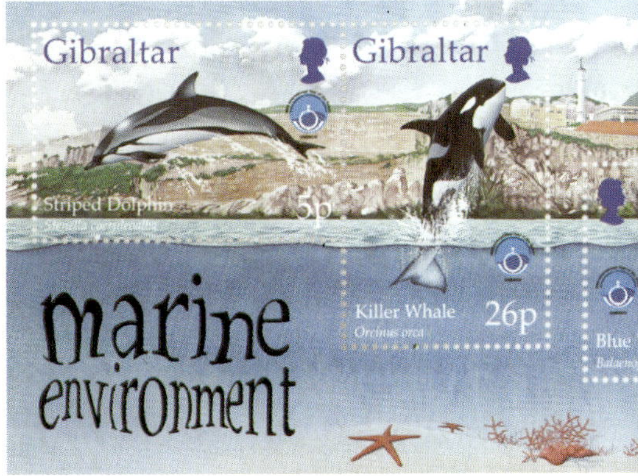

However, the concept really only got under way in the late 1930s, with global celebration of the American constitution (1937) and the New York World's Fair (1939).

In the postwar period, anniversaries of the UPU (1949 and 1974), Rotary International (1955 and 1980), the Shakespeare quatercentenary (1964) and the centenaries of Winston Churchill (1974) and Rowland Hill (1979) were especially popular.

In addition, the United Nations has designated annual events from World Refugee Year (1959) to the International Year of the Ocean (1998), all of which have been widely commemorated. More recently, major international stamp shows, like Pacific '97 in San Francisco and Israel '98 in Tel Aviv, have triggered a spate of stamps around the world.

Mourning stamps come into this category, with extensive issues for John F. Kennedy (1963–64) and Winston Churchill (1965–66) and, most recently, Diana, Princess of Wales and Mother Teresa of Calcutta (1997).

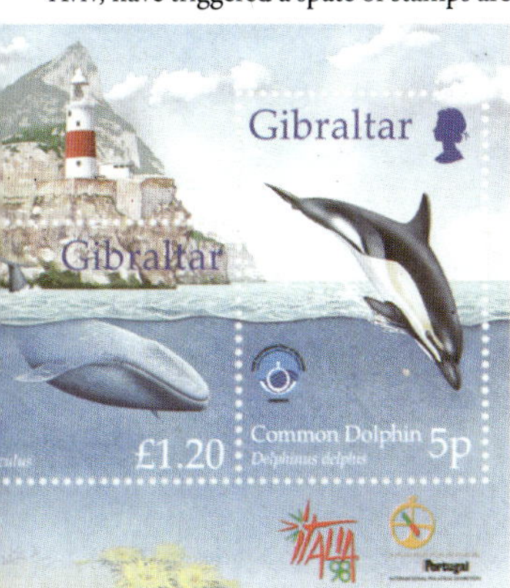

Stamps from Gibraltar for the International Year of the Ocean, 1998.

Stamps Tell a Story

The third branch of thematic collecting offers the greatest scope: the arrangement of stamps in such a way that they develop a theme or concept.

IN EFFECT, the stamps are used to illustrate a story and tend to become merely incidental to the historical research undertaken by the collector. Among the more popular themes are the history of the USA as portrayed on its stamps, or the rise and fall of the Roman Empire illustrated on stamps of Italy and the countries which formed part of that empire.

You might find such subjects too large; perhaps the story of a single city, like London or Paris, would be more manageable. Such a theme would take in not only all the stamps depicting landmarks and scenery, but also those commemorating events and the famous people born there or who spent some of their working lives there.

An excellent topic would be 'Time', with stamps tracing the history of the many different methods evolved for the measurement of time, from the hour-glass to the marine chronometer. Stamps showing the Greenwich Meridian and the International Date-Line would be relevant. The story would embrace all the different calendar systems, and the differences between the Gregorian and Julian calendars could be illustrated with covers from Tsarist Russia to western Europe appearing to arrive before they were despatched. The subject would impinge on mathematics and astronomy, and would culminate in the stamps and stationery of 1900 celebrating the dawn of the twentieth century, as well as the flood of stamps, looking back or forward, as we approach the next millennium.

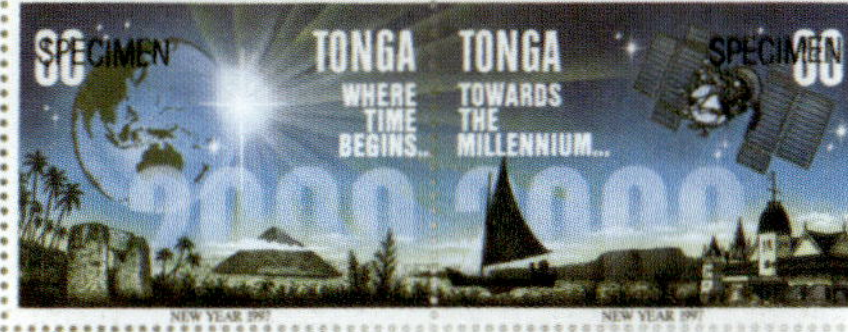

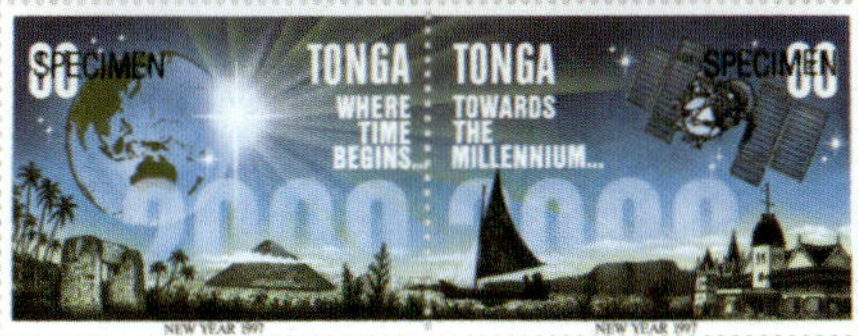

Miniature sheet from Tonga: 'Where Time Begins' and 'Towards the Millennium'.

SPECIALISED COLLECTING
Introduction

The specialist is a collector who concentrates on a single country, or even a specific period, and studies the stamps of his chosen field in great depth.

H E WILL NOT be content with one example of each stamp – mint or used – but will explore in great detail every aspect of the stamps. The differences arising from production over a period of years have already been touched on in The Anatomy of a Stamp.

It goes without saying that the specialist must become adept at using an ultraviolet lamp, but there are other useful instruments. Conventional perforation gauges may not be precise enough, so the Perfotronic gauge, an electronic, computerised machine giving precise measurements to three decimal places, is an essential. A micrometer to gauge the exact

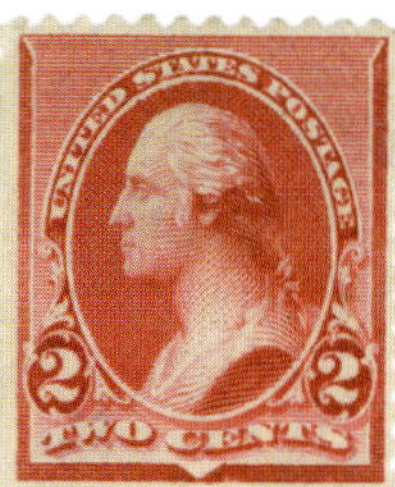

thickness of paper – particularly vital in sorting stamps of the nineteenth and early twentieth centuries into their various printings – is another essential.

The specialist will not be content merely to collect stamps, but will wish to ferret out all the information there is about them. Going beyond the catalogues and handbooks, he will do research in the archives of the Board of Inland Revenue and the Post Office to determine the reasons for the introduction of a new denomination or why a colour change was deemed necessary. It may be necessary to sift through thousands of used stamps to determine the earliest or latest dates of usage.

The ultimate specialisation is the life-long study of a single stamp: the Penny Black (1840–41), the Penny Lilac (1881–1902), Poland Number One (1860–65) and the US Washington 2c (1894–1900) are good examples.

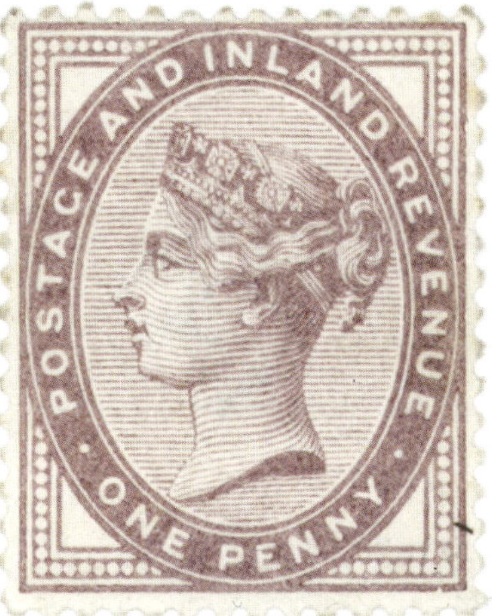

Left: US Washington 2c (1894); above: Penny Lilac (1881).

Machins

The British definitive series in use since 1967 is popularly known as the Machins, after the designer Arnold Machin, RA. The deceptively simple motif of the Queen's profile on a plain background with the value in one corner conceals a bewildering array of technical complexities which makes this arguably the most challenging series of stamps ever issued.

THE ORIGINAL series, launched in June 1967, was denominated in shillings and pence. In February 1971 it was relaunched in decimal currency and continues to this day. Although it cannot compare with such long-running issues as the arms series of Denmark or the Posthorn definitives of Norway it now holds the world record for the number of different collectable varieties.

Even on a simplified basis, going by colour alone, there have been over 120 different stamps, from ½p to £5 and including undenominated first- and second-class versions, since 1971 alone. At one time the higher values were recess-printed and the lower values photogravure, but since 1980 they have also been lithographed. Six different firms – Harrison, Questa, Walsall, Bradbury Wilkinson, De La Rue and even Enschedé of Holland – have been involved in their production. There are major variations in gum, paper, phosphor bands, phosphorescence, fluorescence and perforation. Add to that, booklet panes and composite coil strips with different values side by side or advertising labels attached, and the permutations are almost infinite. Machins take a column in the

Stamps of the World catalogue and occupy over six columns in the 'red' Gibbons; but Volume 4 of the *Specialised Stamp Catalogue*, devoted entirely to the decimal definitives, now runs to almost 800 pages!

The British Machin stamps are an extreme case, but the stamps of every country and every period have their complications, and this is what gives zest to specialised collecting. The serious collector of New Zealand stamps, for example, has to master the intricacies of the experimental papers used in the interwar period, known as De La Rue, Jones, Art, Cowan and Wiggins Teape papers respectively. The wartime stamps are known to have been printed on first fine paper, second fine paper and coarse paper, further subdivided according to whether the mesh of the paper is horizontal or vertical.

British Machin decimal stamps: booklet pane of four 1st class stamps, plus a label celebrating the Queen's 70th birthday.

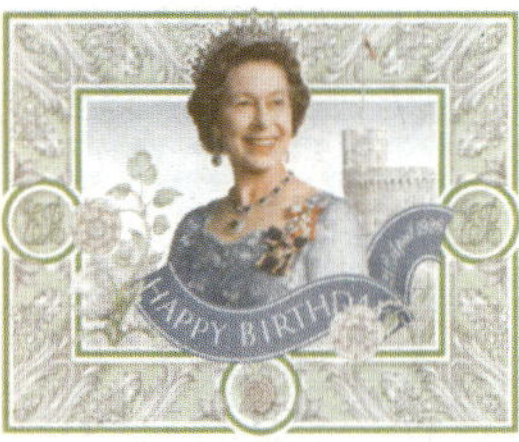

Flaws

APART FROM all the factors in stamp production which make for subtle differences, there are the errors and flaws to contend with. Each printing process is liable to produce its own brand of imperfection. Intaglio stamps may be found with signs of plate wear, or with weak or double entries – portions printed faultily because the plate was not properly treated – and the correction of these flaws may result in re-entries or

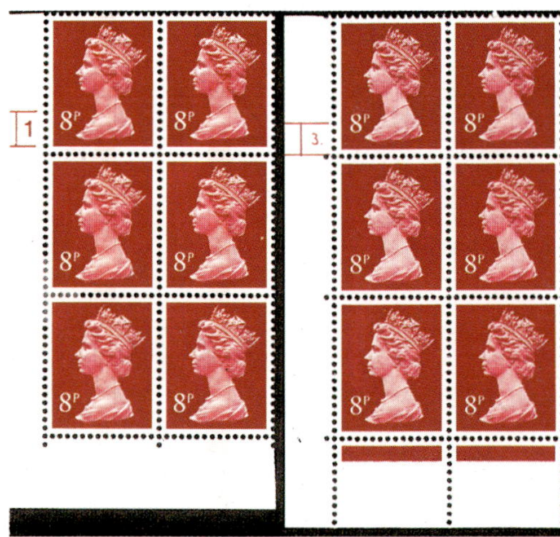

Panes of 8p, 1979–80 showing the differences in printings by Enschedé (left) and Harrison (right).

areas re-engraved or retouched on the plate by hand and therefore slightly different from the original.

Similar flaws may occur through faulty etching of the cylinder in photogravure. In this process a device known as a doctor blade keeps the ink spread evenly, but a slight jump in the blade can result in a coloured or colourless line appearing over several stamps. Such doctor-blade flaws can be quite spectacular. In lithography, creases in the transfers laid on the stones can result in some startling effects, such as the NFW flaw on Newfoundland's 1c stamp of 1911.

British 1½d, 1952 'butterfly' flaw in a positional block.

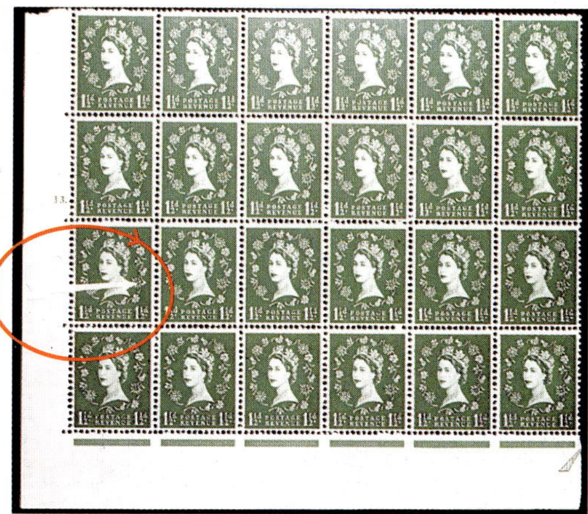

Plating

MINOR BUT constant flaws, frame breaks, weak entries and re-entries serve a useful purpose, enabling the really dedicated philatelist to reconstruct an entire sheet of stamps. Known as 'plating', this became popular with the earliest collectors because British stamps bore corner letters from AA to TL which encouraged them to try to reconstruct the sheet layout.

In reality it was greatly complicated by the fact that many plates were used in the long life of the Penny Red, and even the Penny Black used 11 plates in less than a year. Each of these plates had minute characteristics, such as peculiarities in the letters and stars in the corners, so that specialists soon learn to assign stamps to the exact plate. From 1858 to 1880 British stamps not only had corner letters but tiny plate numbers as well, so plate reconstruction became simply a matter of getting hold of a large enough quantity of stamps.

Nevertheless, the techniques and principles of plating, mastered in the early British stamps, enabled collectors to reconstruct the sheets of early stamps of other countries. The greater availability of reproductions of the proof sheets held by the archives of many postal administrations has assisted this process. There is a vast literature devoted to plating studies alone.

The basis of any plating study is to get hold of the largest blocks and strips you can, especially those with portions of the sheet margins. In many cases stamps from different blocks overlap, and in this manner the plate is gradually reconstructed.

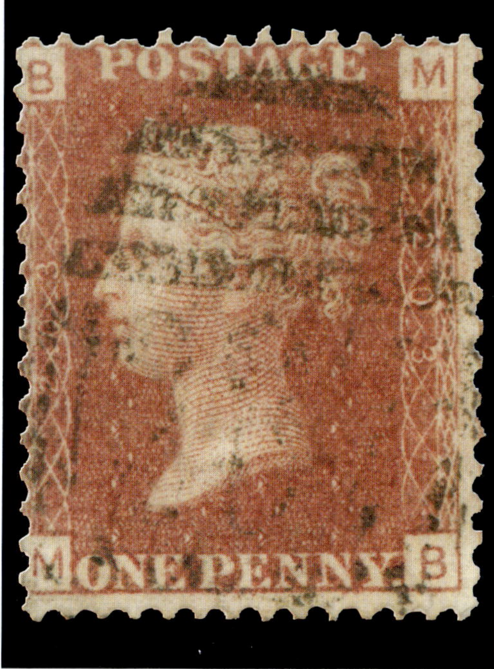

British Penny Red (1864) showing the plate numbers (203) and corner letters BM/MB.

Sheet Margins

PLATING is quite impossible when it comes to most
modern stamps, but the specialist finds plenty of scope
in studying the sheet margins. From 1881 to 1947 British
stamps had control numbers and letters in one corner for
accounting purposes and specialists therefore collect control
blocks and strips.

Control numbers and letters were superseded by cylinder
numbers which identify the printing cylinder used in
photogravure or offset lithography. As sheets are printed two at
a time, side by side, they may be distinguished by the presence
of a full stop after the number, and thus specialists have to
collect 'dot' and 'no-dot' numbers.

Multicolour stamps also have colour dabs, popularly
known as 'traffic lights' and these are also collected in corner
blocks. In recent years many stamps have been printed in
two panes with a 'gutter' (a column of blank paper) between
them. This gives rise to 'gutter pairs' and even 'gutter traffic
light pairs' where the colour dabs also appear between
the panes.

There are many other sheet marginal markings of
considerable interest to the specialist. They include the
printer's name or logo, the plate number (in De La Rue
colonial stamps and in intaglio stamps), registration crosses,
marks and guidelines (especially in bicoloured or
multicoloured stamps requiring two or more passes through
the press), Jubilee lines (marginal rule), arrows to assist counter
staff in folding sheets and perforation guide holes. In some
printings perforations may continue through the sheet
margins; in others there may be a single extension hole or

none at all. In many countries sheet values may include values for each row and this is a further source of variation.

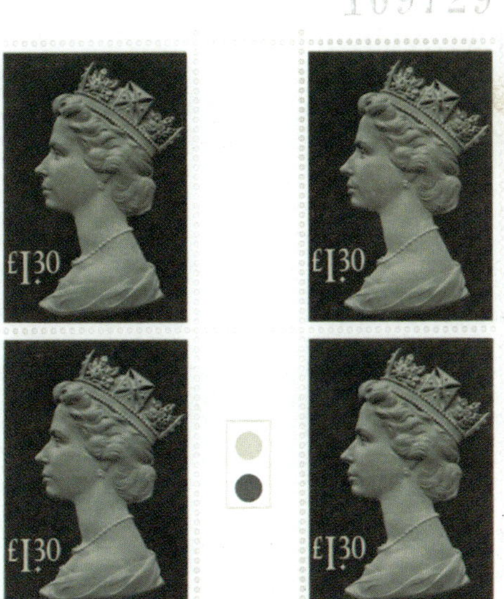

British gutter block of £1.30 stamps, showing 'traffic lights'.

Ancillary Material

The specialist will not be content merely with the stamps themselves but will search for ancillary material associated with them.

A NCILLARY MATERIAL might consist of Post Office notices announcing new postal charges or a change in rates; announcements publicising design competitions; artists' preliminary sketches and finished artwork; proofs taken from the master die at various stages of the engraving; proofs from the printing plate, in black ink or the issued colour; colour trials (testing the effect of various colour combinations); essays (designs which may have been developed to actual printing but which never went into full production); progressive proofs showing each of the colour separations in multicolour printing; imperforate proofs and printers' samples; and stamps overprinted 'Specimen' or its equivalent in other languages, such as *Muster* (German) or *Muestra* (Spanish) for distribution to the UPU or philatelic journalists as publicity material; and even stamps cancelled with a blank circle, black corner bar or defaced denomination for publicity purposes and to prevent postal use.

The issued stamps would be represented by a range of shades, mint and used, in pairs, blocks and strips, perhaps even complete sheets. Changes in gum, watermark and phosphor bands during the lifetime of the issue would be duly recorded. Finally there would be an array of covers, cards and wrappers to illustrate usage, either alone or in combination with other denominations. Unusual postmarks and incorrect or irregular usage would also be shown, where relevant. Presentation packs and folders, first-day covers, maximum cards and other official souvenirs would also be required.

Examples of specimen overprints.

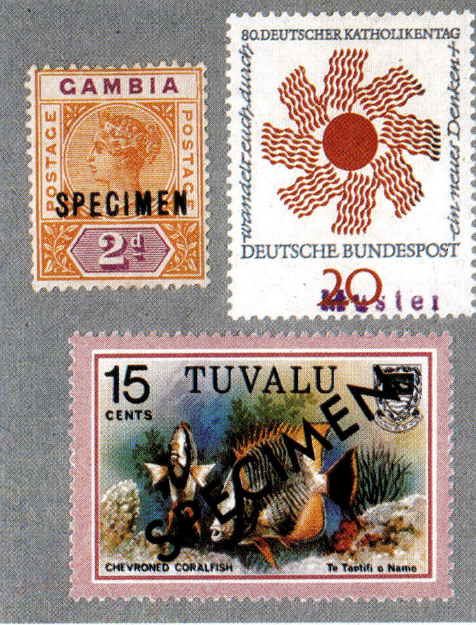

POSTAL HISTORY
Introduction

Postal history material embraces everything from Sumerian clay tablets of 3000 BC to the postcoded envelope retrieved from the office wastepaper basket this morning. It is a rather misleading term as postal services are continually evolving and collectors have to be alert for collectable material associated with the latest developments.

INTEREST in the background to the postal services developed very slowly from the late nineteenth century. Until then, and for many years thereafter, most collectors preferred their stamps in mint condition and regarded the cancellation as an unsightly blemish to be avoided as far as possible. A few discerning individuals, however, paid closer attention to the postmarks on their stamps and began to form small sideline collections of stamps on pieces of envelope bearing complete cancellations.

Postmarks: packet sent from Japan to England via Mailfast.

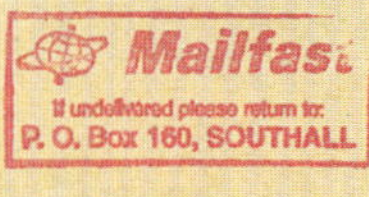

Gradually this idea took hold and several notable collections devoted entirely to postmarks were formed in the early years of the twentieth century. Postmark collecting remained an esoteric subject until the 1950s when greater use of slogan cancellations attracted the attention of many philatelists. Until then it was considered sufficient to have the postmark on a cut-out piece of envelope or postcard, but since then collectors have shown a preference for entires, especially those that have other postmarks as well as mere cancellations.

Earlier sections of this book have shown how postal services were well organised before the advent of adhesive stamps and it was to this period – often, though inaccurately, known as the 'stampless' or 'pre-stamp' period – that collectors turned when they graduated from being mere collectors of postmarks to postal historians.

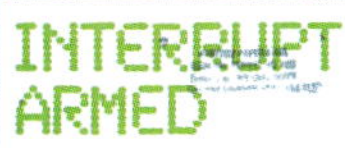

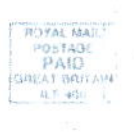

Postmarks: front and back of an envelope sent from Boulder, Colorado, USA, to Tartu, Estonia, remailed at London.

Old Letters

STRICTLY speaking, you do not have to collect this material to be a postal historian, and there are some who are content to study aspects of postal history without actually collecting old letters. But for most people, 'postal history' is synonymous with collecting envelopes, wrappers, postcards and postal ephemera for their postal markings, regardless of whether they then go on to study the historical background.

The first thing that the beginner discovers is that, compared with a straightforward stamp collection, postal history is infinitely more complex and a great deal bulkier. Even a collection of the postmarks of one country, on pieces clipped from kiloware, would rapidly fill an album, while a serious collection of a country's postal history in all its aspects, entailing thousands of entire letters, covers and postcards, might fill an entire room.

Forty years ago, particularly in Britain, old letters could be had by the sackful from wastepaper merchants and property developers as the attics and cellars of old legal and commercial businesses were cleared to make way for office redevelopment. Those were happy days when collectors and dealers alike were largely ignorant of which were the rare postmarks, and pre-stamp

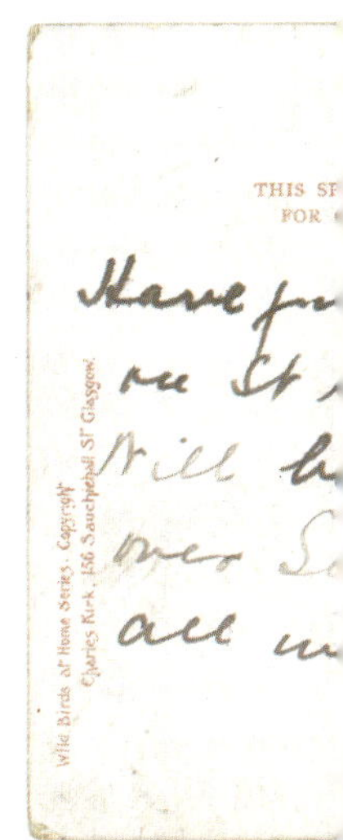

entires were sold for fourpence each or four for a shilling, regardless of their age or postal markings. Up to the 1950s, used postcards of the Edwardian era were a penny each or eight for sixpence. Now there are cards which change hands for four-figure sums, and covers for ten times as much, on account of their rare postmarks.

British postcard with an Edwardian halfpenny stamp (worth a few pence). However, postmarked at the island of St Kilda it is worth at least £200.

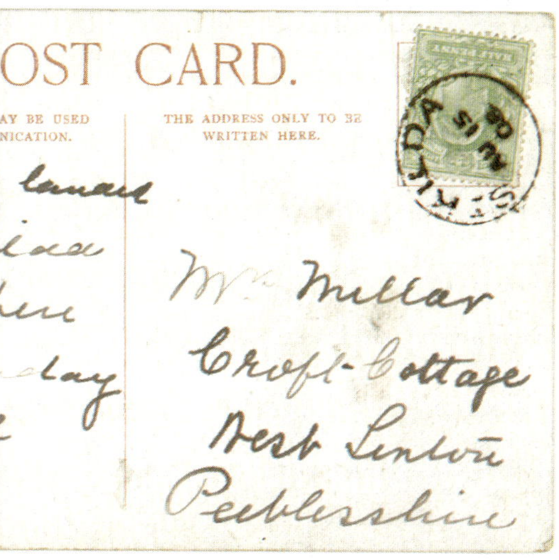

Sea Mail

Certain aspects of postal history attract a large following. They are by no means the only ones but a brief survey of them will give you an idea of the scope of this subject.

MUCH OF postal history concerns the mode by which the mails were conveyed. Airmail has already been discussed, since it has resulted in a large number of stamps and stationery items, but earlier and more traditional forms of mail transportation have left their mark in the album.

Up to the late nineteenth century, mail arriving by private ship was treated as a ship letter, charged at a special rate that included a penny or twopence for the shipmaster. Many seaports round the British coasts had special handstamps inscribed SHIP LETTER and as these are always uncommon (and often extremely rare) they have long been of special interest to collectors.

Their modern equivalent consists of marks inscribed *Paquebot* (the French term for 'packet boat'), adopted by the UPU in 1897. Such marks are often found on mail posted on board ship, franked with the stamps of one country and landed in another, and provide a way of cancelling stamps from abroad. These marks are used all over the world, but are sufficiently uncommon as to excite considerable interest. Apart from marks in French, look out for the equivalent in other languages: *Schiffsbrief* (German), *Buzon Vapor* (Spanish for 'steamer box') or *Per Vapore* (Italian for 'by steamer'). Marks reading 'Received from HM Ships' or 'Maritime Mail' relate to naval mail.

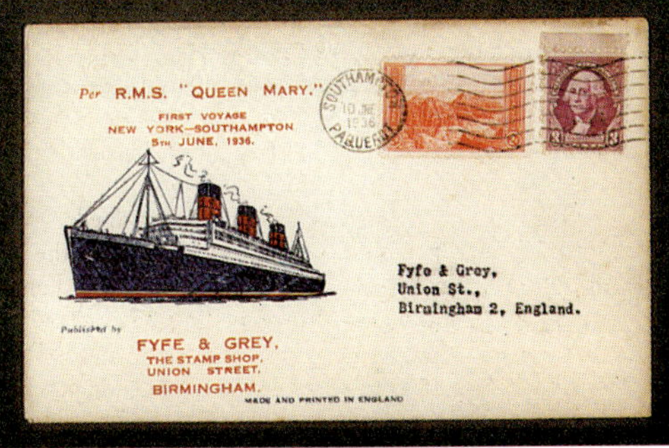

Top: example of a Sea Post card; bottom: souvenir cover from the maiden voyage of RMS Queen Mary, 1936, bearing US stamps and the Southampton Paquebot cancellation.

Railway Mail

TRANSMISSION of mail by railway dates from 1838 and rapidly spread to all countries with a railway system. The processing of mail in transit was accelerated by means of special sorting tenders and carriages. In recent years the number of travelling post offices has declined as more and more mail is transported by air, but the railway mail system has left a rich legacy of postal markings.

These marks were applied as cancellations to stamps on mail posted in the special boxes at the side of the mail trains, and occasionally to items which were misrouted or were back-stamped in transit. The distinctive marks can be recognised by having the names of two or more towns (indicating the route),

Railway letter, Talyllyn Railway Company.

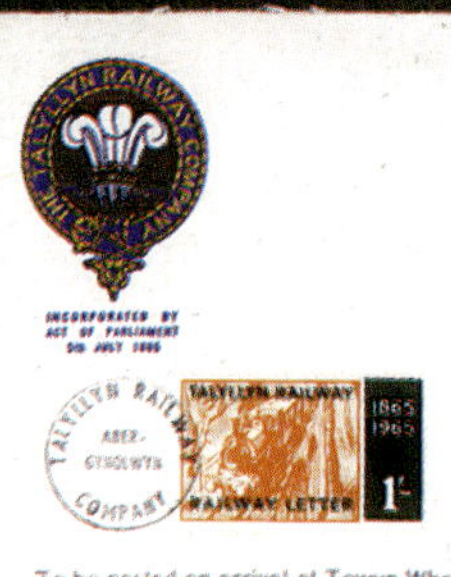
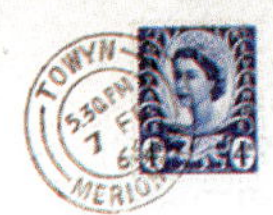

or the initials TPO (travelling post office), RPO (railway post office), SC (sorting carriage) or ST (sorting tender).

Railway mail from other parts of the world may be identified by the words *Ambulant* (French), *Ambulancia* (Spanish), often abbreviated to AMB, *Bahnpost* (German), sometimes including the word *Zug* or *Z.* (train), *Eisenbahn* or *Eisenb.* (German for railway), or *Banen* (Danish and Norwegian). The words *Bahnhof* (German), *Gare* (French) and *Ferrovia* (Italian) indicate posting at railway stations and are not as desirable as items showing train markings. Similarly British postmarks with RSO (railway sub office) merely indicate the status of certain post offices at the turn of the century, and in many cases were nowhere near a railway line but received mail-bags which, at some point or other in transmission, had been handled by rail.

Many railway postmarks have unusual shapes: oval (Germany, Austria and Czechoslovakia), scalloped (French), octagonal (Spanish) or rectangular (Belgium, Netherlands and Luxembourg).

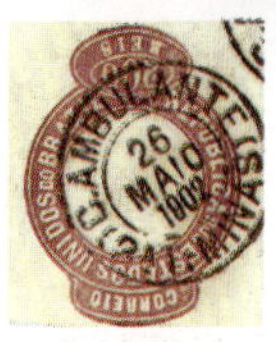

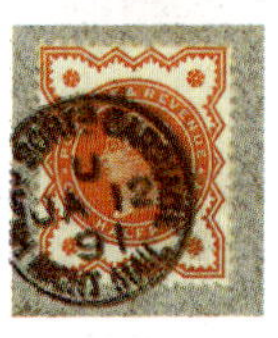

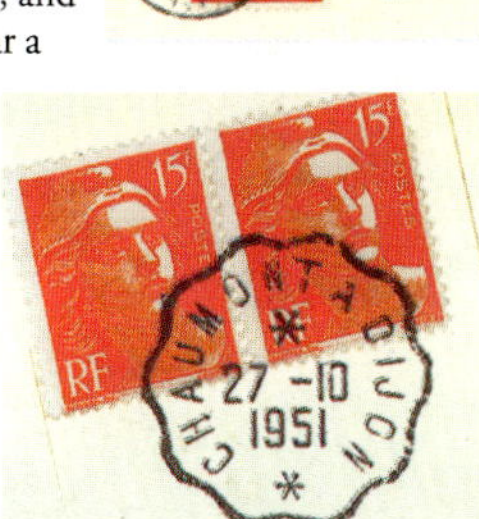

Railway postmarks from Brazil, Great Britain and France.

Military Mail

This mail, sometimes known as forces' postal history, is an enormous field as special facilities for soldiers' and seamen's letters, transmitted free or at reduced rates, have existed in many countries since the eighteenth century.

DISTINCTIVE handstamps showing a crown and inscribed ARMY BAG were used by the British army during the Walcheren expedition of 1799, but regular facilities were not again provided until the Crimean War (1854). Thereafter every war and campaign involving British troops resulted in distinctive postmarks. The Boer War (1899–1902) had many different types, but this was standardised during the First World War. For security reasons the locations of Field Post Offices (FPO) and Army Post Offices (APO) were not

revealed, but as the datestamps bore serial numbers this enables collectors to assign them to particular campaigns.

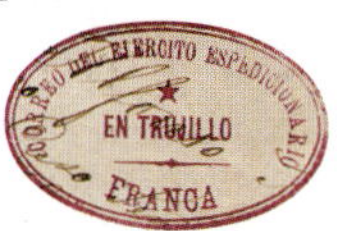

Similar systems have been used by the military forces of other countries. In addition there are cards and covers from volunteer and territorial camps and peacetime manoeuvres, censored mail and the poignant items from prisoner-of-war camps, internment and concentration camps and displaced persons' camps.

Again, for reasons of security, mail landed from naval vessels, especially in the First World War, had 'dumb' cancellations applied to the stamps. At the present time there is a wide range of postmarks and cachets on mail from troops serving with UN peace-keeping forces in the world's trouble spots.

Left: Norwegian field post office in Germany after the Second World War; below: a campaign letter from the Pacific War between Chile and Peru.

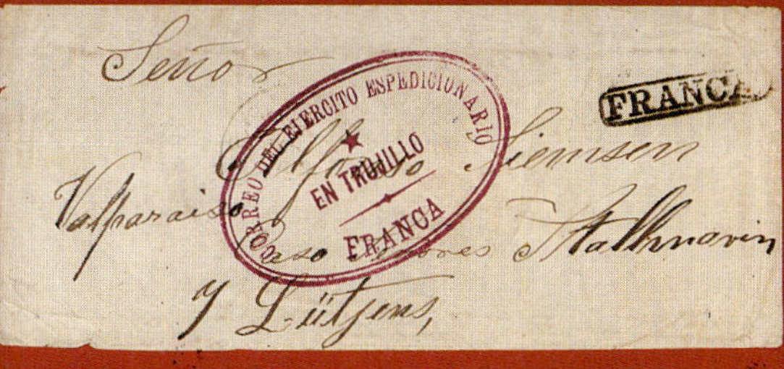

Local Postal History

An interesting collection can be formed pertaining to the postal history of your own town, district or county, starting with postmarks and covers salvaged from your own mail.

OLD POSTCARD albums and bundles of family correspondence will yield many obsolete postmarks and most stamp dealers now maintain a stock of material, usually with a strong local flavour, from legal and business accumulations that often go back for centuries.

In concentrating on local postal history you should try to cover the full range, from the manuscript markings of the early eighteenth century and letters with quaint addresses, or 'free franks' (letters posted by parliamentary privilege – a system much abused by the voters, who would importune their MP for a frank in exchange for the promise of their vote). If you are lucky you may even find a folded letter sheet bearing a Penny Black; the later Penny Reds and Penny Lilacs are still fairly plentiful.

There are the mileage marks used up to 1828 and the undated handstamps of small village offices up to 1860, not to mention counter stamps on registered covers or parcel labels. Most post offices cancelled outgoing mail until the 1960s but

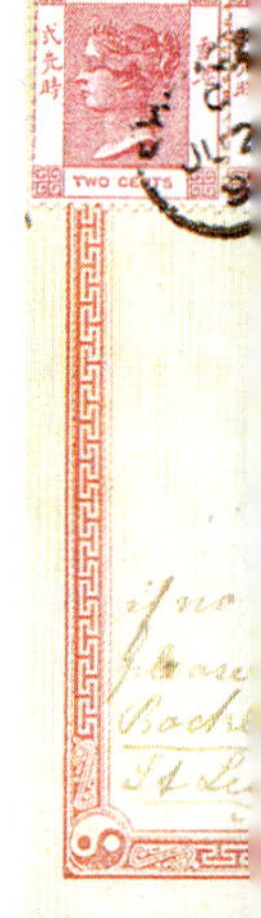

since that time concentration and mechanisation of mails has greatly reduced this. Nevertheless you can still obtain marks from small post offices on certificates of posting. A local collection, garnished with maps, press cuttings and photographs of post offices, is a valuable adjunct to the social history of the area.

Postcard from Chefoo, China to Greenock, Scotland, 1898, via Shanghai and bearing a strip of three 1c stamps of the Imperial Chinese Post (Chefoo) and a pair of Hong Kong 2c stamps (postmarked Shanghai), with Greenock arrival mark applied on redirection to Farnborough.

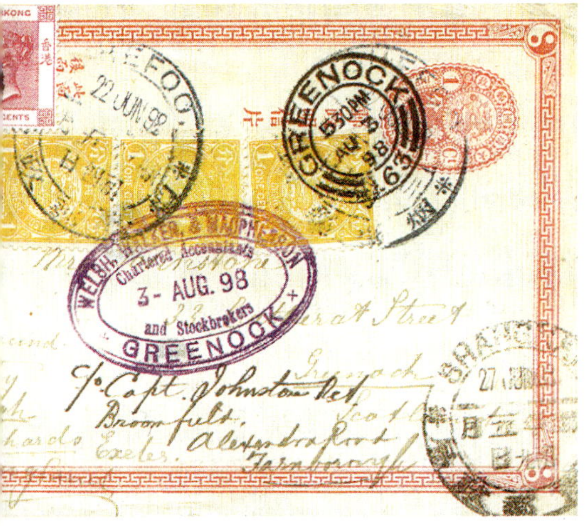

POSTMARKS
Introduction

A postmark is any postal marking: handwritten, handstruck, applied by machine or even printed on an envelope, wrapper or card. Collectors sometimes loosely use the term 'cancellation' as if it were synonymous with 'postmark'. In fact a cancellation is a postmark which has been used to cancel a postage stamp in order to prevent reuse.

THE EARLIEST recorded postal markings of any kind are the red and blue marks on the letters of Egyptian court officials during the Third Dynasty (*c.* 2778 BC) bearing the exhortation 'In the name of the living king, speed!' Examples are preserved in the Cairo Museum. The earliest examples in Europe consist of injunctions to postal officials not to delay important state correspondence.

A formula used in Venice by the early fourteenth century was the Latin *Cito, citissime, volantissime* (quickly, very quickly, very fleetingly). By the sixteenth century the French were endorsing their mail *en diligence* (with speed and care), and it is from this endorsement that French mailcoaches came to be called diligences.

In England letters were often endorsed 'Haste, haste, for life, post haste', sometimes with a drawing of a gibbet as a dire warning to the official who delayed important mail. When the state mails were thrown open to the public a system of marking the amount of postage was adopted: black for postage due from the recipient and red ink or crayon for prepaid letters.

*A Dover Ship letter mark on a letter from Macao to Sanquhar,
Dumfriesshire, 8 January 1796.*

Manuscript Marks

SEVENTEENTH-century letters may also be found with the endorsement 'Post payd' or 'P Pd' written on them in red ink. This system of marking prepaid letters survived until the advent of the Uniform Fourpenny Post (December 1839) and Uniform Penny Post (January 1840 onwards).

In addition to numerals denoting the amount of postage, it became customary to add the name of the town, often reduced to a two- or three-letter abbreviation. This system survived until the 1740s, being gradually superseded by the first handstruck marks.

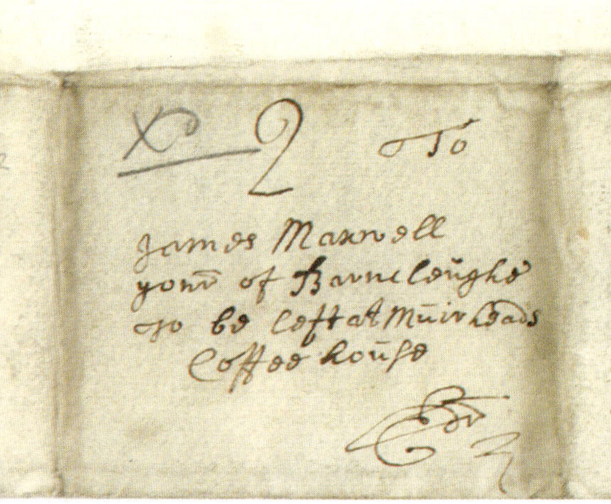

Name Stamps

ALTHOUGH handstruck marks identifying the town were in use in Milan as early as the fourteenth century, this system did not become widespread until the

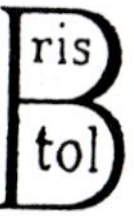
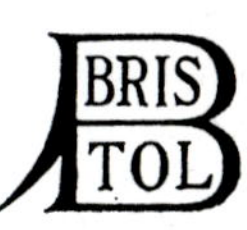

late seventeenth century. Some Irish post offices had handstamps bearing their name by 1698 and this spread to England (1700) and Scotland (1731). The use of undated name stamps continued in the smaller offices as late as 1860. Handstamps showing the distance from London were introduced in England in 1784, spread to Scotland in 1808 and were discontinued after 1828. Many different

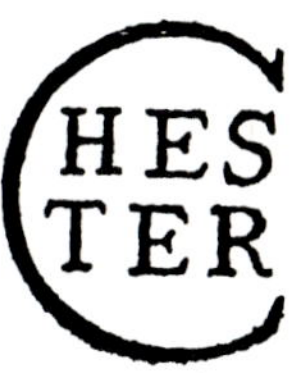

mileage marks might be used at the same office, the computation of distance varying from time to time.

Similar systems were used in many European countries from the early eighteenth century onwards, French postmarks often incorporating the number of the *Département*.

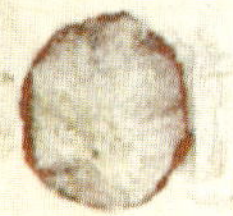

Above: the earliest postmarks for Bristol and Chester; left: early letter showing manuscript endorsements.

Datestamps

THE WORLD'S first postal datestamp was devised by Colonel Henry Bishop, Postmaster General of Britain, who produced it in answer to criticism that letters were often delayed in the post. The Bishop mark consisted of a small circle divided in two with a two-letter abbreviation for the month in one segment and the numerals of the day's date in the other.

These stamps were made of small rods with a semicircular section and were bound together like a wooden clothes-peg. Bishop marks were used in London (1661–1787), Dublin (1670–1795) and Edinburgh (1693–1806), as well as in the American colonies and Calcutta. Although these stamps all followed the same basic pattern they can be identified by variations in shape, diameter, colour and layout of inscriptions.

Exeter and Bristol were the first provincial English towns to use datestamps (1697), employing modified forms of the Bishop mark with the dates shown inside their initial letters. These stamps were confined to Cross Post letters (cross-country mail bypassing London), mail intended for London continuing to go unstamped until the early eighteenth century.

Outside the metropolitan offices (London, Dublin and Edinburgh) dated postmarks did not develop until 1800. Conversely the datestamps of London, Dublin and Edinburgh did not include the town name until the 1850s. A general allocation of datestamps was made to offices transacting at least £1,000 worth of business a year in 1829 and gradually extended. The smallest offices did not get a datestamp until 1885 and it was not until 1905 that *all* offices had a datestamp.

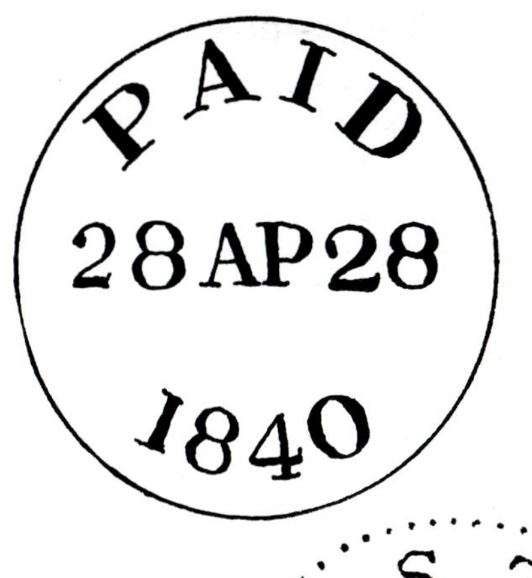

Circular datestamps. Top: London Paid (1840); bottom: Bristol dated mileage mark (1822).

Handstruck Postage Stamps

THE FIRST handstruck postage stamps, indicating the prepayment of postage, were invented by William Dockwra, a London merchant, who devised triangular stamps for a private service, the London Penny Post (1680). Letters handled by Dockwra's offices in London and Westminster were struck with distinctive double-lined triangular stamps inscribed PENNY POST PAID round the three sides. A letter in the centre identified the receiving office. Dockwra's service was taken over by the government in November 1682, Dockwra becoming Controller of the Penny Post. Somewhat similar triangular stamps were used by the government service until 1795.

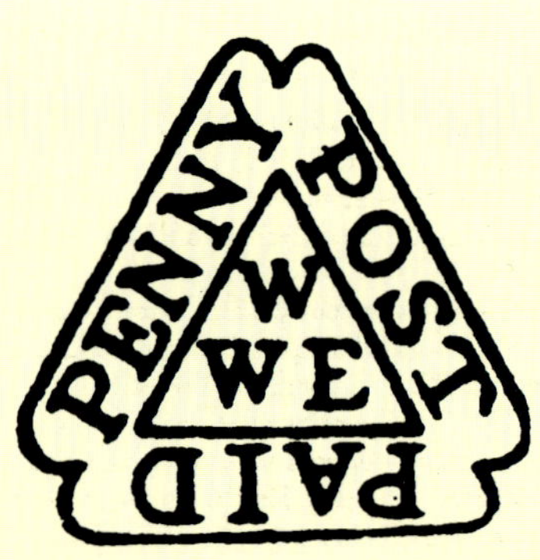

Dockwra also invented marks showing the actual time of posting but these were abolished in 1843 and it was not until 1895 that the time was again indicated in the postmark.

Handstruck postage stamps were also applied to prepaid mail handled by the Dublin Penny Post, established in 1773. A private

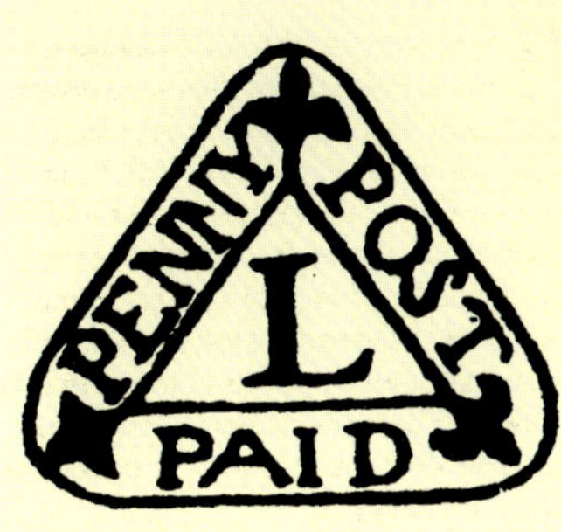

Above and left: Dockwra paid postmarks.

penny post was started in Edinburgh in 1774 by Peter Williamson and continued till 1793 when it was taken over by the Post Office. Handstamps continued to be applied to local penny post mail until the advent of Uniform Penny Postage in 1840.

Similar developments took place in many other countries. In the British colonies, whose postal services were operated by the General Post Office in London, crowned circular stamps inscribed PAID AT followed by the name of the colony were used until the colonies adopted adhesive stamps in the second half of the nineteenth century. Similar handstamps were used in British postal agencies in many countries before they joined the UPU in the 1870s.

Cancellations

FROM 1840 in Britain datestamps were applied to the backs of letters while the adhesive stamps were obliterated by a device known as a Maltese Cross. In 1844 a system of numeral obliterators was introduced, with separate patterns of bars containing numbers which identified each post office: London Inland; London District; England and Wales; Ireland; and Scotland. This system continued into the twentieth century.

In 1853 the first duplex or double stamps were adopted, with a dater and obliterator in a single handstamp. In the 1880s this gave way to combined stamps, with a double-circle case, the office name and an obliterating element (usually thick bars at the sides). Combined stamps are still used occasionally, though nowadays packets too bulky for machine cancellation are usually cancelled by rubber datestamp.

Single stamps, consisting of a single-circle dater, are mainly used for counter work, but also cancelled stamps on registered letters and parcel labels and occasionally on ordinary mail. Pictorial handstamps for special events and the first day of new stamps are now in widespread use.

Cancelling machines were developed from 1857 onwards when Pearson Hill (son of Sir Rowland Hill) devised a machine operated by steam or foot-treadle. Many experiments with machines were short-lived and so their postmarks are scarce. Fully automatic machines developed in the USA in the 1880s and gradually evolved into the high-speed models of today. Cancelling machines have also been adapted for processing bulk postings prepaid in cash, the marks usually being struck in red.

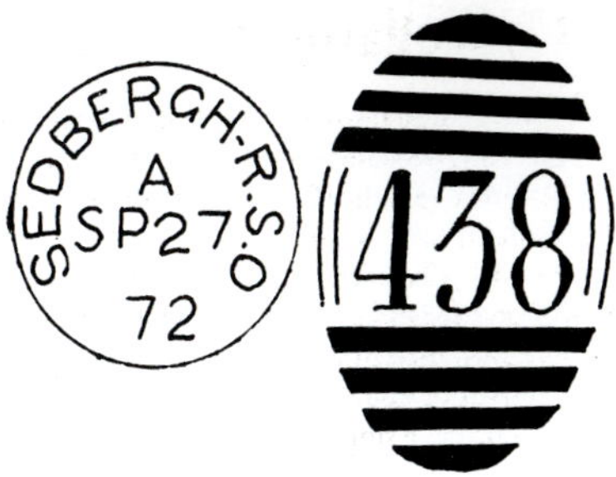

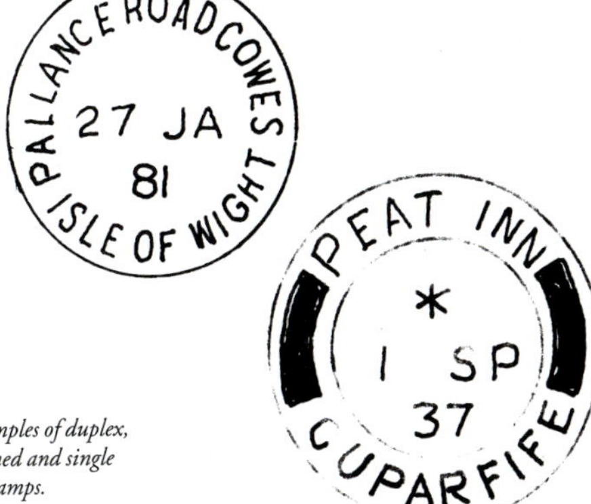

Examples of duplex, combined and single handstamps.

Slogans

ALTHOUGH handstruck slogans were used in London as early as 1661 to advertise the Kent Post, this concept was not revived until the advent of cancelling machines in the 1890s. From 1894 many American offices had cancellations incorporating the Stars and Stripes and it is from the seven wavy lines of this flag that we get the wavy line pattern used in machine marks to this day. Flag cancel marks were adopted by Canada, France, Germany, Italy and New Zealand at the turn of the century.

From this it was an easy progression to placing a slogan in the obliterating element. Slogans publicising contemporary events include Canada's National Exposition, Toronto (1901), the St Louis World's Fair (USA 1902), the Oberammergau Passion Play (Bavaria, 1910), the Brussels Fair (Belgium, 1910) and the Auckland Exhibition (New Zealand, 1912).

The first machine slogans in Britain appeared in December 1917 in connection with the National War Bonds campaign. They were extended to current events in the 1920s and tourist publicity in 1963. Although France and Italy permitted commercial slogans from the 1920s, this was strenuously rejected by the British Post Office for many years. In recent years, however, they have become the norm, a wide range of products and services being advertised in this way.

METER MARKS

METER MARKS, usually struck in red ink, were introduced in 1922 and are now increasingly studied, especially by thematic collectors seeking illustrations of their subjects.

Postage Paid Impressions (PPIs), widely used in the USA, spread to Britain in 1968 but so far have attracted only a limited following.

Meter mark with slogan die in a second colour.

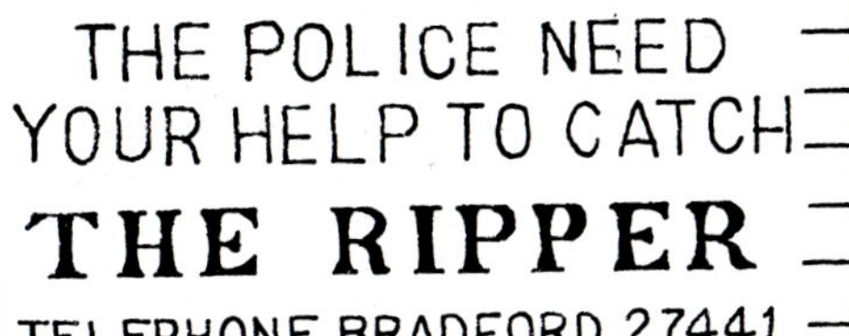

Slogan from Bradford, used in the hunt for the serial killer known as the Yorkshire Ripper – the only time a postmark has been used in crime detection.

CINDERELLAS
Introduction

In the fairy tale, Cinderella was the poor relation who was despised and exploited, but ended up as the belle of the ball and bride of Prince Charming. This is an apt description of the byways of philately, neglected and despised by most collectors for many years, but now attracting a respectable following.

THE CHIEF stigma attached to Cinderellas is that they are not listed in the standard stamp catalogues, and as collectors tended to follow these arbiters of fashion they automatically rejected them. On the other hand, there have always been a few independent spirits who felt that things only became interesting and challenging where the catalogues left off and so they pioneered an interest in the Cinderellas of philately, or revived an interest that had existed in the infancy of the hobby but had long lain dormant.

Moreover, with the trend to greater specialisation, collectors concentrating on a single country have been more inclined to spread their net to include all the odds and ends which the catalogues seldom have the space or inclination to list.

The Cinderellas may be divided into several broad categories: fiscal stamps (known in America as revenues) denoting taxes and duties, bogus and fantasy stamps, stamps for telegraphic services, stamps produced by road, rail, sea and air services, stamps of private local posts, exhibition labels and poster stamps, charity seals and all manner of stickers associated with the postal services.

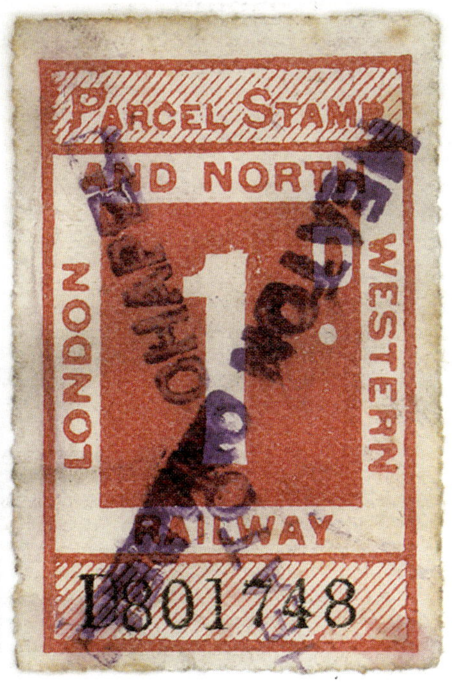

Parcel stamp of the London and North Western Railway.

Revenue Stamps

Adhesive stamps denoting the prepayment of taxes and duties have a much longer history than adhesive postage stamps, having been introduced in Britain in 1694.

STAMPS were originally embossed at the Board of Stamps and Taxes (Somerset House, London) and the regional stamp offices on white or blue paper affixed to parchment legal documents by means of lead staples, secured at the back by small labels. When paper replaced parchment it became possible to emboss the stamps directly on to the documents, a practice which continues to this day, but by that time adhesive stamps were being used for all manner of other taxes – on gloves, wig powder, dice, playing cards, tobacco, wines and spirits, ale, patent medicines, matches at various times and latterly gramophone records.

Adhesive stamps have also been used in the prepayment of entertainment taxes, for the payment of fines and court fees, for passports and consular services such as visas, sales taxes and receipts on all but the very smallest transactions. Adhesive stamps may even be found on old cheques, though later embossed stamps, as in legal documents, were preferred. Airport departure tax stamps, a relatively recent development, now attract serious attention from collectors.

The use of tax stamps for postage (known to collectors as 'postal fiscals') has been sanctioned from time to time. Conversely postage stamps are sometimes overprinted for use as tax stamps, while there are many cases of basic designs being modified for postal or fiscal use. British stamps since 1881 have been 'unified' (i.e. intended for either postage or revenue) and an interesting collection could be formed of these stamps used fiscally on receipts.

Examples of tax stamps.

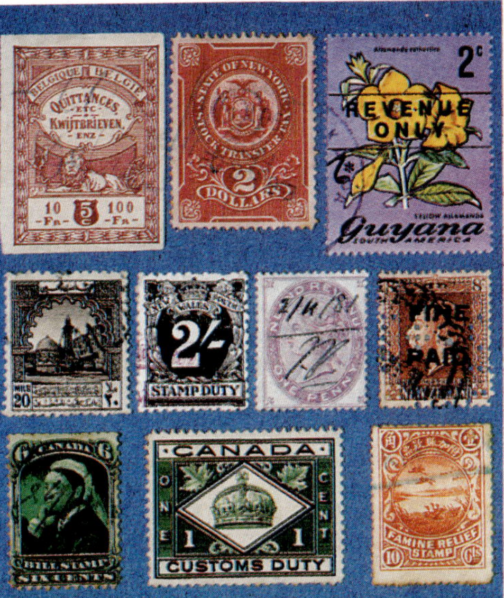

Bogus Stamps

These are stamps of fantasy, sometimes produced for completely non-existent places but more usually inscribed with the names of real places.

THE STAMPS of Counani, Clipperton Island, the Principality of Trinidad and Deh Sedang were produced by confidence tricksters who used them to induce the gullible to invest their money in colonial projects in non-existent countries. Civil war provides a marvellous opportunity for entrepreneurs who are quick to provide the rebels with a postal service – complete with stamps which can then be marketed on the other side of the world where their antecedents cannot be checked. The stamps of the South Moluccas (Maluku Selatan) may have been produced in good faith, but were never issued. Stamps inscribed Azad Hind (Free India) were printed in Nazi Germany for the Indian National Army but never issued – one of the 'might-have-beens' rather than bogus in the strict

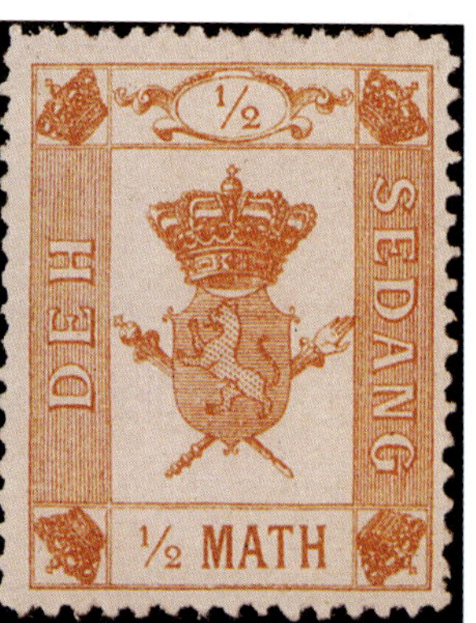

sense. Similarly many of the stamps of Biafra were mysteriously produced in Europe after the Nigerian civil war had ended.

Other bogus issues are more in the nature of propaganda material. Stamps purporting to come from Nagaland, 'royalist' Yemen or 'free' Albania, Croatia and Ukraine during the Cold War belong in this group.

Stamps from the Principality of Thomond or 'the Government of Staffa' (an uninhabited rock) were intended to exploit collectors, as are stamps of the present time purporting to come from Batum and Tuva – places in Russia which, at one time, issued genuine stamps or the Monica Lewinsky stamps of Abkhazia.

Left: bogus stamp of Deh Sedang; below: bogus stamp of the Principality of Trinidad.

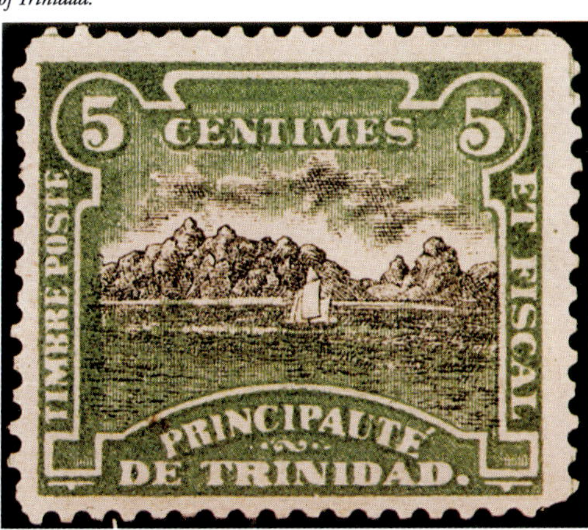

Telegraph and Telephone Stamps

These are stamps intended for the prepayment of telegrams and usually affixed by the sender to the telegram forms, though sometimes used by firms in the payment of telegraphic accounts.

TELEGRAPH services developed in the 1840s and by 1851 distinctive adhesive stamps for this purpose were being issued by the private telegraph companies in Britain. They continued to do this until 1870 when their services were taken over by the Post Office. Ordinary postage stamps were then used until 1876 when, to facilitate accounting, a separate series was adopted. The use of ordinary stamps was resumed in 1881, although separate issues for Army telegraphs were made (1884–1902). The National Telephone Company issued its own stamps, portraying the company chairman, from 1884 to 1891 when they were withdrawn at the request of the Postmaster General.

Telegraph and telephone stamps from Ecuador, Sudan, Great Britain and Spain.

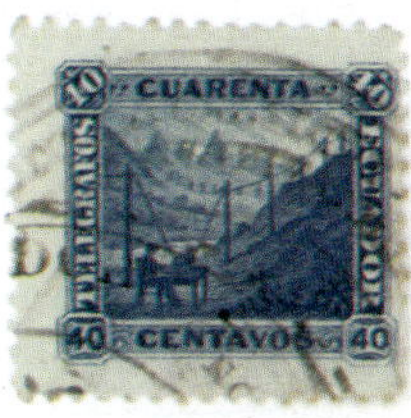
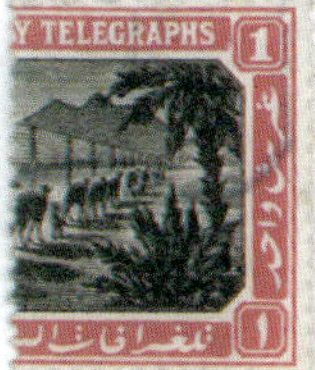

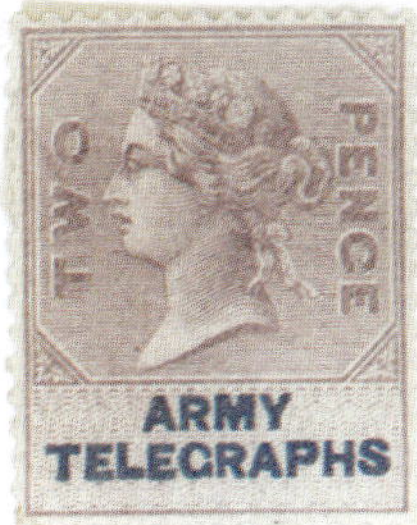

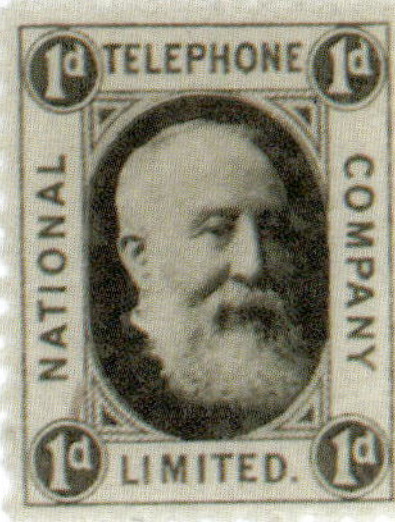

Stamps for both private and government-operated telegraph services have been issued in many countries. In some cases postage stamps were overprinted for telegraphic use; in others similar stamps but specifically inscribed TELEGRAPHS, or its equivalent, were produced. Distinctive stamps tended to be functional in appearance, but Ecuador, Spain and the Sudan issued attractive pictorials. In some cases (India and the Sudan) stamps were either cut or perforated in half, one part being affixed to the telegram and the other to the sender's receipt, meaning that complete stamps exist only in mint condition.

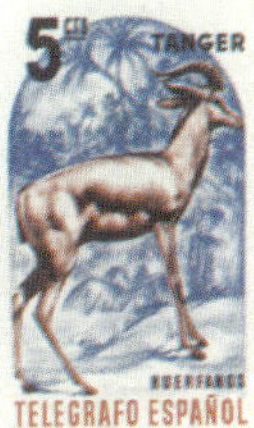

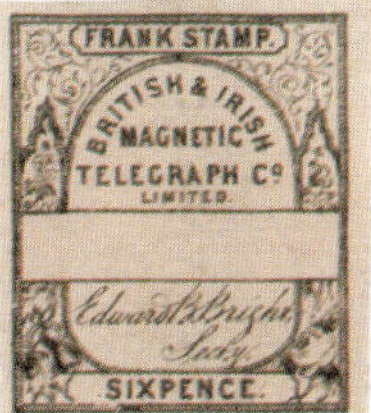

Savings Stamps

People were encouraged to save small amounts through the medium of Penny Banks which flourished in the 1840s. After the Post Office Savings Bank was founded in 1861 they gradually died out, but in 1880 the Post Office devised 'savings slips', small sheets to which a dozen penny stamps could be affixed. When the slip was full a shilling (the minimum deposit allowed) could be deposited in a savings account.

DISTINCTIVE savings stamps, known originally as coupons, were introduced in 1912 and continued till 1936. During the First World War, however, separate issues were made by the National War Savings Committee (ironically, in the light of later developments, these depicted a swastika). Later stamps, simply inscribed NATIONAL SAVINGS, kept this thrifty concept alive after the war and continued until 1976. The earlier symbolic motifs gave way to pictorial designs, including portraits of Prince Charles and Princess Anne.

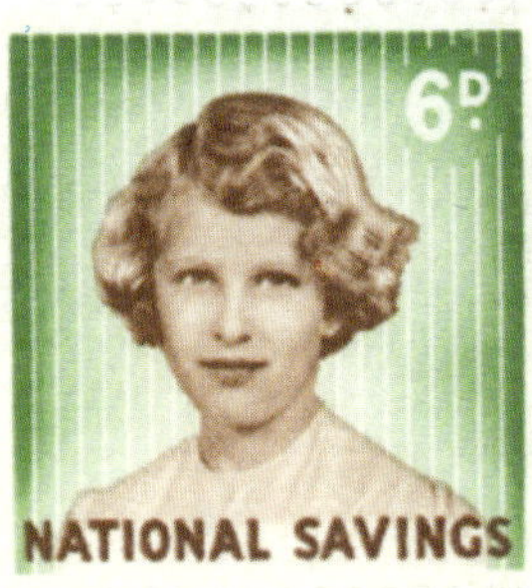

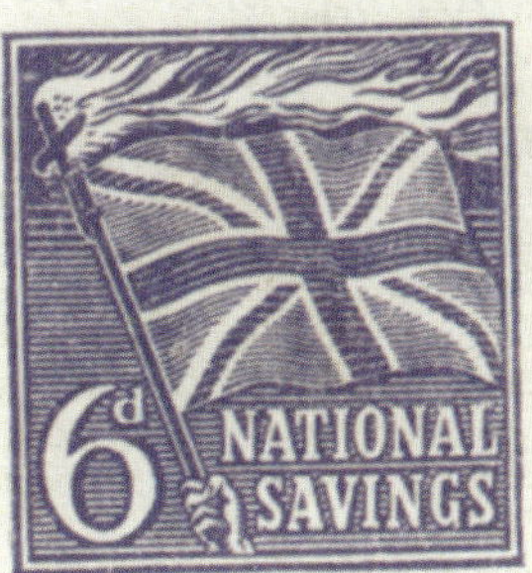

The National Savings scheme was scrapped because it cost too much to administer. However, people had found the stamps useful for regular savings, so the idea has been extended to a wide range of stamps issued by banks and public bodies to help pay for telephone, gas and electricity bills and television licences. There was even a short-lived (and now very elusive) Scottish pound stamp in connection with community charges.

Since 1896, numerous trading stamps have been issued by Sperry & Hutchinson, Green Shield and other discount companies, as well as by cooperative societies and chain stores.

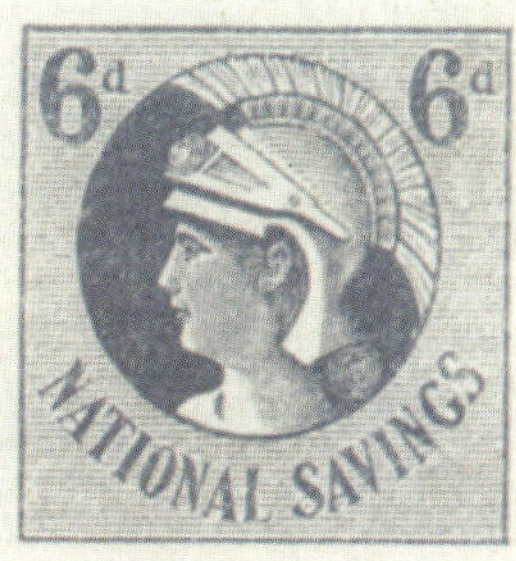

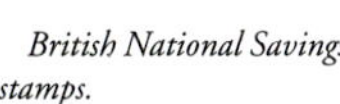

British National Savings stamps.

Insurance Stamps

Insurance stamps for unemployment, sickness and social security benefits date from 1912 in Britain and are now widely used in many countries.

UNTIL RECENTLY, British insurance stamps received scant attention from collectors, mainly because the stamped cards had to be surrendered to the authorities when completed. For that reason used examples seldom came into the hands of collectors, although there was always a devoted band of enthusiasts who made a point of purchasing stamps to be preserved in mint condition. Separate issues were made in Britain for National Health, Health & Pensions, National Insurance and Unemployment Insurance, and there was even a separate series for Agricultural Unemployment Insurance (1945). Ireland operated a similar system and even had stamps to guarantee the wages of building labourers laid off due to inclement weather.

The most elaborate stamps were produced by New Zealand, a new series in various denominations being issued every year. The earliest series (1936) was inscribed UNEMPLOYMENT RELIEF but later issues were more positively inscribed EMPLOYMENT (1937) or SOCIAL SECURITY (1940–58). The most attractive are the Mexican stamps inscribed SEGURO SOCIAL depicting flowers, butterflies, birds and other colourful subjects.

Insurance stamps from New Zealand, Great Britain and Ireland.

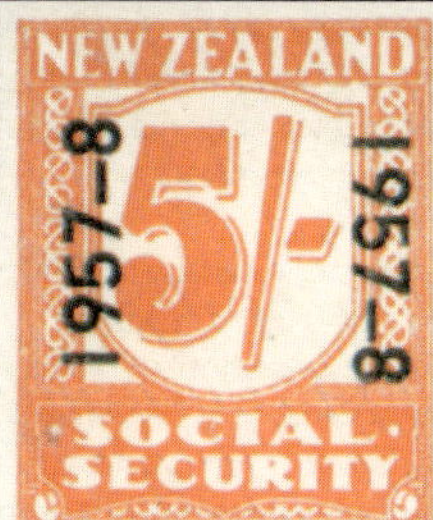

NEW ZEALAND
1957-8
1957-8
5/-
SOCIAL
SECURITY

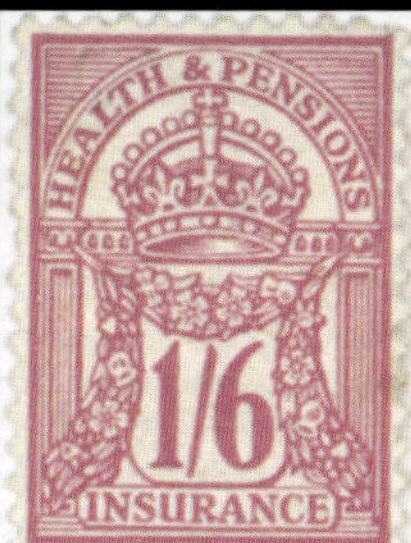

HEALTH & PENSIONS
1/6
INSURANCE

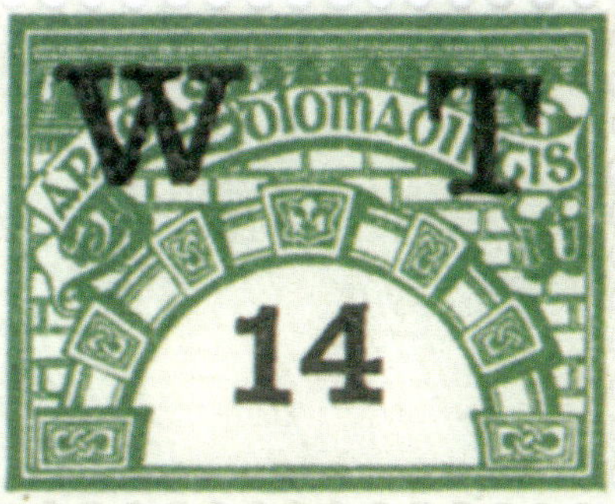

W T
14

Railway Stamps

Distinctive stamps have been produced by the railway companies for many years, mainly for use on parcels but also, in some cases, on express letters.

RAILWAY parcel stamps were first used in Britain in 1855. Even after the Post Office instituted the parcel post in 1883, a high proportion of parcels continued to be sent by rail. Furthermore, as the Post Office was dependent on the railway companies for the conveyance of its parcels, it was obliged to concede to the railways the right to convey railway letters, provided that they bore a penny postage stamp and a special twopenny stamp to cover the rail fee. Special railway letter stamps were issued by many companies and survived until the 1920s. They have been revived in recent years by some of the private light railways operated by preservation societies.

Some of the railway companies had a wide range of stamps for special purposes, such as newspapers, milk churns, farm produce, samples and market baskets. Many were beautifully engraved with

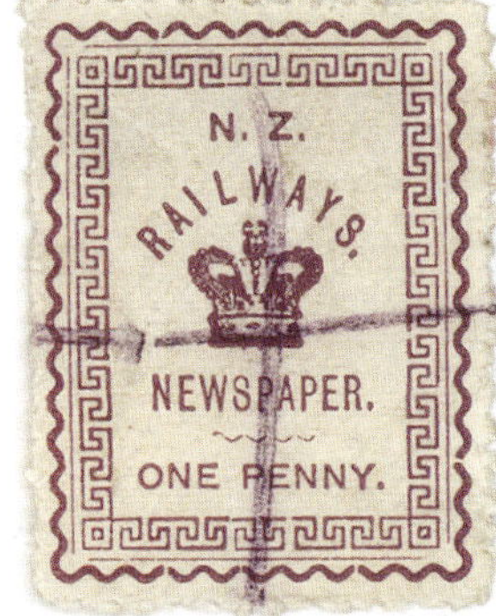

the company's insignia and tiny vignettes of locomotives.

Distinctive stamps were issued by the state railways of many countries. In some, such as Belgium and Bulgaria, the carriage of parcels is a state monopoly in the hands of the railways, and special railway stamps are issued under the authority of the Post Office.

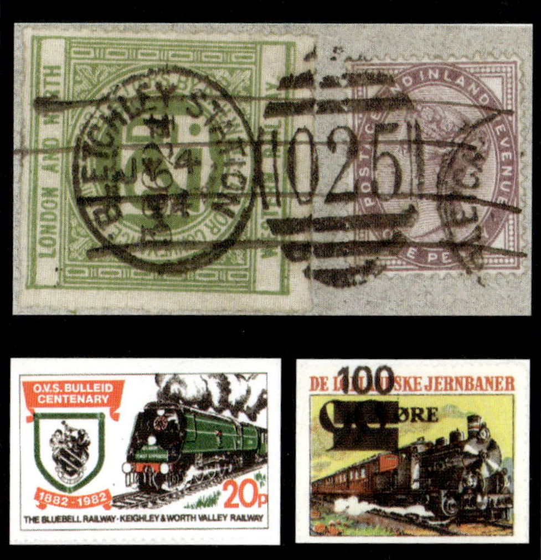

Railway letter and parcel stamps from New Zealand, Great Britain and Denmark.

Courier and Freight Stamps

Deregulation of postal services in recent years has greatly increased the number of companies operating local or national networks for the rapid transmission of documents, packets and parcels.

FREIGHT-HANDLERS have long issued their own stamps. Many bus companies and ferry or coastal shipping lines have, or had, distinctive labels for parcels received and delivered en route, and some survive to this day. But the tremendous growth in the courier industry in the past 20 years has given rise to a large number of different labels for parcels

Strike post cover, 1971.

and express mail. At the same time, Parcelforce has developed its business to keep pace, and likewise issues a wide variety of barcoded labels which, while not regarded as stamps in the strict sense, merit inclusion in a collection of freight issues.

Many of the services in existence today developed out of the attempts to circumvent the postal strikes which engulfed Britain in 1962, 1964 and, especially, 1971. Indeed, the stamps of these strike posts are now a popular collecting theme in their own right.

Barcode courier label of Securicor.

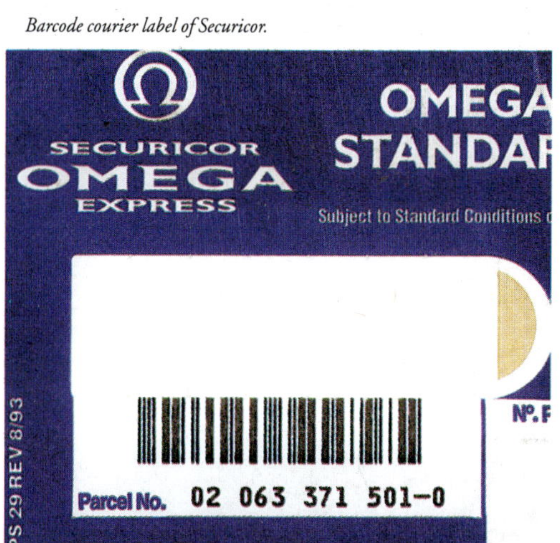

Stamps of the Local Posts

In many countries certain aspects of the post were left to private enterprise. In these cases distinctive stamps were produced but because they were not issued by government authority they are excluded from the standard stamp catalogues. Some of these categories are listed below.

CARRIER STAMPS

IN THE USA, between 1842 and 1863, when general town delivery was taken over by the US Post Office, numerous carriers operated local services and issued their own stamps. In fact, the stamps of the New York City Despatch Post (1842) were the first to appear anywhere in the world outside Britain.

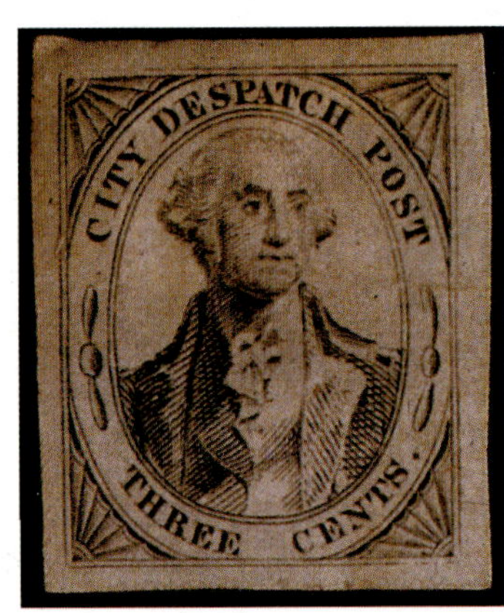

New York City Despatch, 1842.

LOCAL POSTS

UP TO March 1900 local services in Germany were in the hands of over 200 companies, all of which issued their own stamps. Similar services operated in many parts of Denmark, Norway and Sweden.

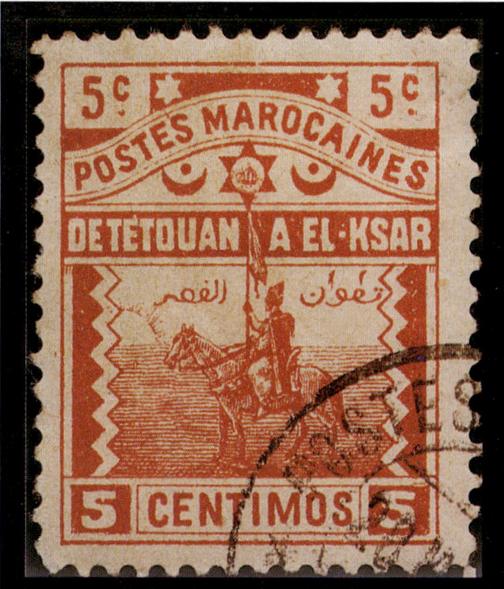

Local stamp from Morocco.

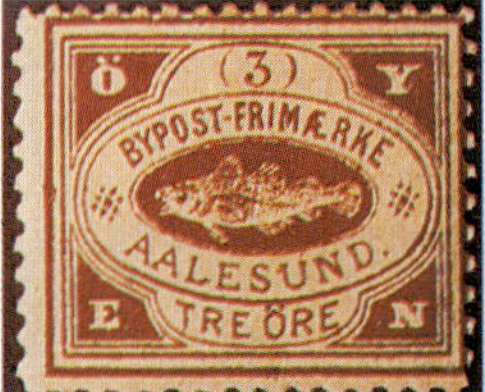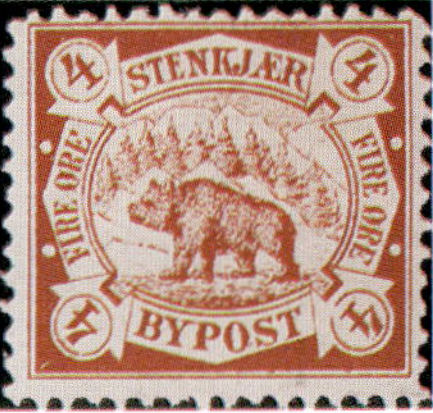

Local stamps from Aalesund, Stenkjaer (above) and Breslau (below).

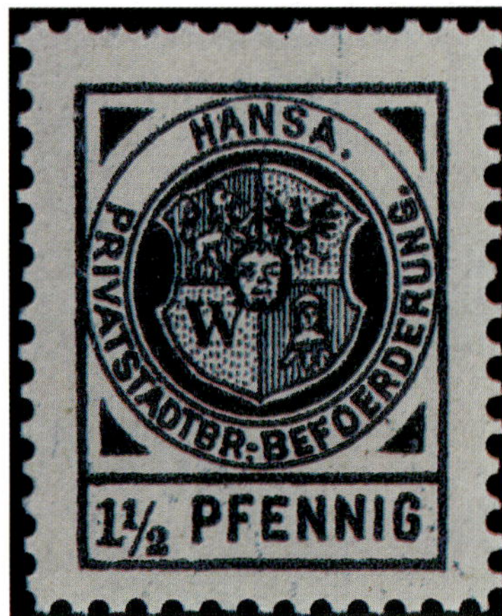

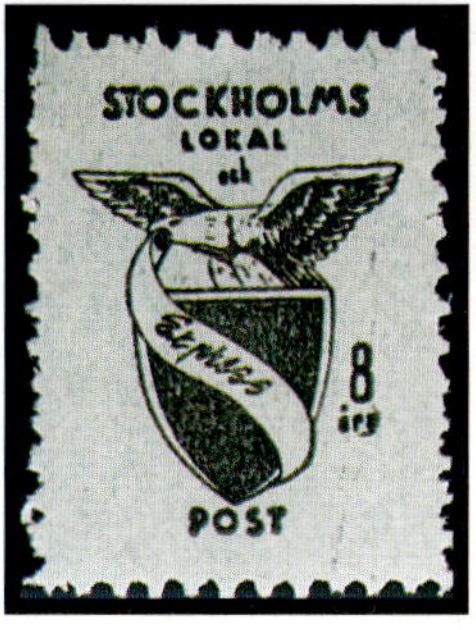 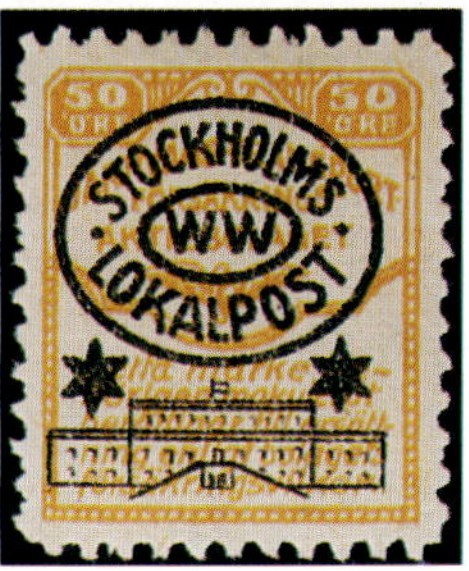

Local stamps from Stockholm.

CIRCULAR DELIVERY STAMPS

IN 1865 various circular delivery companies in Britain began issuing stamps, usually of farthing or halfpenny denomination, for services that undercut the Post Office. They were suppressed in 1867, but three years later the Post Office was forced to introduce a halfpenny rate for printed matter including circulars.

CHRISTMAS CHARITY POSTS

UNDER THE terms of the Telecommunications Act of 1981 scout and church groups are permitted to operate local delivery of greetings cards between 25 November and 1 January each year. Over 200 organisations have taken advantage of this and issue distinctive stamps each year.

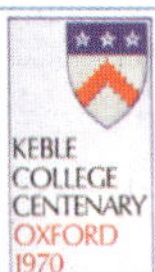

COLLEGE POSTS

MANY OF THE colleges at Oxford and Cambridge issued their own stamps from 1871 to 1884 when the practice was stopped. Keble revived the idea in 1970 to celebrate its centenary.

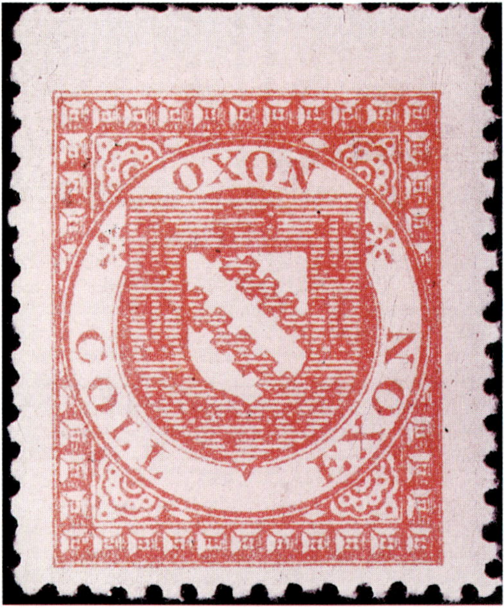

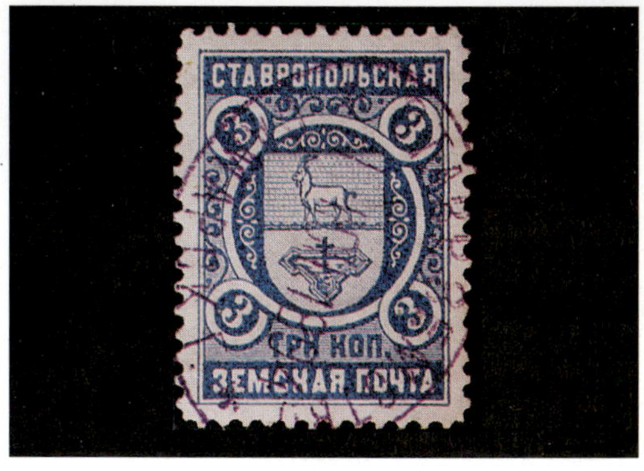

ZEMSTVOS

A NETWORK of local posts operated in the *zemstvos* (regions) of Tsarist Russia and issued stamps from 1864 until 1917, when they were suppressed at the Revolution.

DEREGULATION OF POSTS

THE TREND towards the privatisation of postal services in many countries has led to restrictions on the state monopoly of mail-handling. Already about 20 private services are functioning in Sweden and almost as many in the Netherlands, while Germany is in the process of phasing out the state monopoly altogether. Many collectors are now watching these developments keenly, with a view to building up collections of the local issues of the new millennium from the moment they appear.

Left: Keble and Exeter College stamps; above: zemstvo *stamp from Stavropol.*

Publicity and Charity Labels

Advertising labels, sometimes called poster stamps, were extensively used at the turn of the century to publicise current events and celebrate historic anniversaries. This branch of the hobby even rejoiced in the name of erinnophily (from German *Erinnerung*, 'commemoration', and Greek *philos*, 'love').

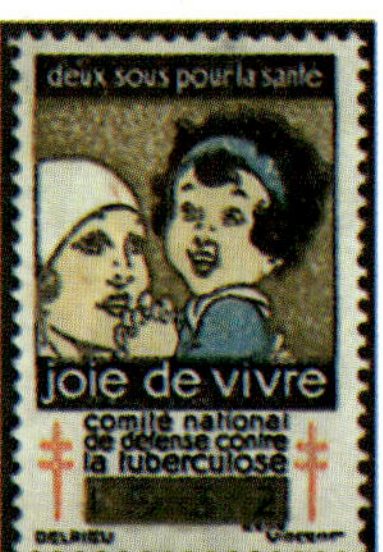

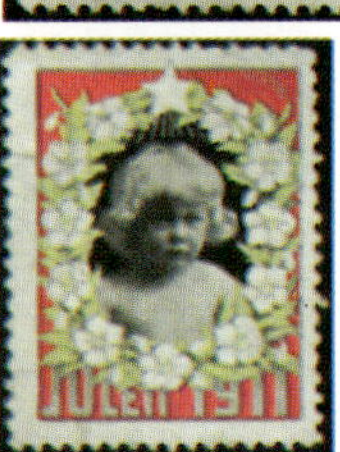

A LTHOUGH largely overtaken by commemorative stamps on the one hand and pictorial postmarks and meter marks on the other, labels still attract a strong following,

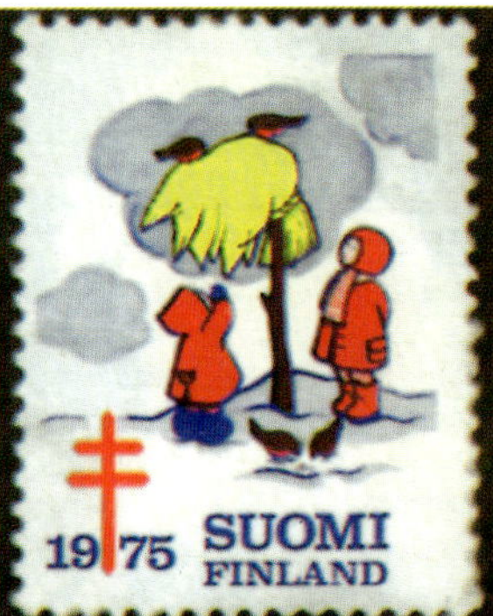

especially those connected with stamp exhibitions.

Christmas seals were invented by a Danish postal official, Einar Holboell, in 1904 to raise money for an anti-tuberculosis fund. The idea soon spread to other Scandinavian countries, France, the USA and Canada. They enjoy semi-official status in the Scand-inavian countries to this day, often produced and issued by the postal administrations. In many cases different designs are used for each label in the sheet. In South Africa they are produced in booklets sold over post office counters. Many charities now issue their own labels for use on Christmas or Easter greetings cards.

A particularly interesting group consists of propaganda and patriotic labels, issued by the different participants in wartime.

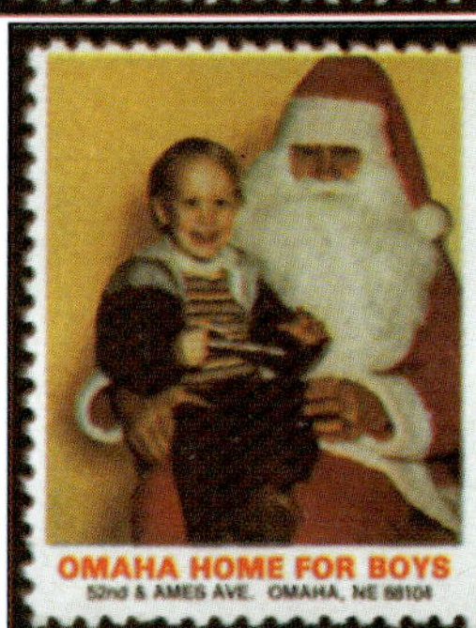

Christmas seals from France, Denmark, Finland, the Faroe Islands and the US.

Postal Stickers

All postal administrations produce stickers in connection with various services. Although not postage stamps, they are official issues, and form an aspect of the study of the postal services.

REGISTRATION LABELS

ARGUABLY THE largest category of postal stickers consists of registration labels, pioneered by the German states in the 1860s and formally adopted by the UPU in 1881, although

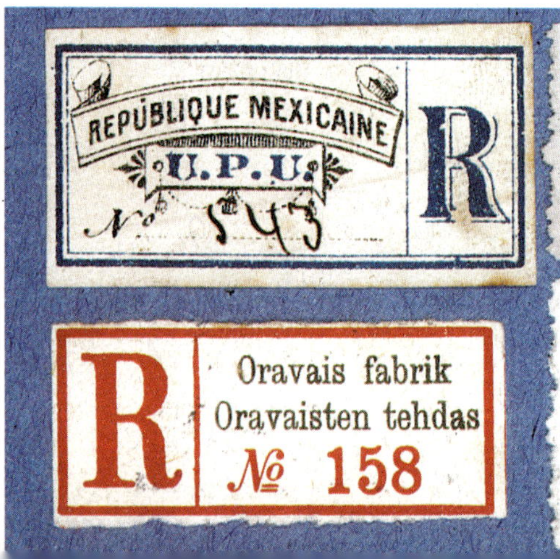

not used in Britain until 1907. Until recently every post office had its own distinctive labels, so that the number of different labels is astronomical.

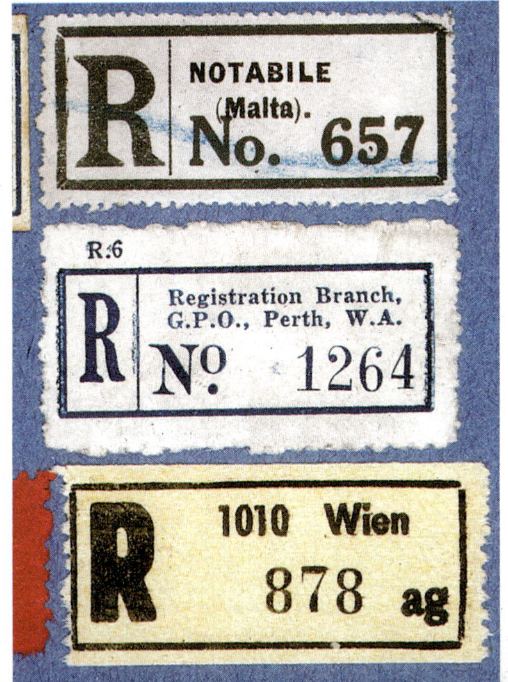

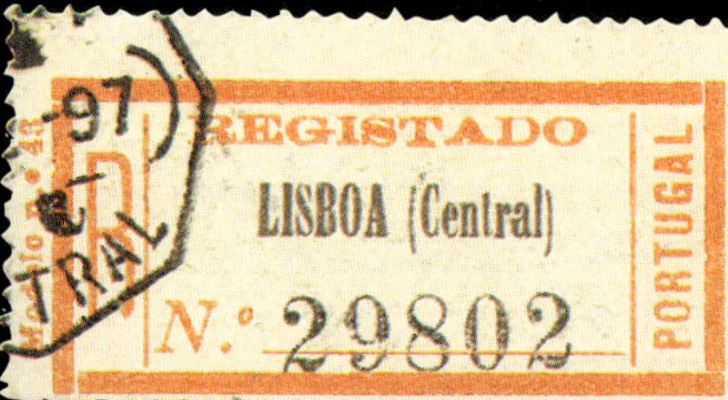
REGISTADO
LISBOA (Central)
N.º 29802
PORTUGAL
Taxpost
UÇAK İLE
PAR AVION

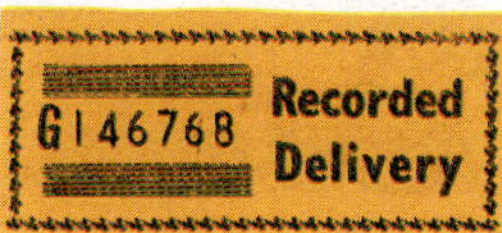

Great Britain: Recorded Delivery label.

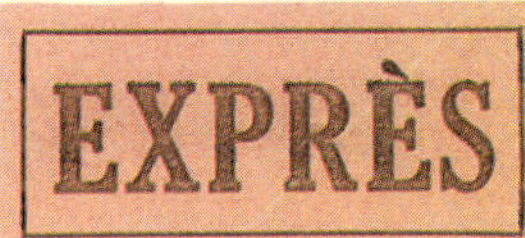

French label for express mail.

PARCEL LABELS

BETWEEN 1883 and 1916 every post office in the British Isles had its own parcel labels. They were superseded by parcel datestamps, but are now keenly sought after by local postal historians. Similar systems operated in many other countries.

AIRMAIL LABELS

FRANCE pioneered these *etiquettes* in August 1918 and since then a vast range has appeared, both official and privately issued by the various airlines. They continue to this day, though largely superseded in many countries by A-priority labels, predominantly blue in colour like the airmail labels themselves.

OTHER SERVICES

THERE ARE labels for certified and insured mail, express and special delivery, the special handling of fragile, perishable or infectious materials, and labels explaining non-delivery or the reason for a surcharge. There are even Israeli labels warning people receiving parcels to be cautious about bombs!

Left: special labels for registered mail (Portugal), Taxpost (Great Britain) and airmail (Turkey).

RARE STAMPS
Introduction

THE STORIES of spectacular finds of rare stamps, or the astronomical sums which the greatest rarities fetch at auction, are always good for headlines in newspapers. This media coverage tends to create a false impression that old stamps are rare and therefore valuable. Many old stamps are quite plentiful and can still be purchased for a few pence. Conversely there are some modern stamps, even of the 1990s, which are extremely rare. Age alone is not a useful criterion.

Similarly there is a tendency to equate rarity with value. There are quite a few stamps of which only a solitary example is believed to exist, but while some of these would fetch a high six-figure sum were they to appear at auction, there are others which might realise no more than a few hundred pounds. The law of supply and demand affects the desirability, and therefore the value, of stamps in the same way as it applies to any other commodity.

Thomas Tapling (whose incomparable collection is in the British Library) once swapped a unique piece – a pair of ½-anna stamps from the Indian state of Poonch – for an

Right and above: Mauritius 2d and 1d 'Post Office' (1847).

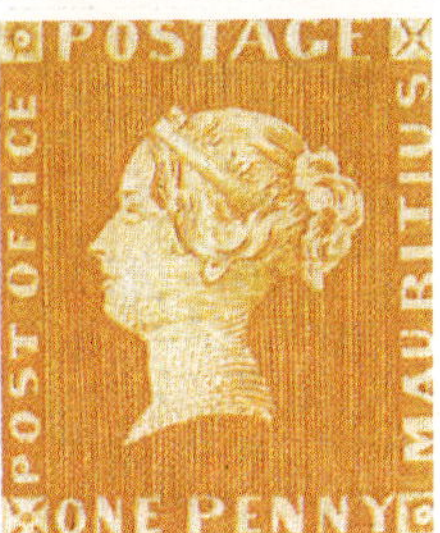

unused Mauritius 'Post Office' 2d. Although the Poonch item is unique, whereas there are four unused and nine used copies of the Mauritius stamp, Tapling had the better bargain. When the Poonch piece came up at auction in 1967 it fetched £320, whereas two years earlier, an unused 2d Mauritius had made £13,500. Today the Poonch item might fetch £5,000, but the 2d Mauritius, now priced at £450,000 in used condition, is beyond price unused. Yet another stamp, of which only three copies exist in used condition, is the Somaliland Protectorate 1 rupee of 1904 overprinted for official use – listed at a mere £650 in Gibbons.

The 'Double Geneva' of Switzerland.

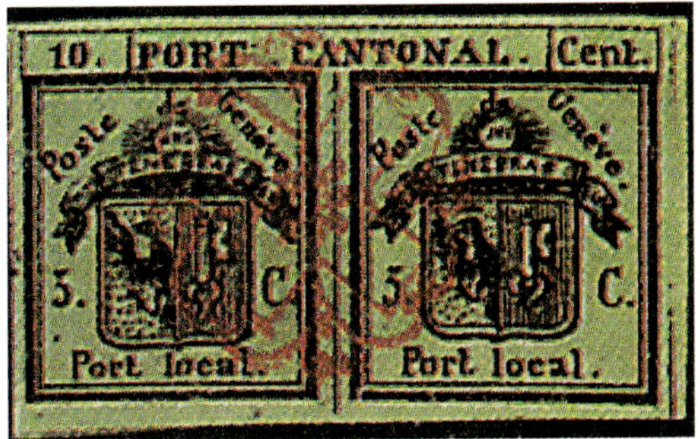

Factors Affecting Value

There are several factors which have to be taken into consideration in understanding what makes a stamp valuable.

NUMBER ISSUED

OBVIOUSLY THE number issued has some bearing on value, but this must still be treated with caution. Far more important is the number that have survived in fine, collectable condition.

There are stamps which were issued in large numbers, the majority of which have been used postally, so very few copies are known in mint condition. This situation applies, for example, to the early stamps of Italy, where a fine used copy

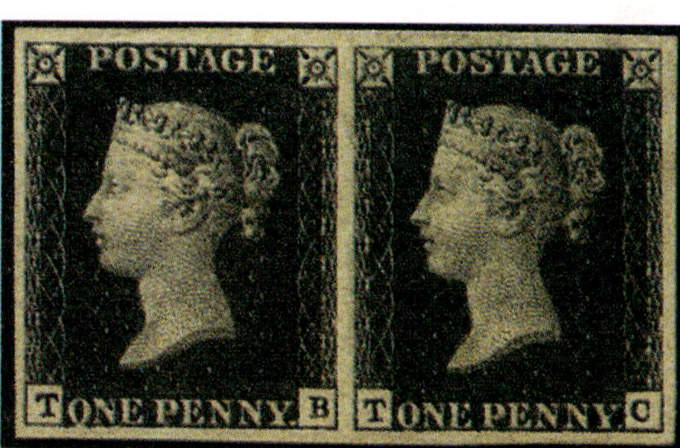

Mint pair of Penny Blacks from the bottom row of the sheet.

may be worth only 50p while a mint stamp may run to hundreds of pounds.

There is a popular fallacy that the Penny Black, the world's first adhesive postage stamp, is very rare if not unique. In fact over 61 million were printed, of which as many as five per cent

Matched pairs of Penny Blacks and Penny Reds from plates 5 and 8.

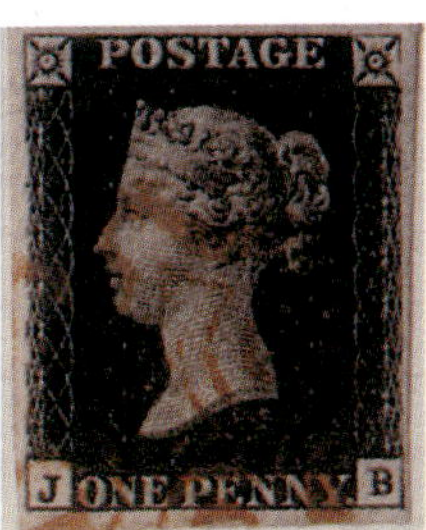
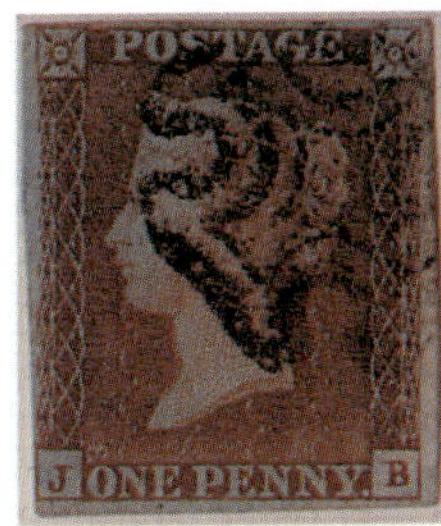
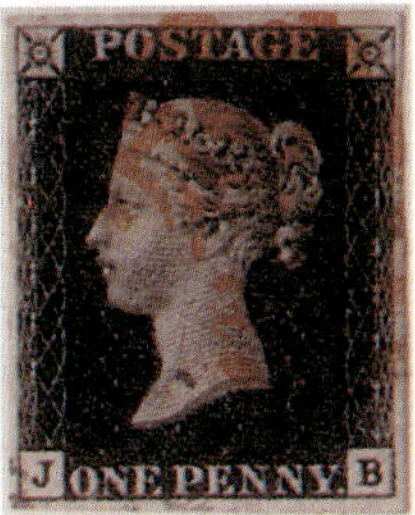

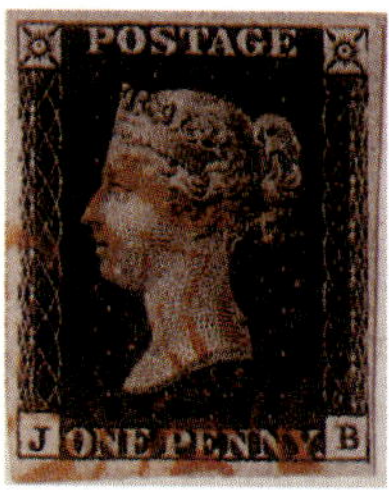

may have survived. No serious collector of British stamps would feel that his collection were complete unless he had at least one example.

Of course, there is a wide disparity in the value of Penny Blacks. The Gibbons catalogues, for example, price the cheapest version of this stamp at £3,000 and £160 in unused or fine used condition respectively, but stamps from Plate 11 (the last to be used) are priced at £4,500 and £1,600 respectively. The catalogue also quotes prices for Maltese Cross cancellations in different colours, the London crosses with numbers 1–12, late usage with the numeral obliterators introduced in 1844, and so on. A Penny Black from Plate 2 with a common cancellation rates £160, whereas one with London cross number 1 rates £2,750 – almost 20 times as much.

CONDITION

ALL OTHER things being equal, it is a stamp's condition which determines its value, and yet this is probably the most difficult factor to assess. A list of the terms most commonly used to describe a stamp is given below.

1. Unmounted mint

A stamp in perfect condition, with four full margins (if imperforate) or well centred with all its teeth intact (perforated). The surface will have a fresh colour, with no sign of rubbing, and its gum will be immaculate, with no sign of hinging.

2. Mounted mint
As above, but very lightly hinged, or bearing exceptionally minute traces of a previous stamp mount.

3. Unused or Part OG
A stamp which has been heavily mounted in an album, either by hinges or by means of a portion of its own gum, but still retains some semblance of original gum (hence the abbreviation).

4. Unused without gum
An unpostmarked stamp which has been stuck down at some time, and on being soaked off the album page, has had its gum washed off. Many very early stamps lack gum for this reason.

5. Fine used
A stamp with the lightest possible postmark but otherwise intact, well-centred and of fresh colour.

The best prices are paid for stamps in categories 1 and 5. Many catalogues now include separate price columns for unmounted and mounted mint stamps, and in some cases the differential may be as much as 70 per cent. The same applies to used stamps with heavy or smudged postmarks, or even rare stamps with such blemishes as a slight thin on the back or a small tear. Average used copies of Penny Blacks, therefore, can often be picked up for £20. Two-margined copies (i.e. with the design cut into on two sides) may cost much less.

To hinge or not to hinge? The modern fad for unmounted mint, apart from raising the basic costs of collecting by insisting that mint stamps should be kept in patent strips and not mounted in the traditional manner, has created a veritable industry in the regumming of old stamps. More on this tricky subject is given in Fakes and Forgeries.

Ironically, most museums, more acutely aware of the need for conservation than private collectors, now operate a policy of removing the gum from stamps, realising that this substance is not chemically inert and often poses a very real threat to the paper, especially the very brittle papers of many classic stamps.

Admittedly, the gum serves no real academic purpose and the museum authorities are unlikely to be worried by the financial aspects of this practice. But it would take a revolution in philatelic thinking to get collectors to remove the gum from early stamps.

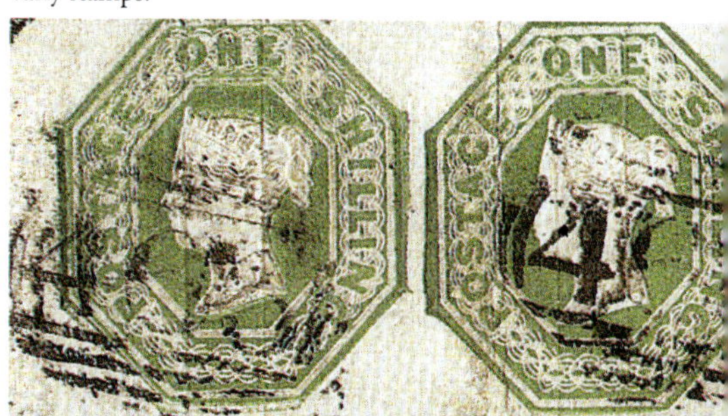

Apart from having unblemished gum, the back of a stamp should not be damaged, thinned or torn in any way. Ideally, imperforate stamps with designs in an unusual shape (circular, octagonal, and so on) should be cut square and are worth a handsome premium in this state. So many copies of the 4 annas indigo and red of India, 1854, were trimmed by native traders (who were anxious to keep the weight of their letters down) that cut square copies are 20 times as scarce. Another reason for classics such as the Ceylon 'Pence' and the British embossed 6d, 10d and 1s stamps being cut to shape is that many of the early collectors trimmed them neatly to fit the printed spaces in their albums. The embossed stamps, printed by hand, are seldom found with good margins anyway, and often impressions of adjoining stamps overlap.

Strip of four British shilling stamps, 1847 showing portions of adjoining stamps and how the stamps often overlap.

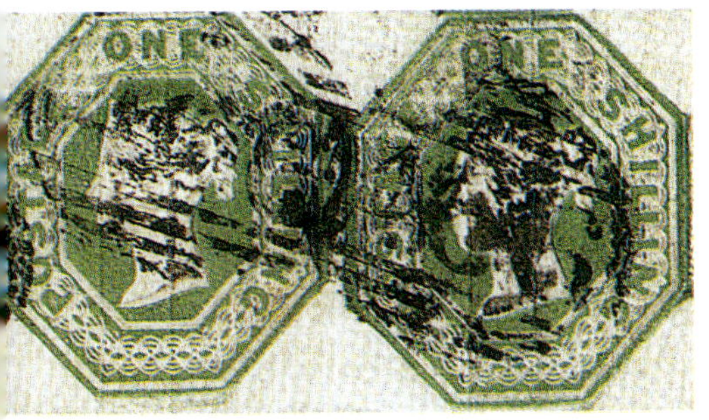

THE SURFACE OF A STAMP

THE SURFACE of a stamp should be freshly coloured, without evidence of fading or bleaching. Foxing or rust stains, occasionally encountered on older stamps printed on paper containing iron impurities, can be removed by the careful use of a little chloramine-T (a form of bleach) in a weak solution, brushed on gently and rinsed well afterwards in cold water. This should only be done in the case of intaglio, lithographed or letterpress stamps on ordinary paper; but *never* on stamps on chalk-surfaced paper or on modern photogravure stamps.

Early intaglio stamps can often be improved by careful brushing with a weak solution of hydrogen peroxide to remove sulphur dioxide damage caused by atmospheric pollution. This sulphuretting can cause ink colours to degrade.

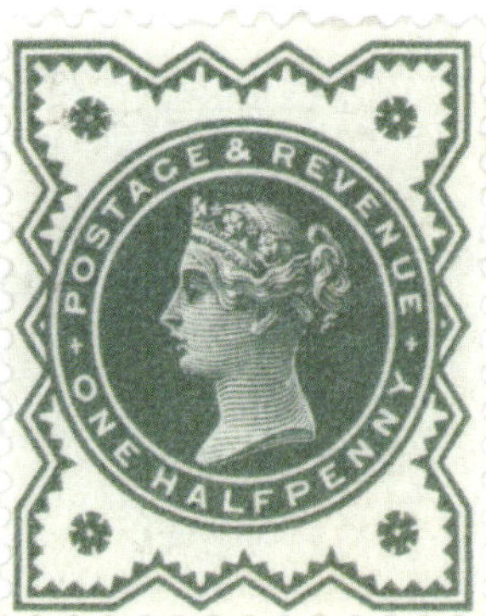

Stamps printed on surfaced paper, particularly those manufactured by De La Rue, with their famous single and double fugitive inks, have to be treated with great care. Unused examples, with full, fresh colours are worth a premium as so many of these stamps (of the period 1880–1930) have rubbed surfaces or faded colurs.

Many De La Rue stamps were printed on ordinary as well as chalk-surfaced paper, so it is important to be able to distinguish them. If silver is applied to a chalk-surfaced paper it leaves a black mark. This can be tested by touching the corner with the edge of a silver coin (any British coin dated before 1920 will do).

Pair of British De La Rue stamps showing the contrast between a stamp in perfect condition and one in poor condition.

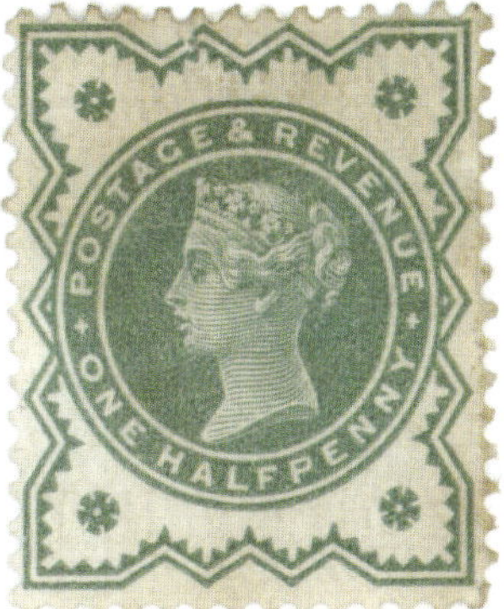

Country of Origin

The law of supply and demand is, to a large extent, governed by the popularity of the country issuing the stamps.

STAMPS attain their greatest popularity in their own country, but much depends on what percentage of the population collects stamps. Many countries have as yet little indigenous philatelic activity; these include the underdeveloped countries, especially those in regions of great temperature and humidity, conditions which militate against stamp collecting. Much also depends on the degree of literacy of the population, their living standards and income and the amount of free time available for hobbies.

The most popular countries from the philatelic viewpoint are those in western Europe, the USA, the older Commonwealth countries (Australia, Canada, New Zealand and South Africa), and in Asia Japan, Taiwan, South Korea, Hong Kong, Singapore and Malaysia. Stamps from former colonies tend to be more popular than those issued since independence. Gold Coast is popular, but Ghana is not. Israeli stamps are popular with Jewish collectors all over the world; similarly Catholics tend to favour the stamps of the Vatican.

At one time the 'dead' countries were not rated, but as many collectors turn away from the constant spate of new issues, the fortunes of Manchuria and Montenegro have revived. Generally speaking, the smaller, more remote and esoteric countries, such as Pitcairn Island and Tristan da Cunha, have a very strong following, even if the number of indigenous collectors could be numbered on the fingers of both hands.

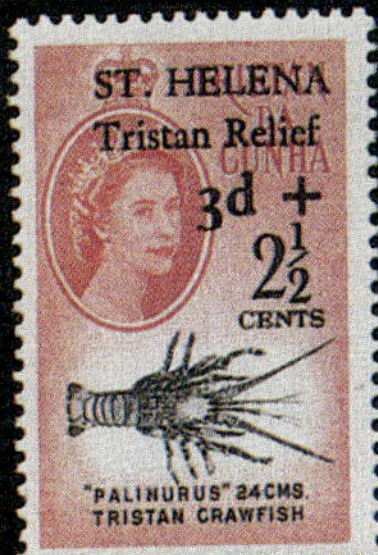
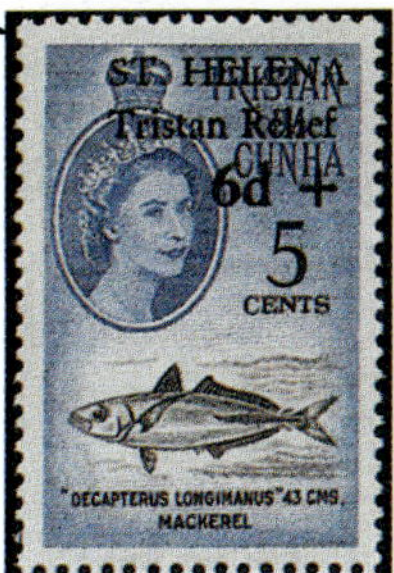
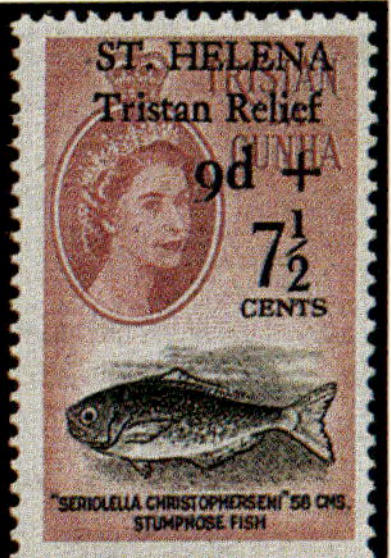
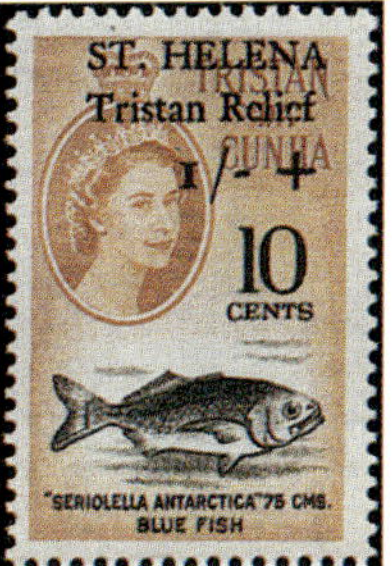

Tristan da Cunha overprinted for use in St Helena, 1961 to raise funds for the islanders evacuated after the volcano erupted. Only 434 sets were sold and now rate £4,000 in mint condition.

Political and Economic Factors

THE POLITICAL and economic stability of a country is reflected in its stamps and there is thus little market for the issues of Albania or former Zaire. Exceptionally, the stamps of former East Germany have risen considerably in value in the past few years as a result of the reunification of Germany.

Germany also furnishes examples of two other phenomena which affect value. The first was the hyper-inflation of 1923, when postal rates changed daily and eventually 50 *billion* marks would hardly pay the postage on a letter. Many stamps of that period are still plentiful in complete sheets, and every schoolboy collection at one time had a fine array of them, from cheap packets. There are still some unconsidered rarities which astute specialists snap up at bargain prices.

The 1 *milliard* marks surcharge on 100 marks purple, issued on 7 November 1923, is popularly known as the Hitler Provisional because it was only issued in Munich, where Hitler staged his abortive *putsch* the following day. Mint examples are priced by Gibbons at 10p but the stamp in the deep reddish purple shade is very scarce in mint condition and now rates £55. Fine *used* stamps are rare. Even the ordinary purple version is catalogued at £26, whereas the reddish purple is a major rarity commanding a figure of £2,750. Only three complete mint sheets of the reddish purple exist and one of these fetched £9,000 at a Sotheby's sale in December 1997.

Hitler Provisional, 1923.

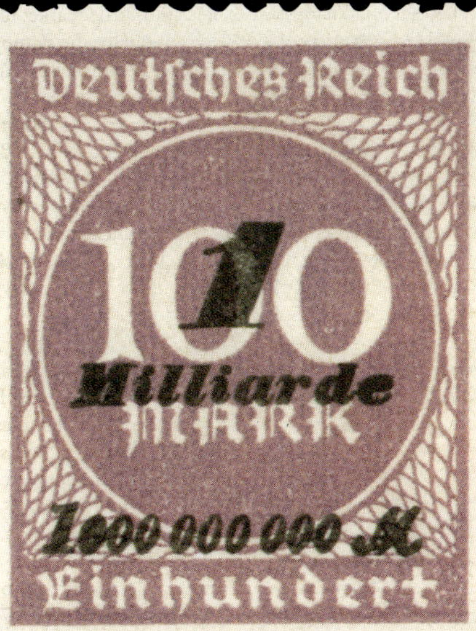
Deutsches Reich
100
1
Milliarde
MARK
1000 000 000 M
Einhundert

In the Right Place
at the Right Time

WHEN I was a schoolboy I had a pen-friend in Germany and this led me to collect German stamps. I purchased mint new issues from a local dealer with my pocket money. In 1951–52 West Germany issued the Posthorn definitives. The set of 16, from 2 to 90 pfennige, had a total face value of 5.15 marks – less than 10 shillings at the then rate of exchange. At the new issue rate then prevailing, I probably paid no more than 12s 6d for the lot, but today that set is catalogued at £1,900.

This is by no means an exceptional example. The Bach pair of 1950 and the St Mary's Church pair of 1951 together cost me about a shilling but today are priced at £125 and £200 respectively.

The reason for the disparity between actual cost at time of issue and the present market level is that, in 1950–51 few

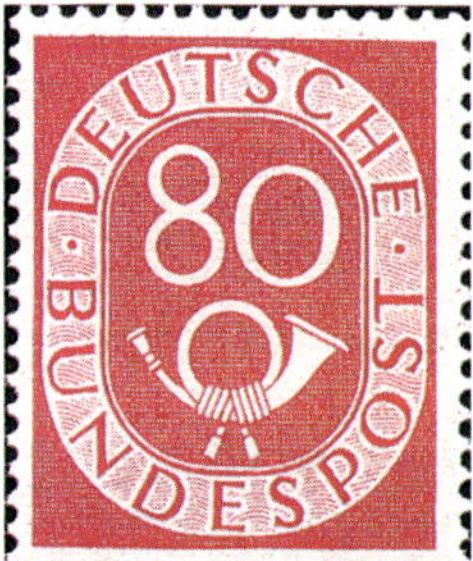

Germans could afford their own stamps. The numbers sold were relatively small and went mainly to collectors abroad. Now, Germany has one of the strongest philatelic markets, with fierce home demand forcing the price of stamps of 1948–52 into orbit.

Interestingly, these remarks apply to the stamps of West Berlin and East Germany in the same period. The Chinese

Friendship trio of 1951, which I bought at the time for less than 2 shillings, is now priced at £350. Berlin's overprints of 1948, especially the mark denominations, are now major rarities. One of my better buys was the Berlin Relief Fund miniature sheet on first day cover which cost me 3 shillings – a week's pocket money – but as it is now worth £2,250 it turned out to be rather a nice investment.

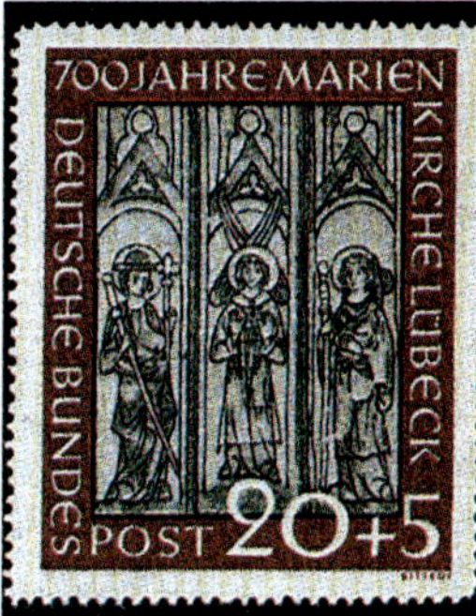

Left: Posthorn definitive 80 pf; above: St Mary's Chuch 20+5 pf; below: West Berlin 10+5, 20+5 and 30+5 pf Berlin Relief Fund.

Great Classic Stamps

Collectors regard 1840–70 as the great classic period, when some of the world's most beautiful – and also most primitive – stamps were produced. All are scarce and some are very rare.

MANY OF THEM were finely engraved, like the British Penny Black and Twopence Blue. Joseph Barnard engraved the first stamps of Mauritius, the first colony to emulate the mother country, in 1847. Barnard, in fact, based his 1d and 2d stamps on their British counterparts but inscribed them POST OFFICE and MAURITIUS at the sides. Most of the 1d stamps were used by Lady Gomm, wife of the island's governor, to invite people to a ball at Government House.

Brazil was the first country in the western hemisphere to issue stamps, the celebrated Bull's-eyes of 1843. The USA

Brazil Bull's-eye (1843).

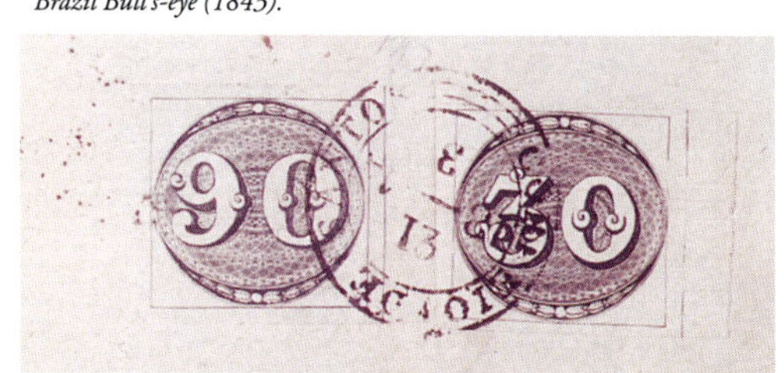

James Buchanan 5c stamp (1845).

followed in 1847, although various postmasters, like James Buchanan of Baltimore, as well as private posts, had issued their own stamps from 1842 onwards.

Geneva, Zurich and Basle introduced stamps in 1843–45, though the federal issues of Switzerland did not appear till 1850.

Germany's first stamp was the *Schwarzer Einser* (Black One) of Bavaria, 1849. In the same year both France and Belgium adopted stamps, known to collectors as the Ceres and Epaulettes respectively.

US 5c and 10c (1847).

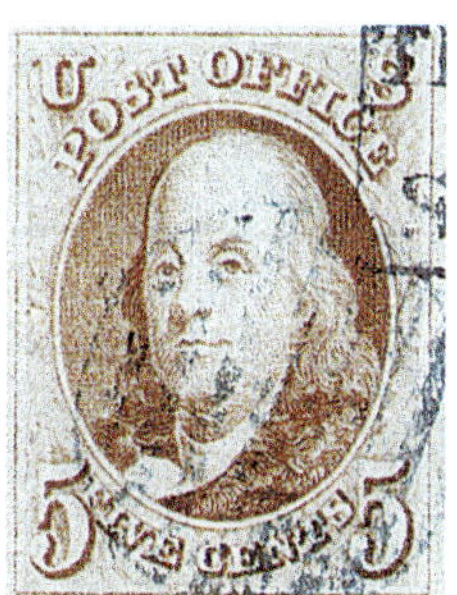
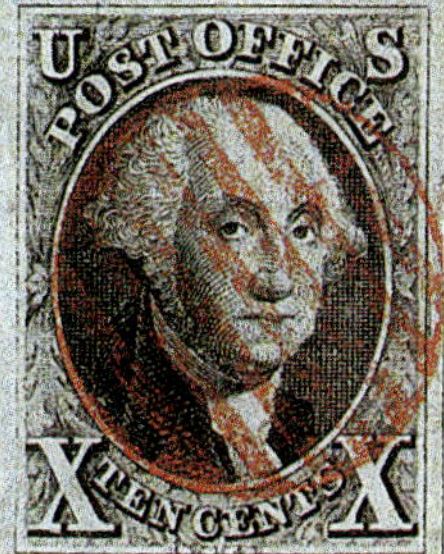

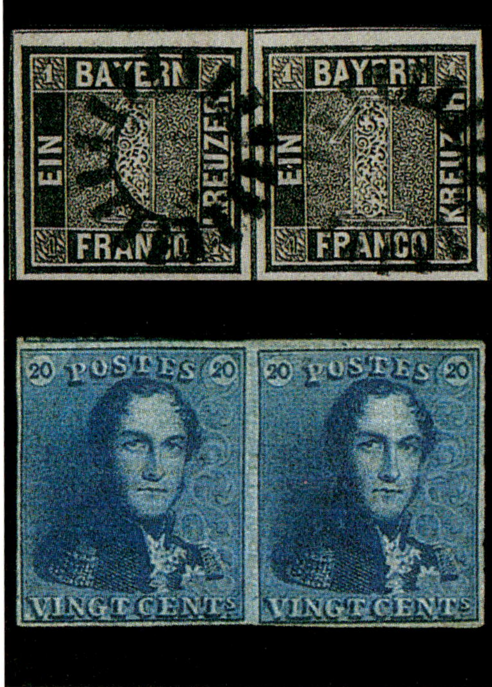

Top: Bavarian 'Schwarzer Einser'; bottom: Belgian 'Epaulettes', both 1849.

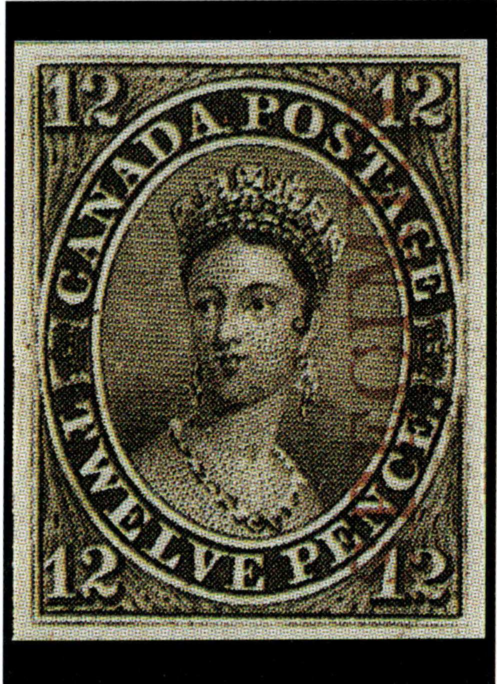

Canadian Twelvepence Black (1850).

The World's Most Valuable Stamp

A world record for a single stamp was established by David Feldman in Zurich on 8 November 1996 when the unique Treskilling (3 skilling) Yellow of Sweden was sold for 2,500,000 Swiss francs plus commission (£1,490,000).

THE 3 SKILLING stamp was issued in 1855, the normal colour being green. In 1885 teenage Georg Wilhelm Backman spent Christmas with his grandmother who allowed him to rummage through an old chest in his search for letters with stamps on them. Georg found several stamps, including the 3sk yellow. A Stockholm dealer, Heinrich Lichtenstein, advertised for 3sk stamps, offering up to seven kronor apiece. When Georg showed the stamp to the dealer, the latter said that it should be green, not yellow, but that he would pay seven kronor all the same.

Colonel Backman lived long enough to see his stamp pass through may hands, fetching ever more astronomical prices each time. Count Ferrary purchased it in 1894 for 4,000 gulden (£400). At the Ferrary sale in Paris (1922) Baron Eric Leijonhufvud paid 35,250 Fr (£694). Claes Tamm paid £1,500 (1926) and Johan Ramberg £2,000 (1928). King Carol of Romania bought it in 1937 for £5,000 and sold it privately for an undisclosed sum in 1950. It appeared in a German sale in 1978 but failed to reach its reserve of 1,000,000 DM. It first appeared in a Feldman sale in 1984 when it sold for SFr 977,500 (£314,309).

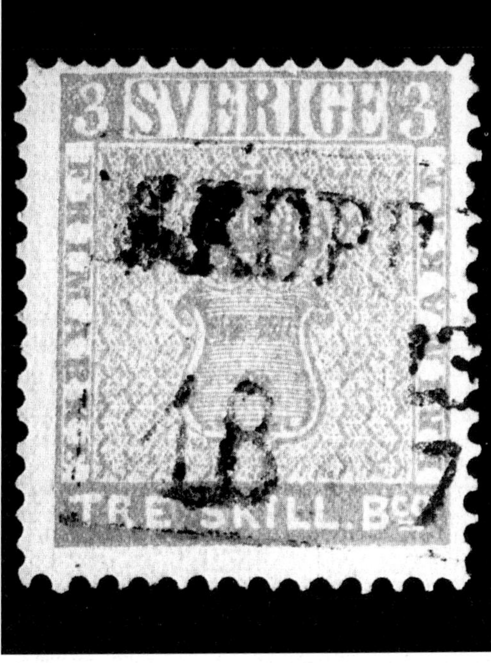

Treskilling Yellow of Sweden, 1855 – the most valuable man-made object on this planet, in relation to its size and weight.

The Primitives

Some of the earliest stamps were makeshifts produced on the initiative of the local postmaster. One of the rarest was the penny stamp devised by William Perot, postmaster of Hamilton, Bermuda, in 1848.

PEROT took the day and month slugs out of his office datestamp and applied it in black or red ink to pieces of blank paper, writing 'one penny' above the year and his signature below. Only three stamps with the date 1848 have ever been found, two for 1849, three for 1853, two for 1854 and one for 1856. Apart from the dates, the stamps differ in the colour of ink or the type of paper used. Of the 11 known specimens, a black one of 1848 and red stamps of 1853 and 1854 are in the Royal Collection.

Apparently Perot hit upon the idea after finding that the coins deposited with unstamped letters in his mailbox when the office was closed seldom tallied. Thereafter he would only accept letters which had been stamped.

The existence of the Perot stamps only came to light in 1897 when an 1854 specimen on a letter of 1855 was found. Several others were discovered between 1898 and 1904. The examples in private hands fetch between £70,000 and £250,000 on the rare occasions they appear in the saleroom.

A penny stamp dating from 1849 by William Perot, a Bermuda postmaster. This is one of only 11 Perot stamps found, and one of only two bearing this date.

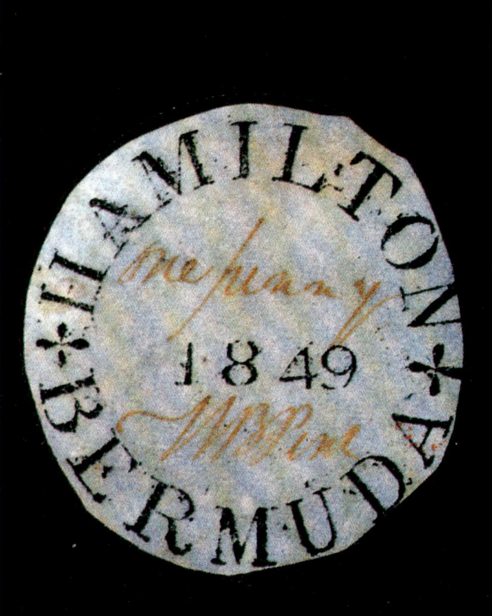

HAMILTON ✣ BERMUDA ✣
one penny
1 8 49

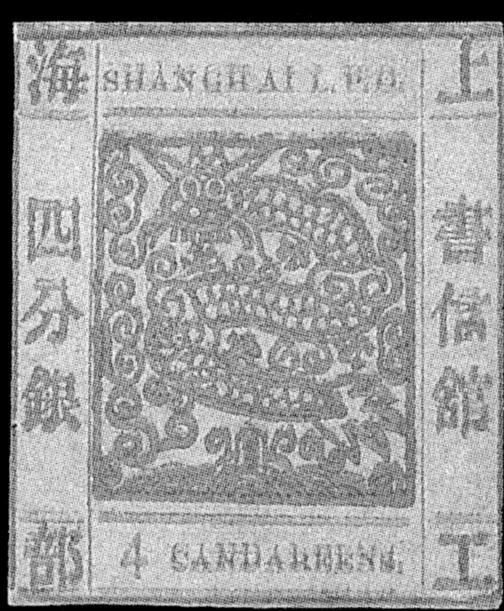
SHANGHAI L.P.O.
4 CANDAREENS

Seeing Double

The first stamps in China were issued by the Municipality of Shanghai, an international community of foreign merchants who organised their own postal service in 1864 and began issuing stamps a year later. This service was suppressed in 1897 when the Chinese Imperial Post was established.

THE SHANGHAI stamps, printed locally, featured a Chinese dragon and were denominated in candareens. The 4 candareen stamp, printed in yellow, is not a difficult stamp to find and averages £120–£150 in mint condition, but is decidedly elusive used (£1,800–£3,500). A solitary example, discovered by John N. Luff, one of the great legendary American philatelists, has a double impression, one colour being slightly lighter than the other with the doubling most noticeable in the upper and lower tablets. Although an entire sheet must have been doubly printed, this is the only example ever to come to light.

Despite being unique (and therefore on a par with the Swedish Treskilling Yellow) it fetched no more than HK$50,000 (about £5,000) when it came up at a Sotheby's auction in Hong Kong in February 1997. Philately is making enormous strides in China and it is likely that this great rarity would fetch a great deal more were it to appear in the saleroom again.

Shanghai 4 candareens, 1865, double impression.

The Siege of Mafeking

The successful defence of Mafeking, besieged by the Boers (1899–1900) made a national hero of Colonel Baden-Powell who founded the Boy Scout movement seven years later.

DURING the siege Baden-Powell had the stock of stamps in the local post office overprinted MAFEKING BESIEGED with new values. Some were stamps of the Cape of Good Hope while others were British stamps which had previously been overprinted for use in British Bechuanaland or the Bechuanaland Protectorate. While some of these siege stamps are not uncommon, only 20 examples have ever been found of the 1s on 4d with the surcharge double. An underrated rarity, it has a current market value of about £3,000.

When the surcharged stamps ran out Baden-Powell issued his own stamps, with his portrait on the 3d and Cadet Sergeant-Major Warner Goodyear on his bicycle on the 1d. These stamps were printed photographically, the earliest instance of this applied philatelically. They are not rare but fetch high prices as forerunners of the Scout theme. The basic stamps in used condition fetch £300–£400 on average, but examples of the 3d with the design reversed are worth 100 times as much. A few horizontal used pairs of the Baden-Powell stamps have been recorded imperforate between and now have a price of £48,000.

Mafeking 1900: 1s on 4d of British Bechuanaland.

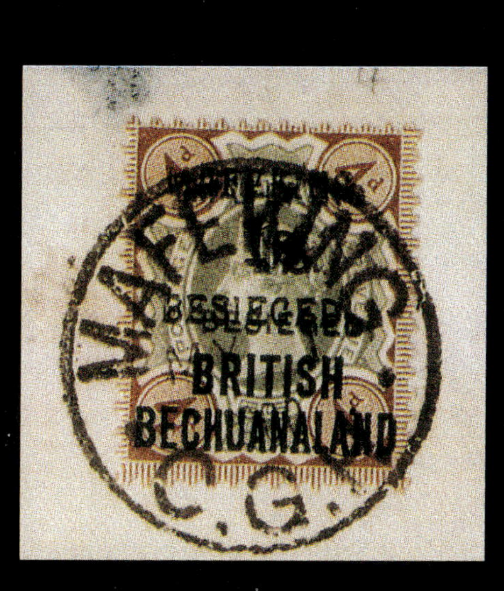

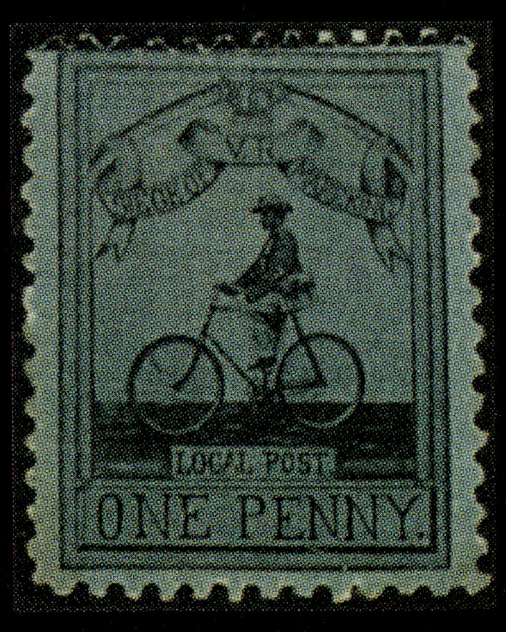

Mafeking 1900: 1d showing Cadet Sergeant-Major Warner Goodyear on his bicycle.

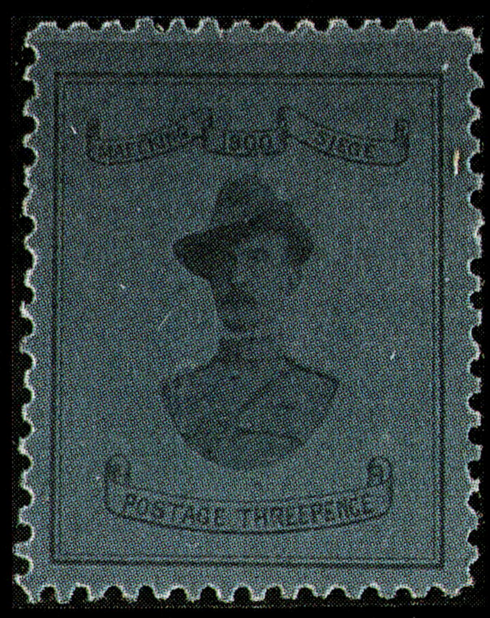

Mafeking 1900: 3d portraying Baden-Powell.

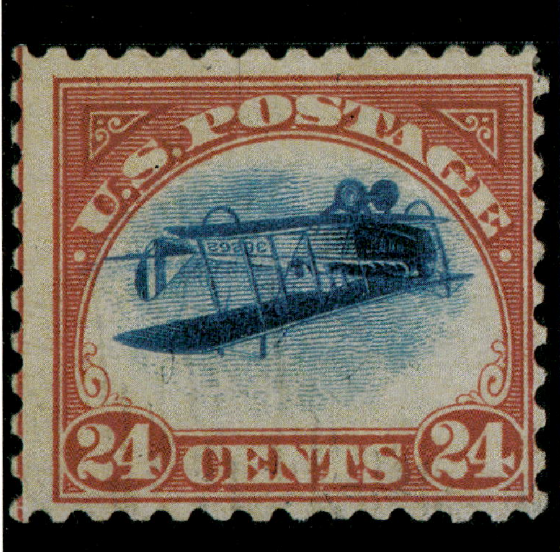

The Inverted Jenny

Many of the great rarities are two-coloured stamps in which the centre is inverted in relation to the frame. One of the most famous is the US 24c airmail stamp of May 1918.

ONLY 15 years after the first faltering flight by the Wright Brothers in 1903, the USA inaugurated a regular airmail service and issued a set of three stamps to cover the principal rates. The 6c orange and 16c green were monochrome, but the 24c had a red frame and a blue centre showing a Curtiss 'Jenny' biplane.

For $24 William T. Robey purchased a complete sheet of 100 from the New York Avenue post office in Washington and immediately spotted that the aircraft were upside down. Robey took the sheet to Eugene Klein, a dealer in Philadelphia, who paid him $15,000 for it. Klein quickly sold it on to Colonel E.H.R. Green for $20,000. Green broke up the sheet, keeping 40 for himself and commissioning Klein to sell off the remaining 60 at $175–$250 each.

By 1958 singles changed hands for $3,000; by 1971 the average price had risen to $16,000. In 1981 a single fetched $115,000 and a block of four $528,000. Green made $1,100,000 for a block of four when it was sold at auction in September 1989. Today Robey's original outlay of $24 is conservatively estimated to be worth more than $10,000,000.

US 24c airmail stamp with Inverted Jenny (1918).

Jubilee Blues

Although stamps are checked at the printers and before issue, some of the greatest finds have occurred over the post office counter.

B RITAIN'S equivalent of the Inverted Jenny is the King George V Silver Jubilee 2½d stamp in the distinctive shade known as Prussian blue instead of ultramarine. On 2 July 1935 A.F. Stavridi purchased a stamp from the sub post office at 134 Fore Street, Upper Edmonton, London, then, realising that the colour was unusual, purchased a few more, as did a friend with him. Having contacted Stanley Gibbons, who knew nothing about an error of colour, he returned to Fore Street and bought the remaining half-sheet of 60 stamps. It turned out that the sub-postmaster had had three sheets (360 stamps) of the wrong colour, while a further three sheets had gone to other offices in London. One of these sheets was acquired by a dealer for 25s and he sold examples to customers at 10d each. By the end of the year singles were changing hands at up to £20.

Although 720 Prussian Blues are in existence, it is still a scarce stamp which fetches about £3,500 mint or used when it appears at auction.

British Silver Jubilee 2½d, 1935 Prussian Blue (above), with a normal stamp for comparison (below).

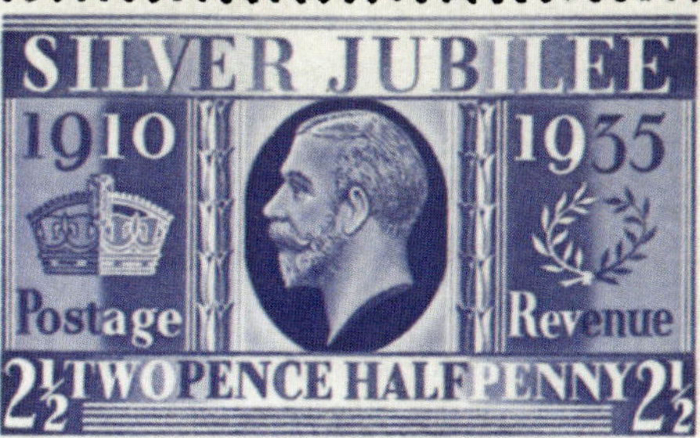

SILVER JUBILEE
1910
1935
Postage
Revenue
2½ TWO PENCE HALF PENNY 2½

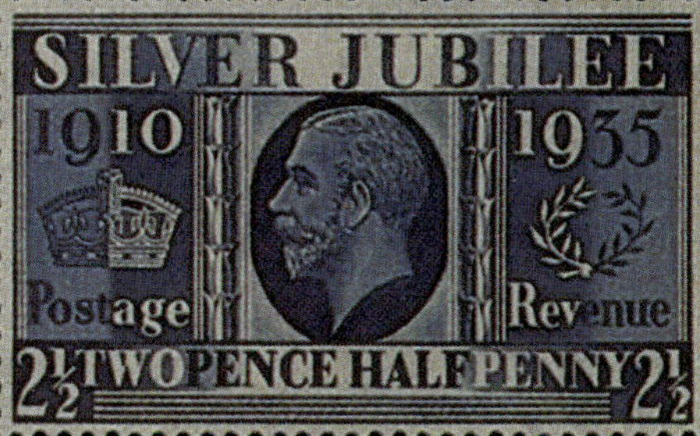

SILVER JUBILEE
1910
1935
Postage
Revenue
2½ TWO PENCE HALF PENNY 2½

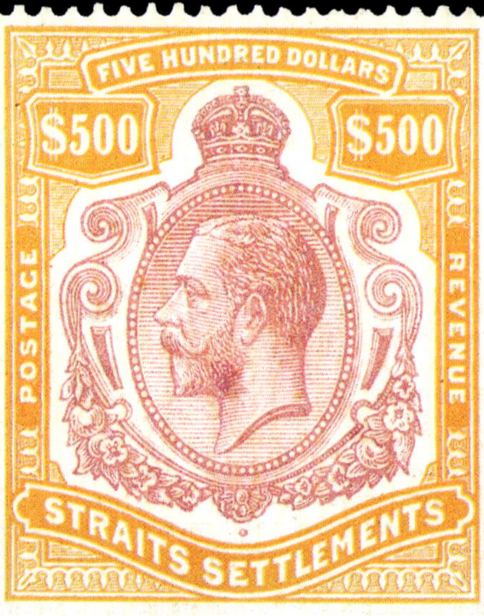
FIVE HUNDRED DOLLARS
$500
$500
POSTAGE
REVENUE
STRAITS SETTLEMENTS

Expensive from the Outset

In the early years of this century several Commonwealth countries had ultra high-value stamps. Although inscribed 'Postage and Revenue' they were clearly intended for fiscal use on valuable contracts. Nevertheless, the inclusion of the word 'Postage' means that they are classed as postage stamps.

IT WOULD be very surprising to come across any of these ultra high-value stamps in postally used condition. Even examples with a fiscal cancellation are scarce, but in mint condition they rank among the major rarities of this century. Kenya had stamps up to £100 in face value, Ceylon (Sri Lanka) up to 1,000 rupees, and the Straits Settlements up to $500. The version with profile of King Edward VII is now rated at £60,000 whereas the George V version is around half that sum, but still not a bad rate of appreciation for a stamp which would have cost the equivalent of less than £50 when it was current in the 1920s.

Generally speaking, the modern stamps likely to turn out the best long-term investment will be those with the highest face value. Britain's Britannia £10 stamp of 1993 (and now obsolescent) may not be a particularly good prospect, but a complete sheet of 25, particularly with plate number 2A in the margins, would probably repay the original outlay handsomely. Similarly, the US Eagle express stamps, with face values up to $14, offer potential, especially in blocks of four showing the plate numbers.

$500 stamp from the Straits Settlements (1921).

FORGERIES AND FAKES
Introduction

A fake is a genuine stamp which has been altered or repaired in some way to make it appear what it is not, for the purpose of deceiving collectors.
A forgery is an imitation of a stamp intended to deceive either the postal administration or collectors. Genuine stamps with forged postmarks or overprints, converting common stamps into valuable rarities, also come into this category.

EARLY STAMP collectors were hampered because there was a dearth of accurate illustrations of stamps in the available stamp catalogues, handbooks and magazines. For that reason they were easily hoodwinked by unscrupulous individuals into paying good money for items which would later turn out to be forgeries.

Pioneer philatelists like W. Dudley Atlee, E.L. Pemberton and the Rev. R.B. Earee launched a campaign in the 1870s to combat the work of forgers. The last-named published a book entitled *Album Weeds,* the classic work on early forgeries which originally appeared in serial form under the heading of 'The Spud Papers' in *The Philatelist* (1871).

Spotting forgeries of the early classic stamps should not be much of a problem to most collectors nowadays, but they still crop up in old-time collections. Most of them are readily detected when compared with the accurate photographs of genuine stamps in auction catalogues, especially the enlarged colour plates of the more important classic stamps.

Forgeries of more modern stamps, however, are often difficult to detect. Where stamps are known to have been forged, the stamp catalogues usually give a warning footnote. In purchasing expensive stamps, it is advisable to exercise caution. The Royal Philatelic Society and other leading bodies have expert committees who, on payment of a fee, will issue a serially numbered certificate guaranteeing the genuineness of a stamp – or not, as the case may be. The leading dealers also offer an expertisation service and guarantee stamps by signing them on the back. The trouble is, these marks of guarantee have themselves been forged, so it is vital to retain the actual expert certificate.

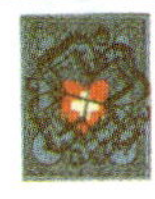

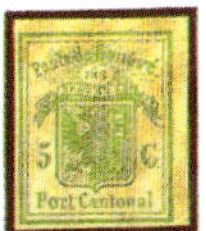

KURT TRÜSSEL, CH-6005 LUZERN
Hirtenhofstrasse 74   Telefon 041-360 60 18

Philatelistischer Experte, Mitglied im
Schweiz. Briefmarken-Prüfer-Verband SBPV

Prüfgebiet: Schweiz ab 1843, ohne Dienst- und Ämtermarken

Luzern, den   22. September 1997

PRÜFUNGS-BEFUND   No   12378

Schweiz: Kt. GENF 1849
Zst.-Nr.:   07
Gestempelt: ungebraucht

ECHT

ERHALTUNG: farbfrisch, vollrandig geschnitten, in einwandfreier Erhaltung.

Dieser Befund wird ausgestellt nach bestem Wissen und Gewissen, jedoch ohne Haftung!

Certificate of expertisation granted by Kurt Trussell of Lucerne in respect of a 5c stamp of Geneva (1849).

Postal Forgeries

A postal forgery is one produced with the intention of defrauding the revenue. Stamps were an early target of counterfeiters, long before a philatelic market existed. Postal forgeries tend to be worth more to collectors than the genuine stamps.

IT SHOULD BE borne in mind that, back in the mid-nineteenth century, competent engravers were common, and the relatively high face value of stamps in relation to the engravers' spending power was an obvious source of temptation. Even the Penny Black suffered the unwelcome attention of a forger, though Rowland Hill dismissed the result as 'a miserable thing which could not possibly deceive any except the most stupid and ignorant'.

This forgery was apparently crudely executed by engraving on a block of wood. More dangerous was a forgery in March 1841 from an electrotype. In both instances, however, the process used for printing differed fundamentally from the original intaglio. Despite this, superficially, and in the poorly gas- or candle-lit sorting offices of the period, such forgeries might easily escape detection.

Britain remained relatively free of stamp forgery because of the intaglio process, the intricate engine-turning of the background and the use of check letters in the corners of the stamp, which differed from stamp to stamp within the sheet.

Other countries, however, which used cheaper printing methods, suffered badly from forgery. France, especially in the aftermath of the Franco-Prussian War (1870–71), Germany at the turn of the century, and Spain from the 1850s onward, provide many examples of forgeries perpetrated to defraud the postal services. Even in modern times forgers have considered it worth their time and efforts. Forgeries of Australia's 2d stamp of 1932 marking the opening of the Sydney Harbour Bridge were foisted on an unsuspecting public, but are easy to detect. The

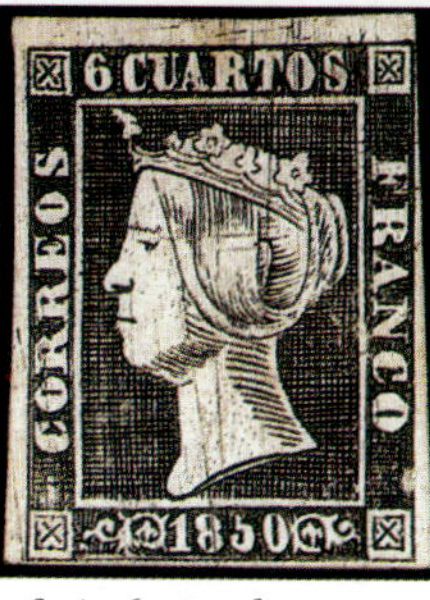

Spain, 6 cuartos forgery.

genuine stamps have a multiple watermark and a perforation gauging 10.5, whereas the forgeries have no watermark and gauge 11.

In recent years British 24p definitives and French Marianne definitives were counterfeited in London and Marseilles respectively. They were supplied to newsagents and tobacconists at a hefty discount and were then sold on to an unsuspecting public.

Spain's 'Penny Black', the 6 cuartos of January 1850, was forged soon after issue. The forgery was quickly spotted on two envelopes passing through the Alicante post office on 2 April and the perpetrator, Vicente Pastor, and three accomplices speedily apprehended. A mint example of the forgery – the only surviving specimen – was discovered in 1929 and sold at auction in Madrid in 1997 for 5,000,000 pesetas, infinitely more valuable than its genuine counterpart.

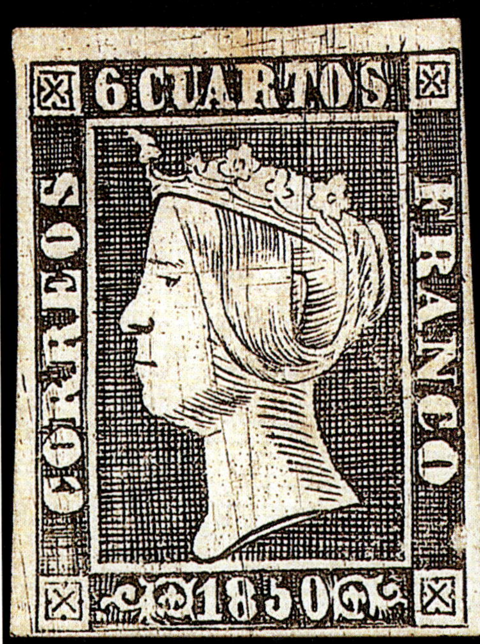

6 CUARTOS
CORREOS
FRANCO
1850

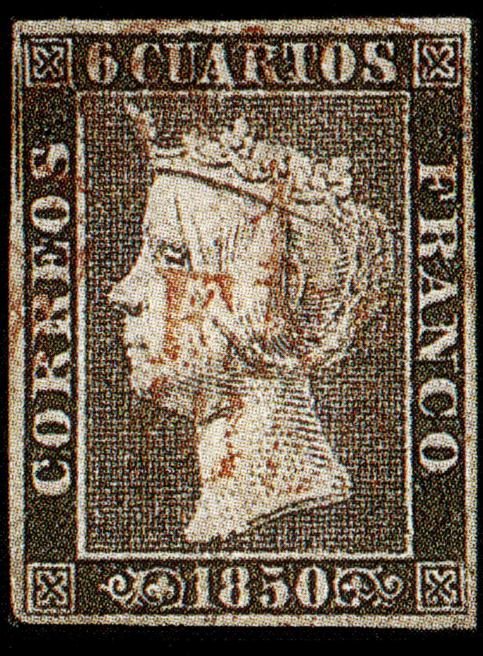

Spain, 6 cuartos, 1850: forgery (left) with a used, genuine stamp (above).

The Stock Exchange Forgery

The most celebrated case of forgery in British philately concerned the 1s green stamp (1867–73 issue). In 1872–73 large quantities of these forgeries were applied to telegram forms by a clerk at the Stock Exchange telegraph office in London.

THE FRAUD might never have come to light but for a lucky accident. The telegram forms were sold to a scrap-paper merchant and should have been pulped, but sacks of them lay in a disused warehouse for 25 years. Workmen came across them and took handfuls of the forms, bearing high-value stamps, to a dealer who sold them on to others. The fact that some of the stamps (from plate 5) had impossible combinations of corner letters alerted Charles Nissen to the fact that the stamps were forged. The matter was investigated in 1899 but no conclusions were reached and no prosecutions resulted.

In 1910 another London dealer, H.F. Johnson, discovered examples of the forgeries purporting to come from plate 6. Not till 1915 did the Post Office repurchase the sacks and discover the full extent of the crime, but by that time all the likely suspects were dead. Most of this material was destroyed in 1940, so that the existing examples on the market are those from the original find in 1898. Today a genuine 1s green in used condition is worth £15, whereas forgeries fetch four-figure sums at auction.

British 1s green, forgery on fragment of telegram form with the Stock Exchange cancellation.

Apart from the impossible corner letters, the forgeries are on unwatermarked paper. Impressions are fairly good, apart from some weakness in the corner ornament. Remarkably, the perforation was accurate.

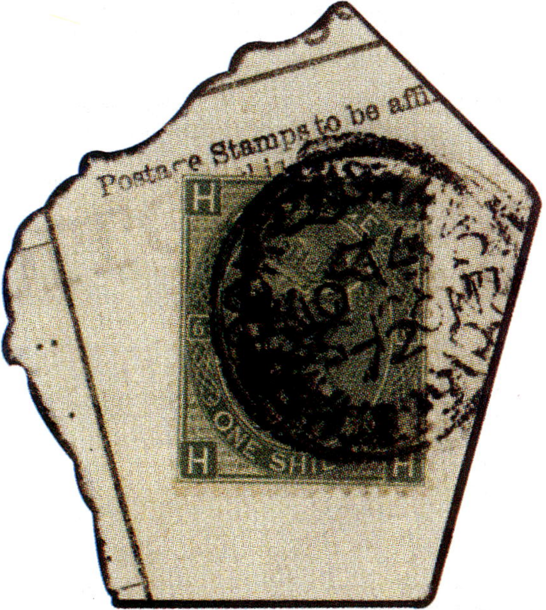

Propaganda Forgeries

Stamps have been forged by governments as well as criminals, as part of the psychological warfare waged during both World Wars.

DURING the First World War, Allied propaganda was disseminated in Germany in the form of circulars and postcards which appeared to have been sent through the post. For this purpose vast quantities of 10pf and 15pf stamps, as well as the equivalent denominations from Bavaria and Austria, were forged in England. The forgeries are very close to the originals, apart from a slight variation in perforation and quality of paper, but there are also minor details in the designs, detectable with a high-powered magnifier.

Both German (Hitler's Head) and Vichy French stamps were forged on behalf of Allied intelligence projects during the Second World War. The latter were used by the French underground to disseminate Allied propaganda material. They are close to the originals apart from details in the shading.

Crude forgeries of British definitives, overprinted LIQUIDATION OF EMPIRE, as well as parodies of the Silver Jubilee and Coronation stamps of 1935–37 were made by the Nazis. In the definitives, the cross on top of the crown was replaced by a tiny star of David, while the circle enclosing the value was transformed into a hammer and sickle, the communist emblem.

France: British forgery (top) and a genuine stamp (bottom) for comparison.

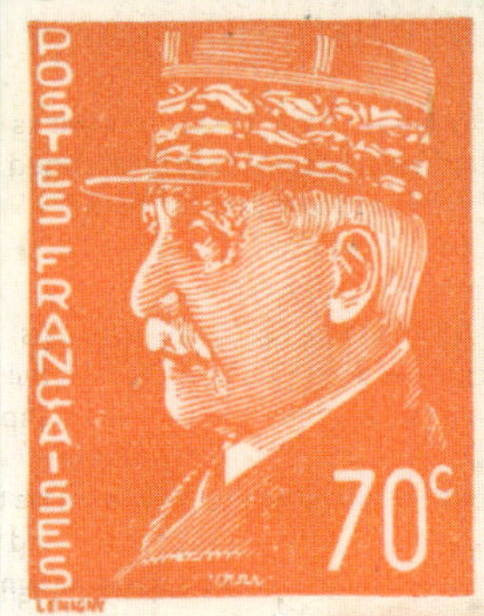
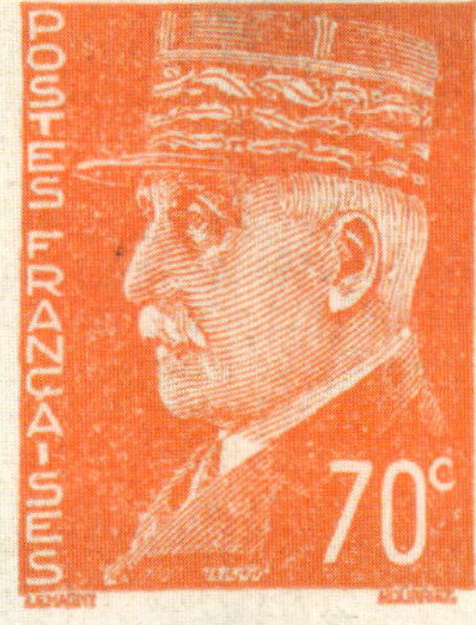

Fakes

There are several ways in which a cheap, common stamp can be transformed into a valuable one. This type of fraud is particularly dangerous because the basic stamp is genuine. Below are summarised the different methods used by fakers.

GUM

MANY GENUINE old stamps have lost their gum through being stuck down in old-time collections or repeatedly hinged with stamp edging which could only be removed by soaking off. While an unusued stamp with part original gum or none at all still has some value, the modern fad for unmounted mint has encouraged the regumming of stamps. This can often be detected because the faker has used the wrong gum or a magnifier reveals tell-tale brush strokes, denoting gum applied by hand whereas the original might have been machine gummed.

COLOUR

A COMMON stamp may be transformed into a rare error of colour by chemical action or even exposure to sunlight. Traces of the original pigmentation usually show up under high magnification, and in addition such examples tend to fluoresce differently from untampered stamps under ultraviolet light.

PERFORATION

A COMMON gauge of perforation can be carefully trimmed off and the stamp reperforated in a rare gauge. Such stamps inevitably look somewhat smaller than the genuine article, so accurate measurements of the teeth of the perforations will usually reveal this fraud.

A variation of this applies to American stamps which, from the outer edges of the sheet, were imperforate on the outer side. Nowadays specialists like to acquire stamps with one or more adjoining sides showing straight edges, as well as stamps from the middle of the sheet perforated on all four sides; but old-time collections (up to the 1940s) abhorred straight edges, and this encouraged the application of fake perforations to remedy this defect.

Similarly, nineteenth-century British stamps are often found with wing margins, very broad margins on one side or the other, owing to the manner in which De La Rue perforated the vertical gutters between the panes. To many old-time collectors these wing margins were unsightly; besides, they did not fit comfortably in the printed spaces in their albums. So they had them trimmed off and reperforated. Stamps to the value of 3d, 6d, 9d, 18d, 1s and 2s with upper left-hand corner letters D, E, H or I (to left and right of the gutter), and 4d and 8d stamps with letters F or G, should have a wing margin. If they have not, it is a sure sign of reperforation. This form of fake detracts considerably from the value of the stamp.

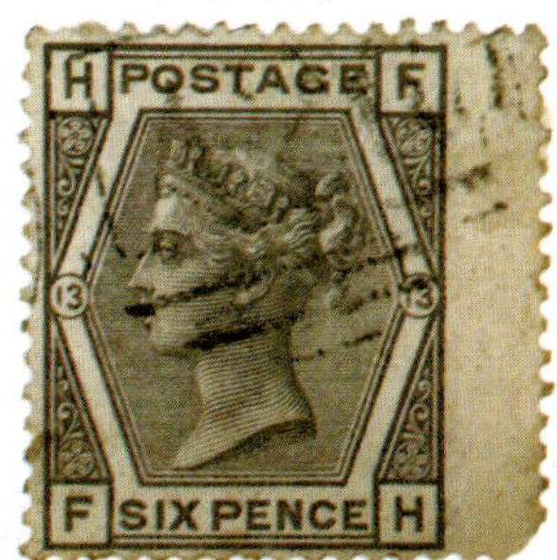

British Victorian stamp with wing margin.

Fake Postmarks

There are many instances of stamps being common or virtually worthless in mint condition, but excessively rare in used condition. This disparity in value has encouraged the application of fraudulent postmarks.

THE CLASSIC example of faked postmarks comes from the Korean Empire whose first western-style postal service was established at Seoul on 18 November 1884. On 4 December an attempted coup resulted in the destruction of the post office and the abolition of the service which was not revived until 1895. Vast quantities of stamps, printed in Japan, later came on to the philatelic market and are by no means expensive. Only a handful of genuinely used stamps of November and December 1884 are recorded, with the result that a mint copy of the 10 mon is worth £7.50 whereas a genuinely used specimen can fetch £2,500.

There are many rare postmarks which transform a common stamp into a valuable commodity. British Edwardian ½d stamps are very cheap, but examples on covers bearing the experimental cancellations associated with the Christmas advanced posting experiments of 1902 and subsequent years are worth many hundreds of pounds, and this has encouraged the forgery of the rarer marks (notably those from Douglas, Isle of Man).

Reprints of stamps of Heligoland were made by an enterprising Hamburg dealer from the genuine plates after the island was ceded to Germany in 1890. To lend authenticity to his products he had forged cancellations applied to them.

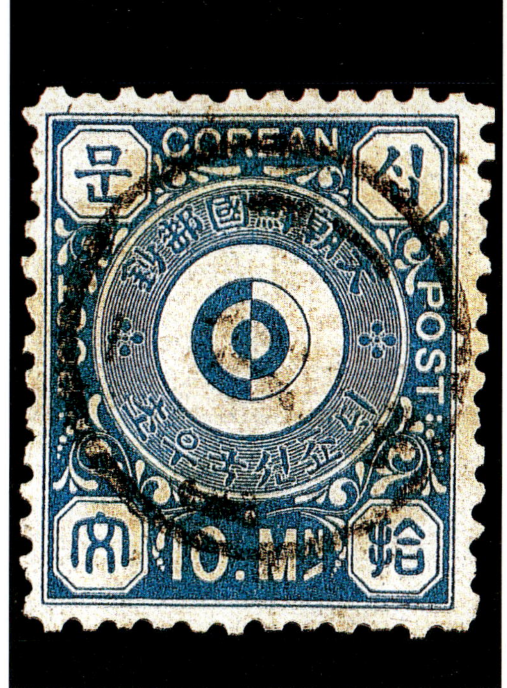

Korean Empire: 10m 1884 with genuine postmark.

Forged Overprints

Stamps converted in face value or purpose by the application of a surcharge or overprint are often more valuable than the original stamp, and inevitably this has encouraged forgery.

FORGING an overprint is infinitely easier than forging an entire stamp, mainly because the vast majority of overprints were applied by letterpress and it would be a relatively simple task to obtain letters and numerals of the correct font.

Forged overprints can sometimes be detected because the colour or quality of ink used differs from that in the genuine overprints. More often, however, it will be minute differences in the lettering itself that gives the game away. A high-powered magnifier with a scale calibrated to a tenth of a millimetre is a useful tool in detecting minor differences in the size or spacing of lettering.

Similarly enlarged photographs or even photocopies of questionable stamps, alongside similar copies of genuine stamps, often show up discrepancies very clearly.

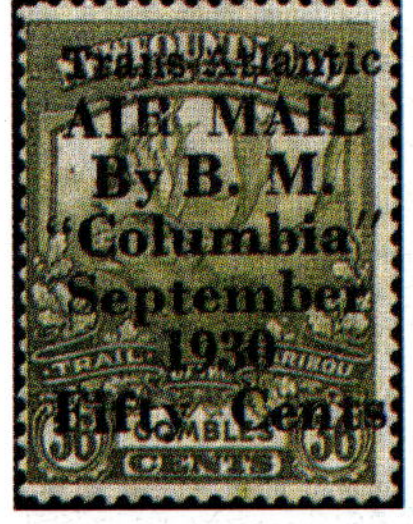

Newfoundland, 1930 'Columbia' airmail overprint, worth £4,500. The unoverprinted 36c stamp is worth £9, so beware of forged overprints.

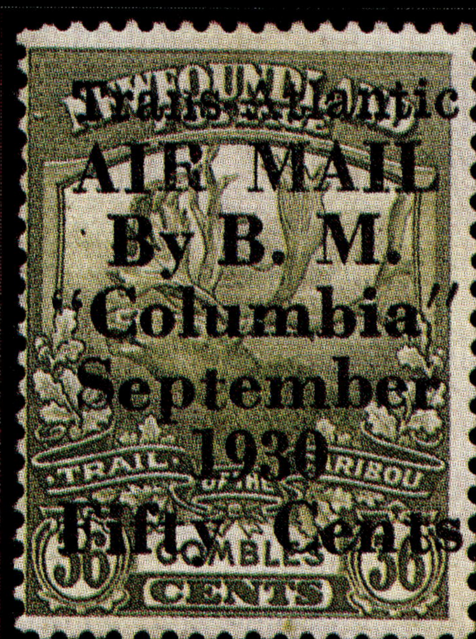

COMPENDIUM
Guide to Inscriptions

A & T Annam and Tonquin
Akahi Keneta Hawaii
Amtlicher Verkehr Wurttemberg
AO Ruanda-Urundi
Allemagne/Duitschland Belgian
  occupation of Germany
Avisporto Denmark
Bayern Bavaria
Bohmen und Mahren Bohemia and
  Moravia
Braunschweig Brunswick
Cechy y Morava Bohemia and
  Moravia
Ceskoslovensko Czechoslovakia
Confed. Granadina Colombia
Continente Portugal
Coree Korea
Cote d'Ivoire Ivory Coast
Dansk Vestindien Danish West Indies
DDR German Democratic
  Republic
Deutsch Neu-Guinea German New
  Guinea
Deutsch Ostafrika German East
  Africa
Deutschosterreich Austria
Deutsches Reich Germany
Dienstmarke Germany
Drzava Yugoslavia
Eesti Estonia
Eire Ireland
Escuelas Venezuela
España Spain
Estados Unidos de Nueva Granada
  Colombia
Estero Italian overseas offices

Etablissements de l'Inde French
  Indian Settlements
Etablissements de l'Oceanie
  French Polynesia
Filipinas Philippines
Francobollo Italy
Freimarke Prussia, Wurttemberg
FSM Micronesia
G & D Guadeloupe
General Gouvernement Poland
Giuba Jubaland
GPE Guadeloupe
Grossdeutsches Reich Nazi
  Germany
Gultig 9 Armee German
  occupation of Romania
Guyane Francaise French Guiana
Haute Volta Upper Volta
Hellas Greece
Helvetia Switzerland
HH Nawab Shah Begam Bhopal
Hrvatska Croatia
Hrzgl Holstein
Irian Barat West Irian
Island Iceland
Isole Jonie Ionian Islands
Kamerun Cameroon
Kalaallit Nunaat Greenland
KGCA Carinthia
Kongeligt Post Denmark
KSA Saudi Arabia
K.u.K. Austria, Bosnia
Latvija Latvia
Liban Lebanon
Lietuvos Lithuania
Litwa Srodkowa Central Lithuania

Ljubljanske Pokrajina Slovenia
Losen Sweden
Magyar Hungary
Maroc French Morocco
Marruecos Spanish Morocco
Mejico Mexico
Militarpost Bosnia
Modenesi Modena
MViR German occupation of Romania
Nippon Japan
Nlle Caledonie New Caledonia
Norddeutscher Postbezirk North German Confederation
Norge/Noreg Norway
Nouvelle Caledonia New Caledonia
Nouvelles Hebrides New Hebrides
NSB Nossi-Be
NSW New South Wales
Oesterreich Austria
Offentlig Sak Norway
Orts Post Switzerland
Ottomanes Turkey
Pacchi Postale Italy
Pakke-Porto Greenland
Poblacht na hEireann Ireland
Poczta Polska Poland
Pohjois Inkeri North Ingermanland
Postat e Qeverries Albania
Poste Estensi Modena
Poste Shqiptare Albaina
Postgebiet Ob. Ost German Eastern Army
Postzegel Netherlands
Preussen Prussia
Provinz Laibach Slovenia
R Jind
Reichspost German Empire
RF France and colonies
RH Haiti
Rialtas Sealadac na hEireann Ireland
RO Eastern Rumelia
RSA Republic of South Africa

Russisch-Polen German occupation of Poland
Sachsen Saxony
Scrisorei Moldavia and Wallachia
SH Schleswig-Holstein
SHS Yugoslavia
Shqipenia, Shqiptare Albania
Slesvig Schlewsig
Slovenija Slovenia
Slovenska Slovakia
Slovensky Stat Slovakia
SO Eastern Silesia
SPM St Pierre and Miquelon
Suidwes Afrika South West Africa
Suomi Finland
Sverige Sweden
SWA South West Africa
TEO Cilicia, Syria
Tjanste Sweden
Tjeneste Norway, Denmark
Toga Tonga
Toscano Tuscany
UAE United Arab Emirates
UAR Egypt
UG Uganda
UKTT Southern Cameroons
Uku Leta Hawaii
Ultramar Cuba, Puerto Rico
UNEF Indian forces in Gaza
UNTEA West New Guinea
Valles d'Andorre Andorra
Van Diemen's Land Tasmania
Venezia Giulia Trieste
YCCP Ukraine
Z Armenia
ZAR Transvaal
Z. Afr. Republiek Transvaal
Zeitungsmarke Austria
Zil Eloigne Sesel Seychelles Outer Islands
Zuid West Afrika South West Africa
Zulassungsmarke German military parcels

Foreign Alphabets

ALTHOUGH the Universal Postal Union now stipulates that country names should appear in the Roman alphabet as well as local script where applicable, many older stamps do not have such dual inscriptions.

Generally speaking stamps with Arabic inscriptions were also inscribed in French or English so should present no problems. On the other hand, some stamps from the Indian princely states have inscriptions only in a wide range of local languages. Stamps of China and Japan, using Chinese characters, may usually be recognised by the state emblem: a starburst sun (China), five-petalled orchid (Manchukuo) or a chrysanthemum (Japan).

The main problem facing collectors is the use of Greek or Cyrillic alphabets. To the uninitiated they often appear the same, and indeed Cyrillic is basically a modified form of Greek, but contains a number of distinctive letters. This is true of the various branches of Cyrillic, as used in Russia, Ukraine, Bulgaria and Yugoslavia. The main inscriptions are listed below.

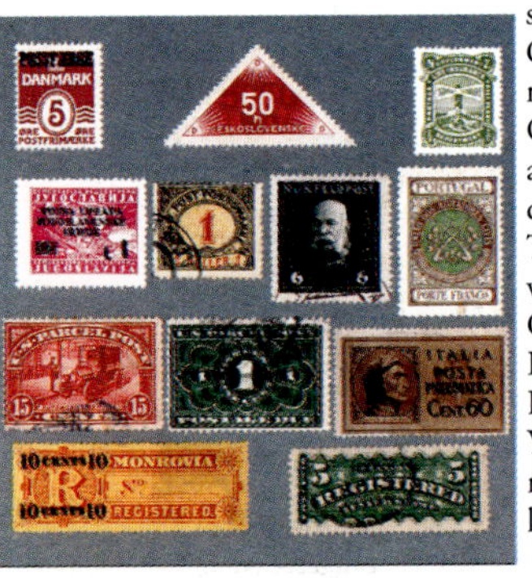

CYRILLIC

АВИОПОЧТА	Russia (airmail)
АСОБНЫ АТРАД	White Russia
БАКУ	Baku
БАТУМ	Batum
БИЉЄТА	Montenegro (stamp)
БОСНА	Bosnia (1918)
БЪЛГАРСКА	Bulgaria
БЪЛГАРИЯ	Bulgaria
БУЛГАРИЯ	Bulgaria
ВЄДЦЄНСКАЯ	Wenden
ВОСТОЧНАЯ	Russian Levant
САНТИМ	Bulgaria (*centime*)
СССР	USSR
СКРИСОРИ	Moldavia
СРБИЈА	Serbia
СХС	SHS (Serbs, Croats and Slovenes)
СТОТИНКИ	Bulgaria (*stotinki*)
ДОИЛАТА	Postage due
ДРЖАВА	Yugoslavia
ЕДИНАЯ ROCCIЯ	South Russia
ЕРМАК	Ermak (Don Government)
НОВУ	Montenegro
ЈУГОСЛАВИЈА	Yugoslavia
КАРПАТСКА УКРАІНА	Carpatho-Ukraine
КИТАЙ	Russian POs in China
КОП	Russia (*kopek*)
КРАЉЄВСТВО	Yugoslavia
ЛЕВА	Bulgaria (*leva*)

МАКЕДОНИЯ	Macedonia
МАРКА	Russia (stamp)
МОНГОЛ ШУУДАН	Mongolia
ОСВОБ ВОЙНА	Bulgaria, Balkan Wars
ПАРА	Serbia (*para*)
ПОШТЄ ЦРГОРЕ	Montenegro
ПОЧТА	Russia (postage)
ПОЧТОВАЯ МАРКА	Russia (postage stamp)
РСФСР	Russian SFSR
РОССІЯ	Russia
РОССИЯ	Russia (since 1991)
РУБ	rouble
РУССКАЯ ПОЧТА	Russian Western Army
ТАКСА	Bulgaria (postage due)
ТЬВА	Tuva
ХЄЛЄРА	Montenegro (*heller*)
ХЄРЦЄГОВИНА	Herzegovina (1918)
ЦРНА ГОРА	Montenegro
УКРАІНА	Ukraine
ЮЖНА БЪЛГАРИЯ	South Bulgaria (1885)

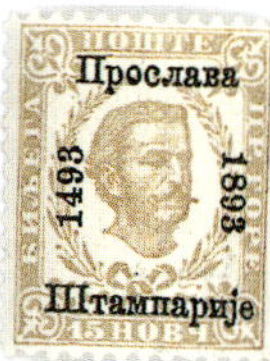

GREEK

ΓΚΙΟΥΜΟΥΛΤΖΙΝΑΣ	Gumultsina
ΔΕΔΕΑΓΑΤΣ	Deadeagatz
ΔΡΑΧΜΗ	Greece (*drachma*)
ΕΔΕΥΘΕΡΑ ΠΟΛΙΤΕΙΑ	Ikaria Free State
ΕΛΛΑΣ	Greece (Hellas)
ΕΛΛΗΝΙΚΗ ΔΗΜΟΚΡΑΤΙΑ	Greek Republic
ΕΛΛΗΝΙΚΗ ΔΙΟΙΚΗΣΙΣ	Greek Occupation
ΗΠΕΙΡΟΣ	Epirus
ΗΡΑΚΛΕΙΟΥ	Heraklion
ΙΟΝΙΚΟΝ ΚΡΑΤΟΣ	Ionian Islands
ΚΟΙΝΟΝ ΝΗΣΙΩΤΩΝ	Dodecanese Islands
ΚΡΗΤΗ	Crete
ΔΕΠΤΟΝ / Α	Greece (*lepton/a*)
ΛΗΜΝΟΣ	Lemnos
ΜΥΤΙληυηˢ	Mytilene
ΠΡΟΣΩΡ ΤΑΧΥΔΡ	Provisional Government (Crete)
ΠΡΟΣΩΡΙΝΟΝ ΤΑΧΥΔΡΟΜΕΙΟΝ	Provisional Government (Samos)
ΡΕΟΥΜΝΗΣ	Rethymno
ΣΑΜΟΥ	Samos
ΣΔΔ	SDD (Greek Military Administration, Dodecanese Islands)

Glossary

Below are some of the terms used by collectors. For fuller details see Philatelic Terms Illustrated (Stanley Gibbons, 1986).

Albino
Colourless impression, usually in embossing.

Backstamp
Postmark on the back of an envelope, applied in transit or on arrival.

Bantams
Reduced-size South African stamps, printed during the Second World War.

Bilingual pair
Stamps printed alternately in two different languages.

Bisect
Stamp cut in half for use as a stamp of half the value.

Cachet
Mark applied to cards or covers, other than the postmark and often private or unofficial in nature.

Cancelled to order (CTO)
Stamps postmarked in bulk, usually for sale to collectors at a discount and often recognised by having gum still on the back.

Centred
Stamp whose design is equidistant from the edges of the perforations on all four sides.

Changeling
A stamp whose colour has changed radically due to exposure to moisture or sunlight.

Coils
Stamps printed in continuous rolls, often differing in watermark, perforation and gum from sheet stamps.

Combination cover
Cover bearing stamps of
two or more postal
administrations.

Controls
Letters and numerals found
on British sheet margins,
1881–1947, for accounting
purposes.

Cut-square or Cut-out
Imprinted stamps cut from
postal stationery; collected thus
in America but entire items
preferred elsewhere.

Demonetised
Obsolete stamps that have
been declared invalid for
postage use.

Die
The original piece of metal on
which a stamp design is engraved.

Dominical label
Label attached to Belgian
stamps, 1893–1914,
instructing the postman not to
deliver mail on Sundays.

Duty plate
Plate used to print the 'duty'
(the value) in conjunction with
a key plate.

Error
Stamp deviating from the
normal in some respect,
e.g. missing colours or
perforations, inverted colours
or centres, double
or inverted overprints.

Essay
Preliminary design, not
subsequently used.

First-day cover (FDC)
Cover bearing stamps postmarked on the first day of issue.

Flaw
Defect in the printing plate or
cylinder, resulting in a constant
blemish on the same stamp on
every sheet.

Graphite lines
Black lines on the back of some
British stamps, in connection
with electronic sorting trials at
Southampton, 1957–59.

Imperforate
Stamps issued without any means of separating them.

Jubilee lines
Lines of printer's rule reinforcing the edges of the plate and first used in the British 'Jubilee' series, 1887.

Key plate
The plate which prints the general design. A second plate, known as the duty plate, adds the country name and face value. Widely used in Britain and other colonial powers for the stamps of their overseas territories.

Killer
Cancellation designed to obliterate the stamp very heavily.

Meter mark
Mark applied by postage meter and often used by firms and other organisations. Invented in New Zealand (1904) and used internationally since 1922.

Miniature sheet
Small sheet containing a single stamp, pair or block, usually with decorative margins.

Mint
Unused stamp with full, original gum on the back.

Overprint
Printing applied to a stamp some time after the original printing, to convert it to some other purpose.

Perfins
Stamps perforated with the initials of firms.

Phosphor bands
Almost invisible lines on the face of stamps, to facilitate electronic sorting.

Pneumatic (tube) post
Transmission of mail in capsules driven by compressed air along a tube.

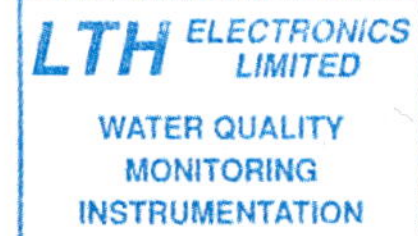

Pre-cancels
Stamps used in bulk postings, with marks previously applied to prevent reuse.

Provisionals
Stamps overprinted to meet a shortage of regular issues, or by new countries pending a supply of distinctive stamps.

Remainders
Stocks of stamps left over after an issue, sometimes sold off cheaply to the philatelic trade.

Reprints
Stamps printed from the original plates, sometimes long after the issue has ceased, and often detectable by differences in the paper, watermark or colour.

Se-tenant
French term meaning two or more different stamps printed side by side.

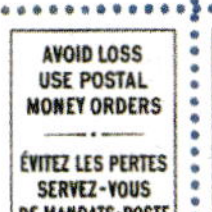

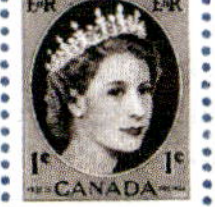

Surcharge
An overprint that alters the face value of a stamp.

Tabs
Stamps with marginal inscriptions or labels (e.g. Israel, Marshall Islands).

Tête-bêche
French term for two adjoining stamps upside down in relation to each other.

Thins
Areas on the backs of stamps where the paper has been thinned by careless removal of stamps from their envelopes.

Vignette
The main motif or central portion of a stamp design, as opposed to the frame, value tablet or inset portrait of a ruler.

Watermark
Translucent impression used as a security device in the paper on which stamps are printed.

Useful Addresses

WHERE TO BUY STAMPS

British Philatelic Bureau
20 Brandon Street, Edinburgh, EH3 5TT (0345 641 641).
Publishes a monthly stock list, available on request. Payment
may be made by MasterCard, Visa or cheque. The most
painless and efficient method of acquiring all new issues of
British stamps and postal stationery by mail order.

Philatelic Counters
London Chief Office, Lombard Street, EC1. Until recently
there were 66 philatelic counters attached to the main regional
post offices but these have been
drastically reduced and currently
operate at the head offices in
Canterbury, Exeter, Leeds,
Leicester, Oxford and Truro.

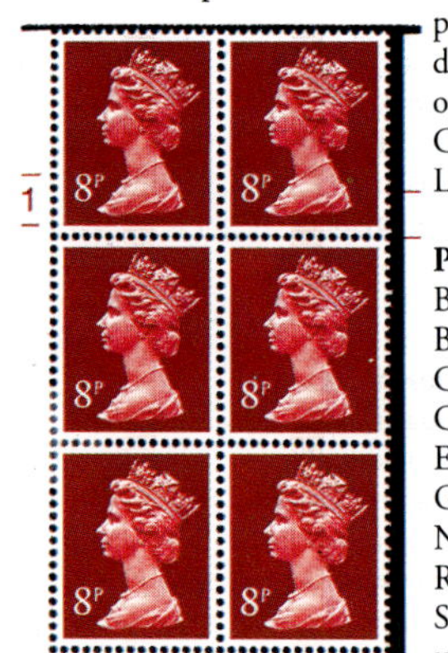

Postshops Plus
Bath, Belfast, Birmingham,
Brighton, Bristol, Cambridge,
Colchester, Coventry,
Croydon, Durham,
Edinburgh, Glasgow,
Guildford, Newcastle,
Nottingham, Portsmouth,
Romford, Southampton,
Southend and Stratford-
upon-Avon.

Collections

Cardiff, Chester, Gloucester, Liverpool, London (Trafalgar Square), Manchester, Windsor and York.

The distinction between Philatelic Counters, Postshops Plus and Collections (often incomprehensible to the philatelic public) appears to lie mainly in the quality of service offered, the level of competence of the counter staff and the range of products available.

Local Dealers

Check the Yellow Pages directory for dealers in your area.

OTHER PHILATELIC BUREAUX

INDEPENDENT postal administrations operate in the Republic of Ireland, Guernsey, Jersey and the Isle of Man. All of them have extremely efficient philatelic bureaux, playing a prominent part in the major British national and international philatelic exhibitions. Methods of payment are the same as for the British Philatelic Bureau.

Guernsey

Philatelic Counter and Postal Museum, Head Post Office, Smith Street, St Peter Port. Friday to Wednesday, 9am–12.30pm; 2pm–5pm; Thursday, 9am–1pm. Free.
Castle Cornet, St Peter Port, has a fine display of postal history as well as the full range of stamps since 1969.
Philatelic Bureau, Postal Headquarters, Guelles Road, PO Box 432, St Peter Port, Guernsey, GY1 3ZE.

Ireland

No postal museum at present, though one is projected.
Exhibits of postal interest in the National Museum, Dublin.
Philatelic Counter, General Post Office, O'Connell Street, Dublin 1.
An Post Philatelic Bureau, General Post Office, Dublin 1.

Isle of Man

The Manx Museum, Douglas contains stamps and postal
  history material. Open daily. Free.
Philatelic Counter, Head Post Office, Regent Road, Douglas.
Philatelic Bureau, PO Box 10M, Circular Road, Douglas, Isle
  of Man.

Jersey

Philatelic Counter and Postal Museum, Head Post Office, St
  Helier, Jersey. Sunday to Friday, 9am–5pm; Saturday,
  9am–1pm. Free.
Philatelic Bureau, PO Box 304, St Helier, Jersey, JE1 1AB.

PHILATELIC ORGANISATIONS

The British Philatelic Centre

107 Charterhouse Street, London EC1M 6PT (0171 251
  5040). Monday–Friday, 10am–5pm.

It houses the following bodies:
  Association of British Philatelic Societies (ABPS)
  British Philatelic Trust
  The Philatelic Traders' Society
  Stampex Ltd (holds national exhibitions, in spring and
  autumn)

The National Philatelic Society (including an excellent
library)

The ABPS publishes a yearbook and directory giving names
and addresses of all affiliated philatelic societies nationwide,
both specialist and local.

PHILATELIC MAGAZINES

British Philatelic Bulletin (monthly) and *British Postmark
Bulletin* (fortnightly), published by the British Philatelic
Bureau. Available by subscription.
The Philatelic Exporter (monthly) by subscription, PO Box
137, Hatfield, Herts AL10 9DB. The main trade journal.
The London Philatelist (monthly), free to Fellows and
Members of the Royal Philatelic Society, 41 Devonshire
Place, London W1.
Gibbons Stamp Monthly (monthly), published by Stanley
Gibbons Publications. On general sale.
Stamp and Coin Mart (monthly),
published by Trinity Publications.
On general sale.
Stamp Magazine (monthly), published
by Link House. On general sale.

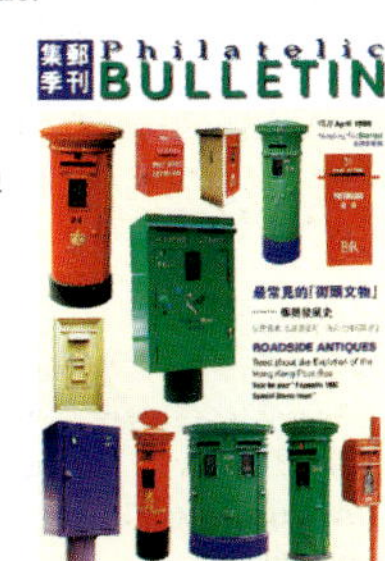

The specialist societies and study
circles publish regular journals, while
the national and some local clubs
produce magazines or newsletters.

Index

C

Canada 21, 65, 66, 72–3, 76, 78, 81, 83, 179, 194, 203
cancellations 152–3
Cape of Good Hope 210
Carol of Romania, King 7, 204
carrier stamps 172
Castle high values 56
catalogues 53, 106–7
Ceylon 219
charity labels 178–9
charity stamps 66–9
Charles I, King 13
Chile 72, 141
China 143, 208–9
Christmas Island 99
Christmas charity posts 175
Christmas seals 178–9
Christmas stamps 62
Churchill, Winston 117
Cinderellas 156–83
circular delivery stamps 175
clubs and societies 32–3
Cocos (Keeling) Islands 99
coil stamps 84, 86
college stamps 176
Colombia 71–2, 76–7
colonial keyplate designs 56
colour 16

colour charts 48
commemorative stamps 58–61
commemorative stationery 94–5
composite stamps 88–9
condition 188–93
Croatia 100
Crown Agents 60
Council of Europe 101
courier stamps 170–1
Courvoisier 25
Cushing, Peter 7
customised stamps 83
Cyprus 109
Czech Republic 21
Czechoslovakia 76–7

D

datestamps 148–9
dealers 43
definitive stamps 54–7
Deh Sedang 160
De La Rue 22, 122–3
Denmark 21, 56, 169, 178–9
Diana, Princess of Wales 60–1, 117
Dockwra, William 150–1
Double Geneva 185

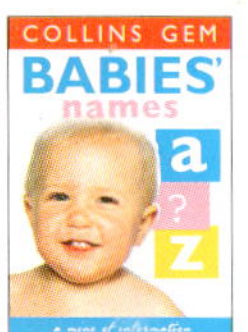
COLLINS GEM
BABIES'
names
a
?
z
a mine of information

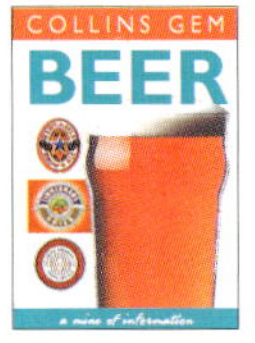
COLLINS GEM
BEER
a mine of information

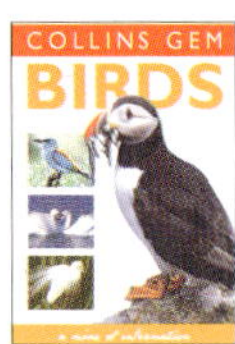
COLLINS GEM
BIRDS
a mine of information

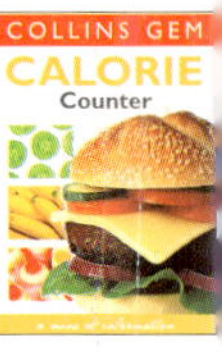
COLLINS GEM
CALORIE
Counter
a mine of information

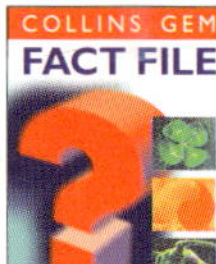
COLLINS GEM
FACT FILE
a mine of information

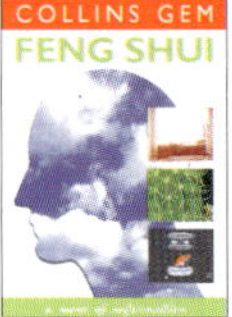
COLLINS GEM
FENG SHUI
a mine of information

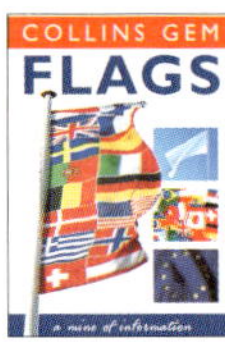
COLLINS GEM
FLAGS
a mine of information

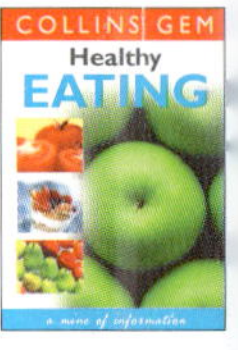
COLLINS GEM
Healthy
EATING
a mine of information

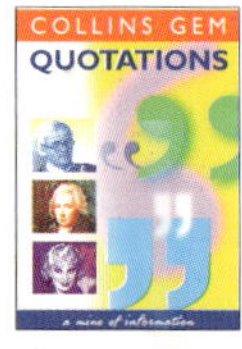
COLLINS GEM
QUOTATIONS
a mine of information

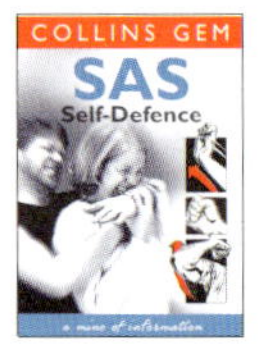
COLLINS GEM
SAS
Self-Defence
a mine of information

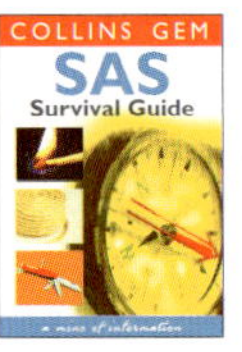
COLLINS GEM
SAS
Survival Guide
a mine of information

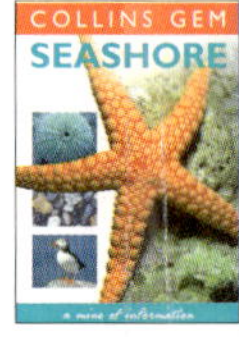
COLLINS GEM
SEASHORE
a mine of information

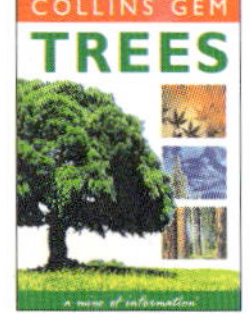
COLLINS GEM
TREES
a mine of information

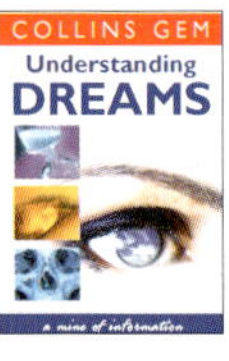
COLLINS GEM
Understanding
DREAMS
a mine of information

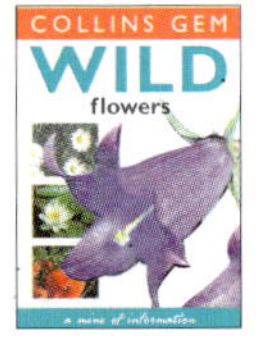
COLLINS GEM
WILD
flowers
a mine of information

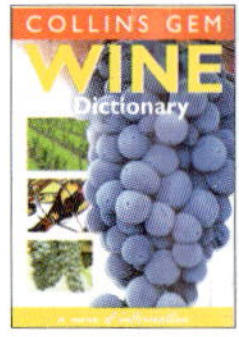
COLLINS GEM
WINE
Dictionary
a mine of information